D1231620

power
money
fame
sex

power
money
fame
sex

A USER'S GUIDE

Gretchen Craft Rubin

POCKET BOOKS

New York   London   Toronto   Sydney   Singapore

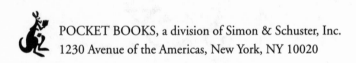 POCKET BOOKS, a division of Simon & Schuster, Inc.
1230 Avenue of the Americas, New York, NY 10020

Copyright © 2000 by Gretchen Craft Rubin

ISBN: 0-671-04128-2

First Pocket Books hardcover printing September 2000

10   9   8   7   6   5   4   3   2   1

POCKET and colophon are registered trademarks of Simon
& Schuster, Inc.

Printed in the U.S.A.

To Jamie and Eliza—
words can't tell how much I love you

ACKNOWLEDGMENTS

My greatest thanks go to my parents, Karen and Jack Craft, who are the best mother and father imaginable—I appreciate them both more all the time. My sister, Elizabeth Craft, set me a great example and encouraged me at every step. Thanks too to my wonderful parents-in-law, Judy and Bob Rubin.

I benefited from the insights and help of Michael Abbott, David Barron, Julia Bator, Michael Beran, Delia Boylan, David Brock, Warren Buffett, Sarah Burnes, Nicole Channing, Jackie Chorney, Denyse Clancy, Betsy Cohen, Tanya Coke, Christopher DeLong, Michelle DeLong, Jana Edelbaum, Courtney Simmons Elwood, John Elwood, Sarah Fain, Lisa Beattie Frelinghuysen, Julius Genachowski, Hannah Griswold, Sebastian Heath, Jamie Heller, Matthew Herrington, Julie Hilden, Andrew Hruska, Reed Hundt, Charlotte Jackson, Paul Kahn, Juliette Kayyem, Susan Kleckner, Becky Lemov, Rick Lerner, Pierre Leval, Blair Levin, Susan Lewis, Tad Low, Kim Malone, Megan Matson, Orlee Mendel, Greg Miller, Marcus Mitchell, Ariel Mosaffi, Elena Nachmanoff, Jennifer Newstead, Michael Nichols, Sandra Day O'Connor, Rusty O'Kelley, Patricia O'Toole, Jenny Roberts, Jed Rubenfeld, Phil Rubin, Michael Scammell, Alison Schafer, Jennifer Scully, Saul Shapiro, Mindy Shultz, Steven Spielberg, Ramie Targoff, Rebecca Todd, Katy Ubaldi, Steve Umin, Jed Weissberg, Amy Wilensky, Fareed Zakaria, Paula Throckmorton Zakaria, and Amy Zegart.

Many thanks to my outstanding agent, Christy Fletcher, and to Michael Carlisle at Carlisle & Company, and to my terrific editor, Greer Kessel Hendricks.

And, of course, thanks to my husband, Jamie.

CONTENTS

fame

sex

introduction

POWER MONEY FAME SEX

Power, money, fame, and sex are social ambitions: they depend on other people for their realization. There is no power without hierarchy, no wealth without comparison, no fame without the gaping audience, no sex in solitude. And because power, money, fame, sex are relative passions, they are insatiable—they're measured against the accomplishments of others, and therefore can never be wholly achieved. "If you desire glory, you may envy Napoleon," the philosopher Bertrand Russell wrote. "But Napoleon envied Caesar, Caesar envied Alexander, and Alexander, I dare say, envied Hercules, who never existed. You cannot therefore get away from envy by means of success alone, for there will always be in history or legend some person even more successful than you are."

Most people agree that the desire for one of these is paramount, but they disagree about which one. "It's all about money," one person insists; another protests, "Money? It's all about sex. Freud, you know." Your own focus depends on your character, your circumstances—even your location.

Each era and place has its ascendant worldly passion. The 1960s was a time of power, of different groups discovering ways to seize and exercise their power. In the 1970s the emphasis slid to sex, to bedroom experimentation, to the oxymorons of open marriage and no-fault divorce. The 1980s was an age of excess and display—preoccupation with money and its trophies. In the 1990s, excess disguised itself in simplicity, and the emphasis shifted to fame: *"Are you somebody?"* Cities, too, assume their character from the worldly passion that perfumes the atmosphere. Power: Washington, D.C. Money: New York City. Fame: Los Angeles. Sex doesn't have its own city; it pervades these three, and all the others.

So who needs a guide to using power, money, fame, and sex? This guide is aimed at two groups of people: *strivers* and *nonstrivers*.

If you're a *striver*, you'll find useful material to spur you on. You can go further than you now imagine by applying the principles outlined here. Remember, the rules don't change, just their context. Today's mail-office clerk is tomorrow's mogul.

If you're a *nonstriver*, this guide will help you precisely because you're *not* plotting your path to a corner office or penthouse apartment. You can use the guide *defensively:* even if you won't use these techniques yourself, you probably don't want them to work against you.

Whether you're a striver or a nonstriver, you've probably noticed that raw merit alone won't secure you your proper share of power, money, fame, or sex. Conscious strategy is sometimes necessary if you're going to keep up with people who exploit advanced techniques. To help you devise your strategy, this guide breaks down the concepts of power, money, fame, and sex and puts them back together so that you—whether you're a claims adjuster or a real-estate magnate or an aspiring starlet—can use them.

Presented here are principles distilled from Suetonius, Tom Wolfe, Sally Quinn, Garry Wills, *Vanity Fair,* and the *Wall Street Journal;* from classics like Niccolò Machiavelli's *The Prince,* a sixteenth-century manual on power, and Sun-tzu's *The Art of War,* a fourth-century B.C. manual on power, and Michael Korda's *Power! How to Get It, How to Use It,* a twentieth-century manual on power. If you haven't yet found the time to read indispensable texts like Thorstein Veblen's *The Theory of the Leisure Class,* Plutarch's *Lives,* Baldesar Castiglione's *The Book of the Courtier,* Daniel Boorstin's *The Image,* or Robert Caro's biographies, read on. Learn from the lives of people like Richard Nixon, Bill Gates, Elizabeth Taylor, Calvin Klein, Larry Ellison, Muhammad Ali, and Jacqueline Kennedy Onassis.

You'll see that distinct patterns and rules emerge. Even though widely separated in time, place, and interests, people reproduce the same methods—mostly without conscious effort. Hugh Hefner and Dennis Rodman applied the same rule of fame (see Chapter 14). Pamela Harriman and Bill Clinton applied the same rule of sex (see Chapter 20). Lyndon Johnson and Barry Diller applied the same rule of power, as did John Sununu and Madonna and Jack Welch (see Chapter 3).

Pay special attention to themes that transcend category and appear throughout the guide:

- **Signaling**—craft the appropriate forms and appearances to create the impression you seek. Act, dress, speak for the role you want—whether of celebrity, tycoon, sexpot, or stud. "Every one sees what you appear to be," observed Machiavelli, "few really know what you are." But at the same time, remember . . .
- *Sprezzatura*—show only a graceful, easy carelessness; never reveal calculation or effort. The appearance of exertion detracts from your achievements.
- **The Principle of Dis-expectation**—to demonstrate your triumph, reverse expectations. Where others make a grand show, use simplicity and modesty to emphasize that you need no outward signals to prove your mastery (or vice versa).
- **The Platinum Rule**—To whom much is given, more is given. It's not fair, but it's true: the momentum of worldly rewards means that those who have much, get more. As French moralist La Rochefoucauld observed, "Fortune turns all things to the benefit of her favorites."
- **The Blues**—this guide doesn't tell you how to achieve *happiness*—just power, money, fame, sex. The worldly passions bring with them their particular blues.

As you read, the guide's principles may seem familiar, or they may seem new, startling—perhaps shocking. You may find that studying the principles set out in *Power Money Fame Sex: A User's Guide* gives you an uneasy, even dirty, feeling. And who wants to admit to being so calculated—aren't you supposed to achieve your goals without effort? or at least without *apparent* effort? (Yes. See the discussion of *sprezzatura*.) Suddenly, simple objects and gestures (a thank-you note, a new office desk, a few names dropped in conversation) are stripped of the mask of civility and spontaneity. Where you once saw naturalness, you now perceive calculation (even if instinctive) and effort. It's unnerving to realize that there's no heroic mystery to great power, great wealth, great fame, great sex—merely straightforward methods pursued to masterful success.

Nevertheless, however sordid, there is a value to understanding the workings of the worldly passions. Once these principles are exposed, their grip slackens. "Ah-ha!" you realize. "Now I understand why my neighbors spent a fortune to decorate their house in a style so minimalist that I thought it was still under construction." Once you see that intimidating rages are a common technique of asserting power, your boss's furies lose some of their terror. (Seeing these principles laid bare may also cause you to reflect, more earnestly than before, on the moral effect of chasing these worldly prizes.)

Certainly, not all the methods described here are admirable. Even though we might wish that artless merit and kindness always triumphed, in fact, sycophancy works, bullying works, self-aggrandizement works. (Note, however, that their opposites also work.) The guide describes what *actually* succeeds rather than what *ought* to succeed. *It's up to you to decide what methods you choose to apply.*

power

CHAPTER ONE

INTRODUCTION TO POWER

What is power? You express your will, and someone else executes it.

To get power, first assert yourself over your own situation. Take charge and take responsibility for decisions within your ambit. Seize control of your time—it's a badge of powerlessness to punch a time card, to apologize for leaving early, to get docked for your absences.

After achieving power over yourself, extend your reach over more people, actions, and ideas, until finally you're shaping the future. One day you're pleased just to be able to send out a letter over your own signature; thirty years later, you're worried about whether you'll be able to prevent your beloved company from being sold to a competitor after you're dead.

Your circumstances, your competition, and most important, the peculiarities of your own character will determine the scope and style of your power. What method will work for you? The gregarious, gift-giving, high-energy model? The unassuming, analytical, behind-the-scenes model? The angry, impulsive, demanding model? No one way is most likely to succeed. It's up to you to decide your technique.

Power comes in two principal types: direct and indirect. Take this quiz to determine which type suits you better.

Quiz: Do you want direct or indirect power?

Pick the answer that describes you. Assume that both responses confer the same financial benefits.

1. You're a lawyer. Which career would you pursue?

    A. Work to score victories on behalf of your own clients.

    B. Teach in a law school so your legal theories would affect scores of future lawyers.

2. Which opportunity is more appealing?

    A. You're asked to join the board of a promising start-up company.

    B. You're asked to write a monthly column for an influential magazine.

3. Which accomplishment would give you greater satisfaction?

    A. To walk past a building with the knowledge that without your contribution, it wouldn't have been built.

    B. To walk down the street with the knowledge that without your influence, the latest fashion craze wouldn't have been launched.

4. If you were outraged by a proposed change in municipal policy, how would you prefer to try to stop it?

    A. Make it clear to the city council that you'll stop doing business in the city if the change goes through.

    B. Appear on a popular local television roundtable to denounce the change.

5. What is your attitude toward providing for your descendants?

    A. I'd like to provide opportunity and guidance for the next generations—for example, by establishing trusts that would provide funds for my heirs, but in such a way that the money couldn't be squandered.

    B. I wouldn't mind bequeathing some money to my descendants, but I'd leave it without strings attached; I'm not interested in trying to control their lives.

Tally your number of *A* and *B* answers.

ANSWER A:

If most of your answers are *A*, you crave *direct power* to shape the outcome of events—for example, as an executive, surgeon, or software developer. You want to be an obvious, indispensable force and to reap clear credit for the fruits of your actions.

    Direct power is found in both the private and public sector.

(Note that in either case, power generally traces back to wealth or control of wealth.)

Powerful private-sector jobs are more widely available, so you're more likely to achieve power there. However, if you're afraid you're stalling out in the private sector, move to Washington, D.C., or the state capital for a government job. If you've achieved significant power in one domain and crave a new challenge, jump from the private to the public, or from the public to the private.

At the extreme, your appetite for direct power provokes you to extend your reach into the future. You strain to preserve your legacy—an impulse that extends to great things and small. Celebrity developer Donald Trump always dreamed of putting his mark on the Manhattan skyline and has succeeded by branding his name on his buildings, in gold-colored letters several feet high. President Nixon's habit of sitting with his feet on his desktop had scarred its

Use your power directly to affect important matters—and insignificant ones, if you choose. Richard Nixon wanted to put his stamp on the Oval Office by leaving his heel marks on the mahogany surface of the desk. (© Bettmann/CORBIS)

mahogany surface. Once, when he was out of the country, the desk was refinished. When he came back and saw the repairs, Nixon snapped, "Dammit, I didn't order that. I want to leave *my* mark on this place just like other presidents."

ANSWER B:

If most of your answers are *B,* you want the *indirect power* to shape people's thoughts. You may not be a necessary part of the action, but you influence what outcome emerges.

You work as a teacher, writer, or filmmaker in order to shape public opinion—by writing op-eds, arguing on TV as a news pundit, hyping this summer's books, leading the latest movement in the academy. You influence what people *think.* John Fairchild, as publisher of the influential magazines *Women's Wear Daily* and *W,* coined the phrase "hot pants" and his magazine identified "the beautiful people," "fashion victim," and "Nouvelle Society"—and by naming these things, invented the *idea* of them. To describe is to create. And when your ideas provoke others to act, your power is limitless. Obscure stock analyst Henry Blodget singlehandedly sent Internet stocks zooming when he raised his year-end price target for Amazon.com from $150 a share to $400. A week later, the stock was at $325. The impact of Blodget's words on the personal wealth of Amazon.com founder and CEO Jeff Bezos may have been indirect, but it was quite tangible. And consider PR man Howard Rubenstein—although he wields indirect power, there's much he can accomplish. Why else would controversial figures like George Steinbrenner, Leona Helmsley, Mike Tyson, Naomi Campbell, Donald Trump, and Marv Albert have hired him?

Professors, management consultants, the clergy, TV commentators, artists, comedians, wield the force of thought. Though the scope of their direct power is quite narrow, they command attention and shape the world of ideas. The ability to direct others' perceptions is the very source, rather than a result, of their power.

Journalists wield enormous power because they set the terms in which the public perceives events; and in response to that power, the profession of "spin doctor" has arisen—another indirect-power profession—to package and create news for feeding to the media.

The *cynosure effect*—the fact that merely your presence in the spotlight makes you a captivating subject—is an important source of indirect power. Why? Because indirect power requires a platform, a bully pulpit of twenty students or thirty thousand readers or forty million viewers. The greater your visibility, the more potent your voice. Don't make the mistake of believing that because this power is indirect, it's less effective. Oprah Winfrey hosts a popular television talk show; the power of her recommendation turned a novel with a first printing of 6,800 into a best-seller with 750,000 in print. You may not have your own TV show, but if you publish a letter in your children's school newsletter that convinces other parents that the school should require the wearing of uniforms, you're exercising indirect power.

Of course, direct and indirect power aren't *really* so easily divisible—each type must partake of the other to succeed, and often a person's power is a blend of both. It's a rare person—and a person of tremendous power—who forcefully combines vigorous, effectual action with influential ideas. Think of Martha Stewart.

• • •

So . . . do you want to be the author of a book, or the editor who decides the book will be published? Would you rather be the teacher who explains evolution to students, or the school-board member who votes to keep evolution in the curriculum? Whether it's indirect or direct power you crave, exploit the power potential of as many sources as possible. To do so, draw upon the eight pillars of power.

CHAPTER TWO

THE EIGHT PILLARS OF POWER

If you're like most people, a taste of power will whet your appetite for more. You begin to dream about what changes you'd make, how you'd spend your time, how satisfying it would be to receive the deference you now must pay to others. But how do you build power? Extend your reach by drawing upon the eight sources of power. To amass maximum power, exploit as many sources as possible—but be sure to match your methods to your personality. If you're shy, don't count on using networking to build your power; if you're consumed with the desire to claw your way to the top, don't count on using the *attraction of presence*. Power comes in many styles, so to achieve your potential, use the methods that best suit you and your circumstances.

1. Maximize the power provided by your institutional position.
2. Use other people as a source of power.
   - Networking.
   - Heir-apparency.
   - Mentoring/Apprenticeship.
   - Proximity.
   - Exclusion.
   - Surrogacy.
   - Sycophancy.
3. Control information.
4. Exploit the *attraction of prowess*.
5. Exploit the *attraction of presence*.
6. Capitalize on your money.
7. Spotlight your fame.
8. Fan the flames of sex.

Special note on method

Techniques of power must be used *mindfully*, in keeping with your station. A strategy that works well for your boss might backfire on you. If he takes a long personal call during a crisis, everyone will comment on his cool; if you took that call, you'd find yourself demoted. If she schedules a meeting early Sunday morning, people are thrilled to be asked to attend; if you scheduled that meeting, no one would show up.

Be subtle. Power strategies tend to work less well as they become more overt. Trying too hard is a sign of weakness; your power should appear to come naturally. You'll find yourself the subject of mockery if you're obviously jockeying for a bigger office, or if you insist that the support staff address you by your last name. Always cloak a power move in a cover of efficiency and necessity. You didn't ask for the extra phone line so you'd have more than your peers; you *need* it because you take more calls. You work out in the office gym at dawn not because you want extra face-time with your boss, but because, like the boss, you like to start your day very early. ("I only need about four hours of sleep a night," you explain modestly.)

1. MAXIMIZE THE POWER PROVIDED BY YOUR INSTITUTIONAL POSITION

Your most obvious power source is your position in an organization, where your position carries automatic rights, responsibilities, and rank. Your goal? To bulldoze ahead as far as possible.

Finally, to your great relief, you've gotten that promotion to "associate director." What now? Grab the prerogatives that accompany your title. Are you now entitled to attend the senior-staff retreat? Is there a parking space that should be reserved for you? Pay attention to details. You observe that your co-associate-director always sits at the boss's right hand during meetings. Next time, arrive early to stake out the seat on the boss's left hand.

Careful distinctions signal your rank in the power hierarchy. The Reagan White House followed strict protocol to determine who sat in which chair around the president. Donald Regan recalled that while he was treasury secretary, "as we sat in a semicircle by the fireplace, facing the president, I occupied the chair that commanded eye contact with Reagan. This chair was mine by virtue of my rank in the Cabinet—it was reserved for the highest-ranking person present. When the vice president attended, or the secretary of state, I was obliged to move to the couch." Each official knew his proper place.

Pay attention to titles, and make sure you have the one you want—even if you have to invent a new one. Maybe, instead of being "senior director of ———" when you're promoted, you want to be "vice-president for ———." Even if you aren't important, you can try to make yourself at least sound important.

Search for ways to expand your turf. Propose that underlings wait for your sign-off before circulating their memos or that your department handle tasks that previously had been sent elsewhere. At the same time, be sure to balance this expansion with delegation; clinging too tightly to the levers of power leads to powerlessness.

Don't assume that merely holding an office automatically grants you all the possible power you might achieve in it. It's up to you to exploit your opportunity. However, it's true (fortunately, for many) that merely holding a significant title does endow you with considerable power. After Silicon Graphics founder Jim Clark found himself outmaneuvered, he noted, "I might not have any power at Silicon Graphics, but [journalists] didn't know that. I was still called the chairman. And most journalists think a chairman of a big company is an important person." The perception of power gave him a power that he exercised through the press.

Remember that the lack of an impressive title doesn't necessarily indicate a lack of power. It's common for someone like a secretary, a human-resources officer, or a nurse to be a power center, despite the lack of high rank.

> **TIP:** Avoid a title that is overlong, has multiple adjectives, or contains more than one prepositional phrase. If possible, reject titles like "Principal Assistant Deputy Under Secretary" or "Associate Principal Deputy Assistant Secretary" (yes, these are actual government titles). And ask yourself whether you really want one of those fashionable, overly cute titles—like "Chief Yahoo!" (Jerry Yang's title at Yahoo), or "Head Coach" (Marty Hanaka's at Sports Authority), or "Minister of Order and Reason" (Martin Tobias's at encoding.com).

2. USE OTHER PEOPLE AS A SOURCE OF POWER

You build power from your relationships with other people. They can contribute to your success, help you get promoted, and make your life easier. (Conversely, if ill motivated, they can sabotage you and block your progress.) Strive to capitalize on every possible connection. Your chief strategy is to align yourself with people who already have power and to draw power from them. Try the seven following methods:

- Networking
- Heir apparency
- Mentoring/Apprenticeship
- Proximity
- Exclusion
- Surrogacy
- Sycophancy

NETWORKING

Exploit other people's power by forging relationships based on mutual acquaintances, schools, political activities, hobbies, employers, clubs, and the like. Once established, these connections pave your way to ask for information, hustle favors, cadge introductions, solicit contributions, and otherwise profit from your acquaintances. You feel a sudden wave of nostalgia for college when you see your former roommate profiled in the newspaper. "I've been meaning to give you a call for such a long time," you explain into the phone.

Don't arrive at cocktail parties, golf games, alumni events, and parties expecting to relax and enjoy yourself. You should be working hard to maintain and expand your base of acquaintances. (Remember, however, always to *act* as if you showed up just to have a good time.) Never underestimate the effectiveness of networking. Its influence often overwhelms merit, which is why the "old-boy" network provokes so much griping. The people who didn't make it into Kappa Kappa Gamma or Skull and Bones or Omega Psi Phi have a reason to be disgruntled.

Your social schedule shouldn't revolve around old pals. Instead, transform professional acquaintances into "friends." Invite them on a ski trip with your family. After hearing that Pop-Tarts are the favorite guilty treat of your new friend the Internet mogul, send over a case to celebrate his latest secondary offering. Plan warm ways to express the spontaneous sincerity of your affection.

Protect yourself by making useful new "friends" out of people who might be in a position to support or oppose you. New York power broker and builder Robert Moses brandished hospitality as a political weapon; he disarmed people by inviting them for dinners and boat rides. President Franklin Roosevelt raised contentious issues informally, around his dinner table, where guests felt uncomfortable disagreeing with him.

Never reveal that your gestures of friendship are inspired by a different agenda, or you'll sabotage the very impression you're working to concoct. Learn from the bad example set by Gwen Cafritz, early in her days as a Washington hostess. She called Congressman Joe Casey's wife to invite the couple to a cocktail party. After she was told that yes, they'd love to come, Mrs. Cafritz continued, "I understand your husband has just been nominated to be secretary of labor." "That's right," Mrs. Casey answered. "Well, if he gets confirmed," added Mrs. Cafritz, "we'd love to have you stay for dinner."

TIP: Enhance your power by bringing together people who want to know each other. Legendary Washington hostesses, like Gwen Cafritz, Perle Mesta, Pamela Harriman, and Evangeline Bruce made themselves power centers by establishing their living rooms as places where the power elite could exchange views.

Join institutions that offer networking potential. Then–Travelers Group Chairman Sanford Weill boosted the flagging prospects of New York City's Carnegie Hall when he took over as chairman, by transforming membership on the board of directors into an outstanding networking opportunity. Soon the number of people clamoring to join (all with a passionate love for music, of course) exceeded spots available.

Although it's gratifying to be the most powerful person in a group, look for ways to spend time with people who have more power than you. As Lord Chesterfield advised his son, "The pride of being the first of the company is but too common; but it is very silly, and very prejudicial." Where should you go—Bilderberg, TED, Davos, Renaissance Weekend, Yaddo, PC Forum?

Diversify your people portfolio by pushing outside your professional and social circle. Studies show that often the people who prove most useful—for example, by providing a lead to a new job—are acquaintances rather than close friends. Cultivate opportunities to branch out.

But while generally you should associate with your equals and superiors, it's also a good idea to maintain at least a few relationships below you; it always helps to know someone in computer support and personnel. And opportunities can flow from the good favor of peers or even subordinates.

HEIR APPARENCY

You gain power if you're tapped as an heir apparent. When super-agent Michael Ovitz, one of Hollywood's biggest players, took over as Disney president, he became the heir apparent to Disney head Michael Eisner—and with that role came enormous potential power. Of course, that power vanished when it became clear that he wasn't going to inherit the Disney mantle after all.

Heir apparency is even more effective if you're an actual descendant in a line of power. Twenty-something Lachlan Murdoch is literally the heir apparent to his father Rupert Murdoch's $13 billion media empire, News Corp., and is treated accordingly, tattoos and all. Although the United States fought a war to be free of hereditary powers, a glance at the Bush family, the Kennedy family, or the Gore family shows that political power flows more easily down a line of descendants.

Power is forward-looking. An heir apparent wields power in the present because he or she will have power in the future (as well as having the ear of the current power holder). That's why a lame-duck politician is crippled, and why your boss might seem reluctant to clarify the issues of retirement timing and line of succession.

TIP: Wondering whether you have power? One sure sign: other people earnestly discuss what kind of mood you're in.

MENTORING/APPRENTICESHIP

Both mentor and apprentice gain from this relationship. As a mentor, you earn the gratitude and loyalty of a subordinate, and you place your stamp on your organization. Mega-director Steven Spielberg admitted that "there is a vanity involved in helping a young person achieve his goal. The vanity is a chance to get started a second time, to project oneself into the young film-maker's own career." Also, your reputation as a helpful mentor will enable you to attract capable people, who will in turn bolster your position.

> **TIP:** Are you widely disliked? Considered arrogant? Abrasive? Then clinching a powerful mentor should be one of your most important goals. Curry favor with someone who can protect you from the consequences of your faults.

As an apprentice, you gain a guide and ally. The support of even one powerful person speeds your way toward success, and that person's protection can keep you secure in a position that might otherwise be precarious. Mentor and apprentice can exchange valuable inside information.

But guard against being dragged down by a mentoring relationship. If you hitch your wagon too tightly to someone else's star, you lose control of your own destiny.

> FOOL: "Let go thy hold when a great wheel runs down a hill, lest it break thy neck with following. But the great one that goes upward, let him draw thee after."
>
> WILLIAM SHAKESPEARE,
> *KING LEAR*

What if, despite your efforts to reach out to a mentor, someone else emerges as the favorite apprentice? Although it's painful to watch someone else bask in the warmth of preference, avoid the temptation to be scornful. Attempts to undermine the favorite are obvious and will only make you look weak.

PROXIMITY

You get power by getting close to, or controlling access to, a powerful person—consider the power of Larry King's booker.

Proximity isn't just a figurative notion; literal, physical proximity to the source cloaks you in power. To solidify his position as sole doorkeeper to President Nixon, and to cut off the power that secretary Rose Mary Woods would gain from her physical proximity, Chief of Staff H. R. Haldeman blocked her from getting the office next door to the Oval Office that was traditionally assigned to presidents' personal secretaries.

Your physical placement shows your position in the pecking order—the closer to the power center, the better. Just as government officials measure their importance by the distance from their car to the president's in a motorcade, the crowd of artists manqués from the Factory knew that whoever rode in Andy Warhol's car was in highest favor.

The power source may differ from place to place, but proximity always matters: Washington types agonize about the location of their seats at the State of the Union address; Hollywood stars worry about their seats at the Academy Awards; New York moguls fret about their seats in the boardroom or at the Four Seasons. Wherever you are, identify the "right" place to be and angle to get yourself in position. Say you're attending a fashion show. You want to be seated front row center, direct middle of the runway. The further back or sideways your seat, the lower you rate.

TIP: When staking out a seat at a meeting, don't assume that the most powerful position is at the head of the table. You're often better off sitting at the middle, where you're closer to others sitting around the table, and therefore more able to talk to and influence them.

Proximity power is exhilarating, because it allows you to participate in events beyond your inherent reach. Dick Morris was an obscure political consultant, but his relationship of intimate trust with President Clinton made him, as *Time* magazine put it, "the most influential private citizen in America."

However, because proximity power is derivative, it's precarious. As with mentoring, if the person from whom you draw power fails, it's easy for you to fail, too. The lives of Gary Hart's staff were blown apart when, just after they'd uprooted themselves to move to Colorado, the exposure of his reckless affair with Miami model Donna Rice tanked his 1988 presidential candidacy. Even proximity to monkey business is risky.

TRUE RULE

If you stake your position on other
people, you're hostage to their fortune.

EXCLUSION

Capitalize on the near-universal desire to be included, and the even
more powerful dread of exclusion: create, control (or, at the very
least, join) the desirable inner circle, the group that includes "everyone that's anyone." This group may be formal (everyone's coming in
on Sunday for the strategy meeting with the boss) or informal
(everyone's hanging out in Pat's office talking about the reorganiza-
tion). Exploit the fact that when that door slams shut, everyone—
like you—wants to be safely inside, not shut out.

The insider group's exclusivity binds its members more closely
together, and because outsiders yearn to be welcomed inside, it
brings them into cooperation
with the group. Or perhaps
those outsiders are safely
lodged in their *own* group.
A group's members define
themselves in contrast
to nonmembers. Insiders,
bound together by some
mutual interest, position,
or style, bolster each other
with mutual admiration and
pride—and disdain for outsiders. Fixed Income looks
suspiciously at Equities;
Equities laughs at Fixed
Income.

It is a terrible bore, of course, when
old Fatty Smithson draws you aside
and whispers "Look here, we've got to
get you in on this examination
somehow" or "Charles and I saw at
once that you've got to be on this
committee." A terrible bore . . . ah,
but how much more terrible if you
were left out! It is tiring and
unhealthy to lose your Saturday
afternoons: but to have them free
because you don't matter, that is much
worse.

C. S. LEWIS, "THE INNER RING,"
THE WEIGHT OF GLORY

Exclusion can be used
with peers or with subordi-
nates. To solidify a group of colleagues around you, create situations
that demonstrate the division between "us" and "them." Flaunt the
group's existence. "A bunch of us are getting together for drinks

after work tomorrow," you tell one of "us" within earshot of several people who aren't. Create an E-mail subgroup limited to "us," to share important information only with the right people.

If you're in charge, use exclusion to bind a group of devoted followers to you. Single out your favorites by loading them with additional work, calling them at home, plying them with personal questions—by making demands, you stimulate loyalty, and by making extra work a mark of favor, you stifle complaints (or, at least, your followers will be complaining only to each other). Soon you've rallied a fiercely devoted group that's working overtime for your benefit. They'll do whatever it takes to hang on to their place in your inner circle. Invent special nicknames for your favored ones. Jack Kennedy signaled his inner circle's boundaries by the childish (why childish, do you suppose?) names he bestowed—journalist friend Ben Bradlee became Benjy, girlfriend Inga Arvad became Inga-Binga, brother Robert Kennedy became Bobby, even though, or maybe because, Bobby disliked it.

Make sure that you and other group members get special treatment—first in line for perks, safe from censure. You're one of the in-group, so your tardiness is overlooked. It's convenient to be safe from official reprimand, and what better proof of belonging?

> **TIP:** To show someone who works for you a special respect, E-mail him or her a document (no one else cc'd) with a note, "I'd really like to have your thoughts on this." The recipient will feel honored to be singled out. Send the note and document to several different people.

SURROGACY

Some positions require stand-ins—which bolster the power of both sides. For example, as a politician, you rely on your staff to represent you; as a staff member, you rely on your principal to grant you a meaningful role. You shake your head, saying, "That won't work; my boss will never accept that," when you (as well as everyone in the room) know that your boss, a "vision person," not only doesn't know anything about this issue but has left it entirely in your hands.

Maybe your boss, like many, shrinks from confrontation. Insinuate yourself into power by taking on the unpopular role of hatchet man, the "bad cop" who allows your boss to play "good cop." Canny presidents usually have at least one person who's willing to play the heavy: think of H. R. Haldeman, Zbigniew Brzezinski, Donald Regan, and John Sununu. Early in his first term, Clinton came under fire for his choice of Thomas "Mack" McLarty as his chief of staff. "Mack the Nice" didn't have the temperament to play the bad cop that love-hungry Clinton needed. In movie making and book publishing, agents, lawyers, personal assistants, and managers make the disagreeable demands so that talent can maintain friendly relationships with industry.

Playing the loyal surrogate to a major player can be a frustrating road to power, because your role often remains obscured. Who really deserves credit for the line, said about the *Challenger* astronauts, that they "slipped the surly bonds of earth to touch the face of God"? (Not Ronald Reagan—and not speechwriter Peggy Noonan either, as it turns out.) In fact, claiming credit is a mark of failure, because the best surrogates never claim responsibility for a boss's achievements. As a surrogate, you're irritated by the fact that someone else's name goes out over your work (later, you'll be unnerved by the fact that your name goes out over your surrogate's work—usually something you haven't even read). Of course, not all surrogates are committed to maintaining anonymity. Political reporter Jack Germond noted of presidential speechwriters that "Somehow we always learned about it when Dick Goodwin or Bill Safire was the ghost."

TIP: Avoid the common tendency of *eye stray*. You're at a crowded cocktail party, and as you chat with a colleague, your eye strays in search of someone more important to corner. Try to disguise eye stray: it's annoying to the person from whom your eye is straying.

SYCOPHANCY

Although sycophancy is often unpopular with third-party witnesses, it is an effective way to get ahead. By toadying to those with more power, or "managing up," you gain power. Direct your efforts and attention to those on the ladder above you and to anyone else who can be useful to you (which, however, can include almost anyone).

For sycophancy to be most effective, scrutinize the character and habits of your target so that you can tailor your appeal. Some pointers:

- Create a need that your target isn't aware of, then satisfy it. "You weren't on the distribution list, Chief, but I raised hell to make sure you got the report." Before, your target couldn't have cared less about the report but now is grateful you fought to get it. This principle (and the others) works outside the workplace as well. In his memoir, Peter Duchin records that soon after marriage to Pamela Harriman, businessman and statesman Averell Harriman remarked, "'Things are great. Why, do you know that Pam even puts my favorite flower by my bed every morning?'" "'Really?'" replied Duchin, "'I didn't know you had a favorite flower, Ave. What is it?'" Harriman stammered, "'Oh . . . I don't know. But whatever it is, she puts it there every morning.'"

- Feed your target's hidden desires. Maybe your target wants to consort with models or athletes or the social elite. You make the necessary arrangements. Reflect the image—fashionable, cunning, life of the party—that your target most wants to project. Does your target want to be considered intimidating? Well read? Comment accordingly.

- Remind your target of how much he or she hates suck-ups and yes-men. Your target, you muse aloud, is impervious to such crude, unctuous strategies.

> DECIUS: "But when I tell him he hates flatterers, he says he does, being then most flattered."
>
> WILLIAM SHAKESPEARE, *JULIUS CAESAR*

- Never miss the opportunity to make an admiring observation. But pay attention—once, at Camp David, President Nixon returned to the cabin and announced, "I shot one twenty-six." Henry Kissinger piped up, "Your golf game is improving, Mr. President." Not the right response. "I was *bowling*, Henry," snapped the president.

TRUE RULE

A flatterer never seems absurd;
the flattered always takes his word.

- Imitation is the sincerest form of flattery, so copy your target in large things and small. Move into the same neighborhood, dress the same way. When Bill Gates drives a Lexus, the Lexus becomes the ultimate car on the Microsoft campus. (Of course, don't copy so exactly that you unnerve your target.) A truly determined sycophant might name a first child after a prized target. (Again, in the wrong context that action might seem . . . creepy.) Follow the same daily schedule—does your target wear Armani? Eat lunch at a nearby diner? Support the opera? Do the same. Watch your target's favorite movies, read your target's favorite books, so you can toss out the occasional reference. President Clinton's well-known fondness for *Meditations* had everyone in Washington reading Marcus Aurelius.

- Preserve your credibility by occasionally disagreeing with or poking fun at your target.

Pursue sycophancy discreetly. If you're too obvious, you'll arouse the resentment of your peers and subordinates. In particular, avoid the "kiss up, kick down" habit that often plagues sycophants. Today's underling may be tomorrow's overling; no need to make unnecessary enemies.

[Mark Antony] never understood that some men go out of their way to adopt a frank and outspoken manner and use it like a piquant sauce to disguise the cloying taste of flattery. Such people deliberately indulge in bold repartee and an aggressive flow of talk when they are in their cups, so that the obsequious compliance which they show in matters of business does not suggest that they associate with a man merely to please him, but seems to spring from a genuine conviction of his superior wisdom.

PLUTARCH, *LIVES*

USING OTHERS AS A SOURCE OF POWER—ILLUSTRATIONS

Situation	DO	DON'T
At a party, you spend almost an hour talking to Peter, who, you discover, is a close friend of Randy, the hottest new producer. You're eager to meet Randy, to tout your latest screenplay.	Five days later, call Peter to say, "I'm having some people over for a barbecue. I hope you can come. Feel free to bring anyone else along."	Five days later, call Peter to say, "I'm having some people over for a barbecue. I hope you can come. And hey, bring your friend Randy, too."
Your boss, who prides himself on being a rowdy renegade, appears one morning at your conservative law firm wearing a garish, ultra-trendy tie.	Say with mock horror, "Wow, you're going to catch some grief for that thing you're wearing around your neck —it's not exactly in sync with the corporate culture around here."	Say, "Love your tie. It looks great."
You and another person have both been hired, and because you're starting a week early, you can choose between an office across from your boss or one on another corridor.	Take the office opposite your boss. (You'll be able to eavesdrop on her phone conversations, see who's meeting with her, and get noticed yourself if you're close by.)	Take the office on the other corridor. (You'll be able to make personal phone calls and slip out early if you're out of sight.)

USING OTHERS AS A SOURCE OF POWER—ILLUSTRATIONS

Situation	DO	DON'T
Your boss asks you to draft a memo analyzing the competition. After a month of frantic work, you hand it in; she makes three stylistic changes, then circulates it over her signature. The memo sparks wide praise.	Tell everyone, "It was great to work with the boss on that memo. I learned a huge amount in the process."	Tell everyone, "I'm the one who deserves the credit for that analysis. I can't believe she put her name on it. She made only a few changes to my draft—just so she could tell herself she played some role in writing it."

3. CONTROL INFORMATION

Apply the three *C*s of information: **create** information (generate and circulate it yourself), **command** information (demand that others create it), and **control** information (act as gatekeeper to control others' access to it). It's a virtuous circle: the more information you have, the more power you wield, and the more power you have, the more information you acquire. The *Platinum Rule*—to whom much is given, more is given—works in the area of information exchange: those who have superior resources are privy to the best new information. Federal Reserve Chairman Alan Greenspan has unparalleled knowledge about the economy, and to whom is he more likely to give the benefit of his views—super-investor Warren Buffett, or you, when you linger to ask Greenspan a question after his speech to the Economic Club of New York?

Being cut out of the information loop is a catastrophe, so fight to maintain your status as an insider. The more sensitive the information you nose out, the better. J. Edgar Hoover derived his extraordinary power from the information he exhumed. Congressmen feared him and presidents wouldn't fire him, because they knew that

Hoover's infamous files held damaging secrets that could ruin their careers.

Be inquisitive. It's 8:30 P.M., and you happen to notice that when your coworker made some furtive photocopies after the office was deserted, she forgot to retrieve the original page from under the copier lid. *Hmmmm.* Why not go see what she left behind? Your boss shut the door to take a call—very unusual. Ask his secretary: "Was it Pat Smith who called? No? Who was it?" You just might find out. When you went to retrieve your document from the printer, you couldn't help but see the heading on the page sent to the other printer: "CONFIDENTIAL: Partners' Salaries and Bonuses." Quietly, accidentally, you add the sheet to your own pile of papers.

Husband your information. Your mentor just told you a juicy piece of information: he's on the brink of firing Dick and promoting Jane. Would your power increase if you broke the news? Maybe, in the short term. But over time, your indiscretion will cost you— with your mentor, who will discover that you can't keep a secret, and with your colleagues as well. You'll eventually get less information, because you'll be marked as a blabberer.

TRUE RULE

The person who tells you secrets will tell your secrets.

An exception to this rule is the deliberate indiscretion, or "leak," as a way to exploit journalists' power; through them, you spin news content, cultivate your relationships with influential writers, and demonstrate your independence from forces that seek to control the disclosure of information. Note that this technique can be risky: alleged leaks from the office of Independent Counsel Kenneth Starr sparked an investigation of the investigator.

Unauthorized leaks can be a tremendous problem for corporations, celebrities, or presidents (remember Nixon's "plumbers,"' who were supposed to plug the leaks?). Political consultant Dick Morris explained how Leon Panetta, as Clinton's chief of staff, was able to plug hostile leaks. First, Panetta identified the probable leaker: Did the reporter praise a staffer in a profile a month after the leak was published? Did the leak echo a view often expressed by a particular staffer? Which reporters regularly quoted which staffers? Once he identified a suspect, Panetta counterleaked. A story (often placed in the *Wall Street Journal*) would anonymously report that a staffer was losing influence or on the way out or out of favor with the President. He stopped the leaks.

A key element of information gathering is *access*. Lobbyists, of course, earn a living from their extensive contacts, but you, too, should work to expand your base. Access gives you a source of information and a platform for persuasion. You hear all the scuttlebutt. You know the people who can give you information or favors. The people who matter return your phone calls.

TIP: Make yourself a repository of the latest scoop, no matter how inconsequential. People will come to you to find out a former classmate's new address, where an ex-colleague decided to work after she quit, which caterer the boss uses. And, at the same time they ask you for information, they'll add to your store.

Insinuate yourself as a gatekeeper to information sources. You've got power if you can provide or cut off other people's information—and you've guaranteed yourself a constant supply.

Create the impression that you're the source of the best information. You send the E-mails to inform the rest of the office about your team's progress, so you're perceived as the leader and spokesperson; you clip articles and send them to coworkers, superiors, and clients with an "FYI" note attached.

4. EXPLOIT THE *ATTRACTION OF PROWESS*

People revere achievement and skill, wherever they appear. Call this feeling the *attraction of prowess*—the gravitational pull that draws people to ability, in any form. Lookers-on revel in high standards of performance, they thrill at triumphs, and they rush to participate.

If you exert the attraction of prowess, you can drive your troops mercilessly and they'll never flag. People long to dedicate themselves to an outstanding, effective leader, and if you prove your prowess, they'll follow you to the uttermost.

The people who work with you admire your quick mastery of new information, your ability to cut through confusion to make a decision, your articulation of a vision that inspires the whole team. You give them the joy of *things done well.* "We worked for weeks on that speech," they tell each other, "but those off-the-cuff remarks were better than anything we drafted!" They take pride in working for someone of your caliber, and they spur themselves to greater heights to meet your expectations. They're confident that their own efforts will be effective, because they've dedicated themselves to your service. As they gravitate toward you, they enhance your power.

The attraction of prowess reaches up and down a chain of hierarchy: the CEO seeks out the outstanding junior associate, just as the junior associate seeks out the CEO. This attraction is felt across unrelated fields: you're a brilliant surgeon, but you feel eager and humble when you go quail hunting with one of the country's foremost guides. You brandish the quail you shot and shyly call the guide to join you for the photograph.

To amplify the effect of the attraction of prowess, strive to acquire exceptional skills. Don't limit yourself to what's professionally relevant, but strike out in bold directions. Emulate those top executives who cultivate an imposing hobby: Virgin Group Chairman Richard Branson flies hot-air balloons; Oracle head Larry Ellison races yachts; direc-

> **TIP:** Confound stereotype. If you're a woman, become a big-game hunter. If you're a man, become a flower-arranging expert.
> (See the *principle of dis-expectation,* Chapter 3.)

tor Woody Allen plays clarinet with a jazz band every Monday night. Other possibilities? Scuba dive with sharks, cultivate bonsai, take up rockclimbing or hang-gliding, hunt cape buffalo in Africa. Actor John Travolta's possession of a fleet of airplanes is made much more impressive by the fact that he himself is certified to fly any of them. Airplane flying is an excellent choice, because flying *seems* difficult and macho but is in fact fairly safe and straightforward. (And, of course, it's expensive.)

Note that the attraction of prowess operates even when your ability is irrelevant. You played college football? You're just the kind of person this investment bank wants to hire. The scratch golfer enjoys a real status in the office regardless of limited intellectual ability. Sometimes, in fact, your prowess seems all the more impressive for being completely unrelated to your regular activities. Think of how actress Geena Davis enhanced her reputation by making it to the qualifying finals for the Olympic archery team. A movie star, *and* a world-class archer!

Not so long ago, people bragged about their lack of prowess in handling office equipment. No one would admit to knowing how to type, and only secretaries, apparently, could plumb the mystery of the simple fax machine. Given today's technology obsession, however, such lack of prowess would make you seem backward and out of touch. Proclaim your mastery of all the latest equipment; you'll get left behind if you can't handle E-mail, the Internet, conference calls, a cell phone. Of course, strive to have enough power that you don't *have* to use these things—someone else takes care of that—but you should never hint that you're baffled by them. Even if Chairman and CEO of Random House Peter Olson refuses to type his own E-mails (he dictates to an assistant), he should never confess that he doesn't know how to use E-mail. Always create the impression that you could handle any function that anyone else is doing.

> **TIP:** Look for ways to highlight (or inflate) your prowess. Richard Wagner reportedly put small mistakes into his orchestrations, such as putting a B natural in place of a B flat in one player's part. Then, as if he could discern the half-tone error, he'd halt a performance at the music's height to correct the mistake.

But I don't have any exceptional abilities, you may be thinking. I'm not an outstanding performer at my job, and I don't have any flashy hobbies, either. Don't worry. Other sources of power succeed as well, so draw on those.

Special note on *foot-washing*

If you clamber to a position of significant power over others, and particularly if you exhibit the attraction of prowess, you'll benefit from people's urge to pay homage. People long to defer—even truckle—to their betters. Call this impulse *foot-washing,* after the gratification that Mary Magdalene felt at kneeling and washing Jesus' feet.

You're surrounded by people who delight in giving you special treatment. Everywhere you go, people want to please you: they drive themselves to the limit to accomplish your commands, they offer conciliatory gestures, laugh at your jokes, allow themselves to be persuaded by you, whisper informative gossip, and literally back away to give you more personal space. Why do waiters at a catered dinner party squabble for the privilege of serving a visiting tycoon? Why does an American woman thrill at the prospect of curtsying to the Queen of England? Why do drivers cheer at the sight of the presidential motorcade sweeping by, even when they've been trapped in traffic for the last hour? They feel the pleasure of foot-washing.

A divine assurance and an imperious complaisance, as of one habituated to require subservience and to take no thought for the morrow, is the birthright and the criterion of the gentleman at his best; and it is in popular apprehension even more than that, for this demeanour is accepted as an intrinsic attribute of superior worth, before which the base-born commoner delights to stoop and yield.

THORSTEIN VEBLEN,
THE THEORY OF LEISURE CLASS

Unlike sycophants, foot-washers have no expectation of reward or reciprocation; they yearn merely to pledge their allegiance to a superior. Accept offers of fealty with grace, and without surprise.

The foot-washing impulse is both noble and base. It is noble because it is an expression of reverence for exalted ideals, such as patriotism or genius or justice, as embodied in an individual. Foot-washing is a way to participate, however humbly—where the only service is to acknowledge and serve the great.

But foot-washing is also base. You shudder at the ardent faces of those who stoop and scrape before you. Perhaps their foot-washing is an expression of thoughtful respect; or perhaps it's nothing more than the blind worship of worldly trappings (wealth, fame, beauty, birth) and the longing to associate with the mighty, if only as an idolater. There is a thrill in subservience.

Foot-washers, in all innocence, often corrupt the very person whom they revere as superior. Few can withstand the smiling crowds, their rapturous delight in every gesture and word, their flirtations. Such admiration tempts out from suppression your least admirable

To us [household servants], then, the world was a wheel, revolving with these great houses at the hub, their mighty decisions emanating out to all else, rich and poor, who revolved around them. It was the aspiration of all those of us with professional ambition to work our way as close to this hub as we were each of us capable. For we were, as I say, an idealistic generation for whom the question was not simply one of how well one practised one's skills, but *to what end* one did so; each of us harboured the desire to make our own small contribution to the creation of a better world, and saw that, as professionals, the surest means of doing so would be to serve the great gentlemen of our times in whose hands civilization had been entrusted.

KAZUO ISHIGURO, *THE REMAINS OF THE DAY*

qualities, until you find yourself indulging every mood of irritation, peremptoriness, promiscuity. If you're not careful, your behavior will degenerate as you become accustomed to the fact that the foot-washers are blind to your faults, or will excuse them, or even deem them wonderful. You begin to change.

5. EXPLOIT THE *ATTRACTION OF PRESENCE*

Just as people are attracted to prowess, they are attracted to *presence*—the quality that combines confidence, self-assurance, ease, and grace. Your presence exerts a magnetic force on the people around you and is therefore a source of power.

Presence can be directed outward or inward. If you possess the rare ability to blast that quality outward, you possess *charisma*. If you're instead equipped to direct it inward, over yourself—your fears, ambitions, insecurities—you've achieved self-possession.

CHARISMA

The most glorious source of power is charisma—but if you're not born with charisma, forget it.

Charisma is the ability to exert an overwhelming personal force; you draw people to you, so that they wish to touch you, follow you, emulate you. Your followers perform beyond expectations; they alter their fundamental values and beliefs; they feel exhilarated, resolute, and eager to sacrifice their personal interests for the sake of you and the goals you've set—even when you offer nothing but blood, toil, tears, and sweat.

What are the qualities of charismatics? Mesmerizing, courageous, articulate, energetic, attractive, artistic, and sexy. Plus that special grace. One journalist described the eighteen-year-old Muhammad Ali, the former Cassius Clay, in 1960, as "the most vivid, the most alive figure I'd ever met. It was like meeting a great actor or an electrifying statesman, some sort of figure that had a glow, an energy inside him, and you knew right away that you'd be hearing about him for years."

Winston Churchill, himself a charismatic, described at length the charisma of his great contemporary "Lawrence of Arabia," T. E. Lawrence: "Here was a man in whom there existed not only an immense capacity for service, but that touch of genius which everyone recognizes and no one can define. Alike in his great period of adventure and command or in these later years of self-suppression and self-imposed eclipse, he always reigned over those with whom he came in contact. They felt themselves in the presence of an extraordinary being. They felt his latent reserves of force and will-power were beyond measurement. If he roused himself to action, who should say what crisis he could not surmount or quell?"

If you have charisma, you don't need institutional position to be effective; however, you might choose, like Martin Luther King, Jr., to combine personal power with organizational leadership. With or without such a base, you have a force that far surpasses your particular organization.

Leaders with this kind of charisma can inspire their followers to pursue profound change. And it's not always change for the good—consider Adolf Hitler.

There is a lesser brand of charisma, whose holders inspire the same near-worship and endless fascination, but without the intense purposefulness provoked by leaders like Mohandas Gandhi. Princess Diana's charisma arose out of her fairy-tale transformation and position, not her revolutionary vision of society or her "good works"—despite what her adulators claim. (Note that Diana's charisma was undiminished by the loss of most of her dynastic role by divorce.)

You can't acquire charisma; it's the product of character or fate or both. Without her fairy-tale life and powerful personality, Diana could not have won her charismatic triumph. She was the ordinary duckling turned into a glamorous swan, the maiden who married a prince. (© Bettmann/CORBIS)

If you are a charismatic, make sure you have writers and historians around you. Jesus' words were recorded by the Apostles. Jack Kennedy's brief period in office was exhaustively memorialized in the paeans of Arthur Schlesinger, Jr., Theodore Sorensen, William Manchester, Benjamin Bradlee, and others. (Their presence in his circle was no accident; Kennedy himself admitted, "Some of us think it wise to associate as much as possible with historians and cultivate their good will"). Harold Ross's reputation as an editor survives because his band of brilliant *New Yorker* writers memorialized him so well. Even Alexander the Great traveled with historians and poets to record his heroic deeds (who nicknamed him "the Great"?), but according to legend, he wept at Achilles' tomb because he had no Homer to immortalize his exploits.

Although charisma is a rare quality that must be inborn and can't be faked, there's nevertheless a considerable industry devoted to trying to teach it. Dale Carnegie's 1936 classic *How to Win Friends and Influence People* has never been out of print. Even decades after it first appeared, a person checking it out from the Library of Congress received the book with a bright pink slip:

> **BOOK—IN DEMAND**
> The long list of Senators and Representatives waiting
> for this book requires that, in fairness to them,
> it be treated as a TEN DAY BOOK i.e.,
> it is to be returned 10 days from this date so
> that it may be delivered to the
> next Senator or Representative on the Waiting List.

Who more than members of Congress would seek, in that well-loved chestnut from a salesman's Middle America, to find the secret to charisma?

Charisma is often confused with the attraction of prowess. Michael Jordan is often described as charismatic, but it was his astounding basketball ability, not his character or message or position, that riveted his fans.

Also, what many people call "charisma" is actually charm—a lesser quality, certainly, but valuable. Charm can be learned, but it requires more effort than merely addressing people by name and remembering the names of their children.

Charm in conversation

1. As William James pointed out, "The deepest principle in human nature is the craving to be appreciated." Ask questions that show not only that you remember where your interlocutor works, but that you know all about her recent triumph; or that you think his opinion is particularly worth seeking out. "You've traveled in Russia, John. What do you think of the current situation?"

2. Talk to people about themselves, and they'll listen for hours. Look people in the face (avoid eye stray, see Chapter 2) and pay

attention. Find a way to be genuinely curious, because if you're like most people, you can't successfully fake interest for long.

3. Don't monopolize conversations. Guard against launching into a long story with no particular point, or including too much detail. "So then in December of 1995—or was it January of 1995? I mean, January of 1996. No, it must have been, actually, November of 1995, because I remember it happened just after my aunt had to go to the hospital, and that was the day before Thanksgiving. So anyway…"

4. Have something to say. Keep up with current events, both momentous (peace-keeping missions) and frivolous (Emmy Awards). Cultivate some specialty—you'll find that a single, narrow interest (skiing, fishing, the Civil War) has surprising broadening powers.

5. Poke fun at yourself. Put others at ease by laughing at your own mishaps—forgetting to bring identification to the airport so you missed that crucial flight; tripping over a curb into a full sprawl in the first five minutes of an important date; being the only man at a wedding who didn't realize that you're supposed to know to wear a tuxedo to a 7:30 P.M. ceremony without any instruction on the invitation.

6. People find nothing more charming than being proven right in a disagreement. Be quick to admit that you were wrong. "Yes, yes, I remember now. You're right, for a while Chris Rock *was* a regular member of *Saturday Night Live*."

7. People are suckers for flattery. A perfunctory "I love your dress" isn't as effective as a more thoughtful comment, however. "You sound like you know a lot about it. Do you have a background in the field?" "Did you play sports in college?" Laugh at other people's jokes.

Charm in presence

1. Exude energy and good spirits. Don't brood over past insults or slights. People are inclined to like anyone who seems to like them, so adopt a friendly attitude.

2. Cultivate *sprezzatura*, an easy manner (see Special Note, later in this

chapter). Don't get flustered over petty uncertainties—who should pick up the check, who should sit next to whom around a dinner table, making introductions. Don't yell at a waitress or a policeman.

3. If nothing else, make sure you're well groomed. Brush the dandruff off your shoulders, suck on a breath mint, wash your hands frequently if you have a moist, sticky handshake. And, although this seems obvious, don't indulge any disgusting habits—if your dinner companion isn't giving each bite of food a loud, suspicious sniff before putting it in his mouth, don't do that yourself.

SELF-POSSESSION

Charisma is the rarest source of power. When presence drives inward instead of outward, it assumes the more common and obtainable shape of *self-possession*—which, although it doesn't evoke charisma's violent attraction, is nevertheless magnetic. Self-possession encompasses self-knowledge and self-control. You recognize your strengths and limitations, and you have command over your own nature. Soon you have an air of distinction, of being destined for great things; others defer to you.

Self-possession protects you. Without it, you're easily consumed by vanities, insecurities, and "needs," and it's no trick for someone to outmaneuver you. Remember: The fewer your apparent needs and desires, the freer you are from others' machinations.

Self-possession liberates you from affectation, intrigue, and posturing. You don't try to safeguard your position by surrounding yourself with weaklings. Maybe you fail as a number-cruncher, or as a savvy politician, or as a glad-hander. "Fine," you say to yourself, "I'll hire someone to do that for me." You're not threatened by the capable people around you, and so your power grows. You're not agitated by the need to dominate. Because you have control of yourself, you can consider the feelings and thoughts of the people around you; this understanding of your colleagues will enhance your power.

Self-possession (or lack of it) matters, because personality matters at every level. It

> **TIP:** Your being at ease puts others at ease. Don't hide your background (religion, race, gender, nationality, education, hometown), and don't talk incessantly about it either. Pretension, not honesty, elicits snobbery.

matters that the billion-dollar conglomerate's CEO dreads conflict, or that the renowned sculptor hates the press, or that the flag-waving immigrant engineer cares passionately about advancing American technology.

For many powerful people, a fateful lack of self-possession condemns them to disgrace; some invisible trip wire—greed, drink, promiscuity, paranoia—waits to destroy them. As President Reagan's speechwriter Peggy Noonan warned, "If the head of the NSC [National Security Council] is not relaxed about his personal powers, beware: He will attempt to show his mastery through some scheme that will more likely illustrate his inadequacies. If the new chief has an ego to beat the band, beware: He'll trip over his vanity, and take the president tumbling with him."

Conversely, attaining self-possession lifts others into triumph. In a 1927 letter, Lord Winterton observed about Winston Churchill, who, at age fifty-two, was certainly no callow youth: "The remarkable thing about [Churchill] is the way in which he has suddenly acquired, quite late in Parliamentary life, an immense fund of tact, patience, good humour and banter on almost all occasions; no one used to 'suffer fools ungladly' more than Winston, now he is friendly and accessible to everyone, both in the House and in the lobbies, with the result that he has become what he never was before the war, very popular in the House generally—a great accretion to his already formidable Parliamentary power."

> There are five qualities which are dangerous in the character of a general.
> 1. If reckless, he can be killed . . .
> 2. If cowardly, captured . . .
> 3. If quick-tempered you can make a fool of him . . .
> 4. If he has too delicate a sense of honour you can calumniate him . . .
> 5. If he has a compassionate nature you can harass him . . .
>
> SUN-TZU, *The Art of War*

USEFUL DEFECTS AND HARMFUL VIRTUES

Presence allows you to harness your defects, as well as your virtues. Many wielders of power exhibit enormous flaws, but successfully compel these faults to contribute to, rather than detract from, their power. Did Richard Nixon become president *despite* his insecurity and mistrust, or at least partly *because* of these traits? As Alexis de Tocqueville put it: "We succeed in enterprises which demand the positive qualities we possess, but we excel at those which also make use of our *defects*." What are your faults? Spendthrift? Excellent. (Copy media mogul Steve Ross, who cloaked profligacy in generosity and won the profitable hearts of Barbra Streisand, Steven Spielberg, and others.) Take offense easily? Perfect. (Copy basketball superstar Michael Jordan, who used other players' insults to motivate himself to play harder.)

Many observers fail to recognize that the same traits—gregariousness, skepticism, zealotry, trust—serve contradictory purposes, at once fueling success and provoking failure. Consider the last lines of George Stephanopoulos's memoir of his work in Clinton's campaigns and administration: "Now I watched from far away, enjoying

Put your faults, as well as your virtues, to work for you. Michael Jordan is quick to take offense; he used his thin skin to keep his supercompetitive nature at its highest pitch. (© Reuters Newmedia Inc./CORBIS)

the show but wondering too. Wondering what might have been—if only this good president had been a better man." Stephanopoulos doesn't contemplate that perhaps Clinton couldn't have been as good a president had he been a "better man": the qualities that brought him down bore him up. After all, the same ego, ambition, and grandiosity that suit people for leadership can disfigure their characters. And what compels us in our leaders? The excesses of Lyndon Johnson or the wholesomeness of Jimmy Carter?

TRUE RULE

Some disgust us with their virtues;
others attract us even in their faults.

Virtues, by the same token, can work to your detriment. One of Franklin Roosevelt's qualities was his tremendous sympathy, but this virtue hobbled him when it kept him from firing incompetent figures in his administration.

Know yourself, and control yourself. Nothing aids you more in the conduct of your life than comprehension of your own weaknesses.

Every excellency, and every virtue, has its kindred vice or weakness; and if carried beyond certain bounds, sinks into one or the other. Generosity often runs into profusion, economy into avarice, courage into rashness, caution into timidity, and so on:—insomuch that, I believe, there is more judgment required, for the proper conduct of our virtues, than for avoiding their opposite vices.

LORD CHESTERFIELD, *LETTERS TO HIS SON*

6. CAPITALIZE ON YOUR MONEY

Money buys power. For instruction on how to use your money to get power, see Chapter 11, "Money for Power or Fame."

7. SPOTLIGHT YOUR FAME

In our media age, fame confers power; yesterday's *éminence grise* today wears fire-engine red and TV makeup. To bolster your power, exploit the spotlight. See Chapter 16 on how to use your fame to acquire power.

8. FAN THE FLAMES OF SEX

Sex can be an effective—though precarious—way to grab power. See Chapters 19, 20, and 21 on how to use sex to bolster your power.

Special note on *sprezzatura*

Whether you're using power, money, fame, or sex, always radiate *sprezzatura*—that is, make the difficult appear easy. Give the impression that your accomplishments are the result of graceful, spontaneous action. Never admit to effort. Your actions must appear uncontrived and nonchalant.

One of the reasons that "preppy" culture continually fascinates—both before and after its 1980s heyday—is its emphasis on *sprezzatura*. As Lisa Birnbach's *The Official Preppy Handbook* noted, "Since Preppies want always to appear capable and comfortable, everything they do or wear must look as if it were done without a second thought. Forget about the time practicing a bow tie knot or forehand topspin return; the important issue is that it looks like a cinch in public." Whether or not you want to emulate the preppy style of dress, you should emulate this quality of ease. Everything—playing the piano, telling a joke, reading a spreadsheet, throwing a party—should come effortlessly.

Never admit to calculation or ulterior motives.

> Everyone knows how difficult it is to accomplish some unusual feat perfectly, and so facility in such things excites the greatest wonder; whereas, in contrast, to labour at what one is doing . . . shows an extreme lack of grace and causes everything, whatever its worth, to be discounted.
>
> BALDESAR CASTIGLIONE,
> *THE BOOK OF THE COURTIER*

> In high school I was athletic and thus, to a certain extent, popular. However, I worked unduly hard at it, at sports, with very little *sprezzatura,* which made me extremely unpopular among the dozen or so really popular, athletic people. Why? Because I made popularity or grace look like something less than a pure gift.
>
> DAVID SHIELDS, *REMOTE*

Learn from the bad example of one indiscreet art patron who confessed to *Worth* magazine that she collected art solely to become a museum trustee. Hide your struggles to master unspoken rules. For example, that job seeker should never have asked his Goldman Sachs interviewer, "How many eyelets should I have on my shoes? I heard of a guy who lost a job because he had the wrong number." Never admit to small-minded concern for such minutiae. (That's *not* to say that such minutiae don't matter. Four, five, or six eyelets are standard; to have fewer or more eyelets is trendy.)

Appear to take for granted your own power, and other people's willingness to serve you. It's all the natural result of your character and inborn ability. Consider the contest between Jack Kennedy and Richard Nixon. Both were natural cutthroat politicians—but Nixon showed the effort, the strain, the patchy TV makeup, and the Madison Avenue techniques; Kennedy was just as much the product of artifice, but he hid it from his audience beneath a cool mask.

Never undermine your exertions by showing visible effort. For example, while addressing people by name is a good way to make them feel appreciated and important, don't pour it on too thick. Overusing the comma-name-comma construction—"Let me give you an example, Pat, of how I make my decisions"—reveals your seeming friendliness to be affected, and therefore, insincere and overworked.

● ● ●

Once you've achieved some measure of power by drawing on the eight sources discussed above, you realize that your power must be *felt* in order to be *perceived*. But how do you make your power evident to the people around you? You must demonstrate your power.

CHAPTER THREE

DEMONSTRATIONS OF POWER

You must assert your power for it to be perceived. That process is often complex and subtle, but fortunately there are also quick, direct ways to brandish your power. The following thirteen methods are among the most popular.

However, although effective, some methods described below provoke hostility and should be used sparingly. Note, too, that when people see a naked assertion of power, they resist, and therefore the one wielding it loses effectiveness. For instance, gratuitously cc'ing the boss on an E-mail you've sent to a colleague to demand that a late report be on your desk by Friday is such blatant power-grubbing that you're sure to make an enemy.

Change your strategies as your power grows. As you move up in rank, methods become more sophisticated, so avoid the more obvious ploys—at least until you've accrued so much power that people must accommodate any outrage. When you first started, you checked and double-checked your E-mails before sending them out; now you feel free to mark your outgoing E-mails as "high priority," even when there's no real urgency, to emphasize that recipients must drop every-thing to answer you immediately; once you've acquired a *lot* of power, you'll no longer do anything so obvious; you won't need to.

Power strategies must also adapt to changing times. Twenty years ago you would have left your jacket draped over the back of your chair to create the illusion that you were working late; two years ago you would have programmed an E-mail message to mail at 4:00 A.M., to create the illusion you were still busy at your desk. Now that those ruses fool no one, you'll have to invent something new. (Until, of course, you have enough power that you make a show of leaving early.)

If you're looking for a quick way to signal your power, try one of the methods described below, or even better, use several methods in combination. Never rest. It's not enough to gain a foothold and to show off what you've achieved; you must continually work to maintain and expand your power. Demonstrating your power offers a critical advantage—because power begets power, your *perceived* power snowballs to build greater actual power.

THIRTEEN WAYS TO DEMONSTRATE YOUR POWER

1. Impunity
   - Prodigious or unnecessary spending
   - Intimidating rages
   - Arbitrary punishment and reward
   - Imposition of your idiosyncrasies on others

2. Ceremony and privilege

3. Consumption of resources

4. Rewarding friends and punishing enemies

5. Steamrolling the competition

6. Travel

7. Time

8. Safety

9. Speech

10. Office

11. Telephone

12. Cash

13. Power masterstroke

1. IMPUNITY

Demonstrate your power by flaunting the fact that, whatever the rules for everyone else, *you* can get away with anything. You're free to indulge in misdeeds and personal whims where others must be cautious and considerate—you're too powerful to be punished. There are several effective ways to advertise your impunity.

Spend a fortune, and charge it to the company or government. Most people aren't able to charge excessive expenses to their employer—but you do. Make this strategy even more effective by spending on important people, in the form of gifts or parties or perks.

<u>Sample power move:</u> To mark the 1961 opening of the Robert Moses Power Dam, Moses ordered extravagant hospitality, including chartered planes, excursions, and a reception featuring a fountain of martinis and a fountain of manhattans—all at government expense.

<u>Sample power move:</u> Occidental Petroleum head Armand Hammer used that corporation to bankroll his personal philanthropies and to buy works of art. Occidental also subsidized his annual birthday party, his personal lawyers, his bodyguards, his Boeing 727.

Indulge in intimidating rages. Most people must keep their more unpleasant qualities in check, or face the repercussions. You don't. Show that you don't have to exercise normal self-control and, at the same time, drive others to yield to you to avoid your anger.

<u>Sample power move:</u> Legendary Hollywood studio head Lew Wasserman's anger was so ferocious—he'd yell until saliva spilled from his mouth—that men were known to faint or throw up from the terror of a tongue-lashing. This threat contributed to the absolute authority he maintained.

<u>Sample power move:</u> Hollywood powerhouse Dawn Steel warned a prospective employee, "The last [assistant] left because I called her a cunt. Would that be a problem for you?"

Mete out arbitrary punishment and reward. Generally people feel an obligation to keep up at least a semblance of justice, rationality, and proportionality; you feel free to be inconsistent, arbitrary, and impulsive. Keep everyone around you in a constant state of uncertainty.

[Sulla's] rapacity was great, but his generosity was greater; he gave promotion for no apparent reason and was just as unreasonable in the way in which he would insult people . . . we may conclude that he was by nature savage and unforgiving, but was capable of controlling his natural severity by considerations of self-interest.

PLUTARCH, *LIVES*

Sample power move: Movie producer Don Simpson fired assistants who put cream in his coffee when he was dieting, or who put nonfat milk in his coffee when he wasn't, or who toasted his bagels for too long, or who used the wrong kind of mustard.

Force your idiosyncrasies and convenience on other people. Show them that they must endure whatever you do. They can't assert their modesty, or squeamishness, or their own convenience, because only your preferences matter.

Sample power move: Lyndon Johnson compelled aides to talk to him while he was on the toilet. He made them strip and swim nude in the White House pool during breaks from meetings. He'd call a halt to his White House staff's policy work so they could spend a half hour on a desperate hunt for a specific brand of peanut brittle.

TIP: Demonstrate your impunity by bringing a child to an adult event. Show up at a formal wedding with your toddler or bring your newborn grandchild to a lecture. Would anyone dare ask you to leave?

Sample power move: Media mogul Barry Diller once refused to begin his luncheon speech until everyone had finished their meal because he didn't like to hear the "clinking" of silverware while he was talking. It was worth the wait to hear him speak—to an appropriately hushed room.

Demand that your day unfold according to your habits and schedule, no matter how inconvenient or expensive the accommodation.

Sample power move: For more than two decades, by contract, Elizabeth Taylor refused to work during her menstrual period.

But don't make the mistake of overestimating your impunity (see Chapter 4's discussion of "a sense of invulnerability"). Learn from Leona Helmsley and her notorious declaration, "Only little people pay taxes." She learned otherwise when she was sent to jail. Talking in a similar vein about his nightclub Studio 54, Steve Rubell confided, "It's a cash business, and you don't have to worry about the IRS." Soon after he was raided by a team of government agents known for throwing tax evaders in jail for long sentences. Carefully gauge what liberties your power permits.

2. CEREMONY AND PRIVILEGE

Ceremony and privilege reinforce your power, by illustrating the deference that is your due. (Some are so important that they're discussed in their own sections, which follow.) Privileges such as the key to the executive washroom, the reserved parking space, the best seats at a black-tie benefit, or the umbrella suspended over your head the moment you step outside are exclusive, add to your personal convenience or pleasure, and give you a conspicuous status signal. Be sure to display the prerogative of your position: the gavel, miter, toque, or lab coat.

> Sample power move: In the Nixon White House, H. R. Haldeman ordered the civilian guards, who sat as they watched over the inner White House hallways, to spring to attention whenever a member of the White House senior staff passed.

> Sample power move: During World War II, when even King George VI tried to subsist like his ordinary subjects, Winston Churchill insisted on unlimited rations and a full hot bath each evening.

Some privileges come about informally, by tacit understanding, but are followed with iron discipline nevertheless. There was a time when investment bankers at Morgan Stanley didn't feel comfortable wearing suspenders to work unless they'd reached the upper echelons. At *Vogue* under the intimidating direction of Anna Wintour, junior staffers weren't to speak unless spoken to (one young editor

Government Perk Quiz

Many high government officials could earn far more if they jumped to the private sector; the perks and honorifics of office assuage the pain of lost income. The thrill of discovering that you can decorate your office with your picks from the National Gallery's undisplayed art treasures, or realizing that flags will be flown at half-mast if you die, makes it easier to take the pay cut. Match the prerogative to the government office.

a. Portal-to-portal car service

b. Free airport parking in a VIP space

c. Mailing at public expense

d. Free use of the Kennedy Center's presidential box

e. Personal signature printed on currency

f. Private access to first-run movies

g. Lifetime office subsidy

i. Current president

ii. White House aides

iii. Congressmen, justices, diplomats

iv. Secretary of the Treasury

v. Congressmen

vi. Cabinet officers, top White House staff, the Chief Justice

vii. Former presidents

Answers: a-vi; b-iii; c-v; d-ii; e-iv; f-i; g-vii.

was scolded by Wintour's assistant after she greeted Wintour in the elevator).

Don't make the mistake of thinking that you can win appreciation and respect by relinquishing the privileges of power. Ceremony and perks amplify your aura of dignity and *gravitas*. Because people prefer an aura of greatness and mystery around their leaders, preserve some inaccessibility.

Without the trappings of power, you lose some of the substance of power. As part of his crusade against the "Imperial Presidency,"

Jimmy Carter (he was sworn in as Jimmy instead of his baptismal name "James") renounced some of the traditions of the office: he silenced the playing of "Hail to the Chief" at his arrivals; he carried his own garment bag. But these well-intentioned renunciations diminished his stature. Carter thought the American public would appreciate a common-man approach, but they didn't; Ronald Reagan's reaffirmation of pomp and circumstance—he had such reverence for the Oval Office that he wouldn't take off his coat in that room—was welcomed.

> For be a man's intellectual superiority what it will, it can never assume the practical, available supremacy over other men, without the aid of some sort of external arts and entrenchments, always, in themselves, more or less paltry and base. . . . Such large virtue lurks in these small things when extreme political superstitions invest them, that in some royal instances even to idiot imbecility they have imparted potency. But when, as in the case of Nicholas the Czar, the ringed crown of geographical empire encircles an imperial brain; then, the plebian herds crouch abased before the tremendous centralization.
>
> HERMAN MELVILLE, *MOBY DICK*

Initially, Bill Clinton repeated Carter's mistakes by trying to act the part of the regular guy; he stripped away some of the dignity of his office, for example, by wearing jogging shorts so that undignified (and unflattering) bare-legged photos appeared on the evening news. Eventually his staff realized that, as aide George Stephanopoulos put it, "maintaining a slightly regal aura in office is as effective as the populist touch during a campaign . . . We started playing 'Hail to the Chief' at all public ceremonies." In his second term, of course, maintaining presidential dignity was to become a much more serious problem than hiding chubby legs.

You may not always succeed, but do what you can to aggrandize your entitlements. Chief Justice Warren Burger worked to improve his transportation privileges—he did manage to expand the Supreme Court's limousine service and security force, but he was turned down repeatedly when he asked to use the presidential Air Force planes.

What can you do? You might not be able to demand limousine

service, but you can move to a bigger office when you get a promotion. Explain that you don't eat meat, and in fact, don't like to watch anyone eating meat, so can everyone's lunch be vegetarian only? *Thanks.*

At the same time, never allow yourself to be seen quibbling over privileges or proper ceremony: insisting on the dignity of your office makes it appear that you haven't earned it. Then–House Speaker Newt Gingrich invited ridicule—and he got it—when he groused that President Clinton snubbed him on the Air Force One flight to Israel for Prime Minister Yitzhak Rabin's funeral. Gingrich's complaints? He was forced to use the plane's rear stairs, and Clinton didn't invite him up front to talk. Gingrich looked even worse when he confessed that he'd triggered a government shutdown in part to spite President Clinton for these slights.

Once granted a prerogative, exercise it with confidence. Grab a seat at the head table; refuse to let your assistant go home before you do—you couldn't possibly take the time to print out a document yourself. Initially, Bill Clinton's traditional presidential military salute had a tentative look; finally National Security Advisor Anthony Lake spoke to him about it. Then his gesture became more assured.

A satisfying privilege of power is that you never need introduce yourself. No business cards and name tags; everyone knows who you are. In fact, your name carries so much weight that many people don't address you by name; instead they use your title, such as Boss, Coach, Governor, Chief, or your initials, the way Supreme Court clerks refer to the Justices, or even by the initials of your title, the way White House aides refer to the President of the United States as POTUS. (Of course, the use of name substitutes also signals intimacy, which is an added bonus.)

3. CONSUMPTION OF RESOURCES

Consume resources: staff, office supplies, other people's time. A flurry of assistants and apparatus signals your power—both because you show that you demand and receive more than other people, and because you demonstrate that you're (apparently) working harder and producing more than other people. Appearance is everything, so be sure that your actions are visible.

Remember: don't *ask, tell.* Be polite, of course, but your message is "I'm going to need a fax on a separate phone line at home. Please arrange for someone to install it tomorrow," not "Does the company ever arrange for people to get a fax machine at home? Because if so I think that might be useful for me." And remember to insist that you *need* these things. You're not interested in self-aggrandizement, you merely want what's functional and efficient.

TIP: No prerogative is beneath your notice—even a simple "the" is worth defending. THE Metropolitan Museum of Art insists on approving any invitation listing the museum as location, to ensure that no one has the temerity to drop the "The" in front of The Museum's name. And scrupulous observers of British form insist that only the proper highborn folk get the honorary "The" before their title (capitalization of "The" is optional, except for The Queen and Queen Elizabeth The Queen Mother). And "the" makes anything sound more important: The Donald, The Yale Law School.

Use your imagination. Requisition a dictaphone, a cell phone, a laptop, a new computer program, a ticket admitting you to a high-price conference—if you're the only one who needs these things, well, you must be working harder than everyone else. (You're cutting edge, pushed to the limit.) You announce that you must have a high-speed data line set up in your office. Your coworkers are astonished; they can't imagine why you need that, and in any event, they'd never have had the temerity to make such a request. You make a favorable impression simply by asking, and if you prevail,

Checklist:

First make sure you're keeping pace with your colleagues; then try to think of additional ways to consume resources. Some suggestions:

• Salary, benefits, and bonus—ask for more money and perks than you think you deserve. Your demands will become the basis for negotiation, and in any event, it's human nature to prefer those who place a high value on themselves.

• Administrative support—the bigger your staff, the better. With extra hands you can do more, and soon you'll need even more additional staff. Remember, resources consumed by your staff count as resources consumed by you, so encourage them to make their own demands.

• A multitude of stationery printed with your name and title—business cards, "with the compliments of" notes, formal stationery, sticky notes, buck slips (what are buck slips? long, narrow slips of heavy-stock stationery, with your name at the bottom and company logo at the top, an absolute necessity in Hollywood). Once you have every type of stationery imaginable, demand that it be engraved instead of printed.

• Transportation services—don't fly coach if your colleagues are flying business or first class.

• Access to perks like the gym, executive dining room, tickets to basketball games or Broadway shows or wine tastings—even if you don't take advantage of such things, assert your claim to them. (Added bonus: giving away those tickets demonstrates that you can afford not to take advantage of such perks, and that you've got even better things to do.)

you've demonstrated your worth gauged by the resources you've commanded. You silently congratulate yourself on your victory, and after all, that indispensable high-speed data line will come in handy to check your private portfolio's stock values.

Demand that arrangements be altered to suit your specifications—your arcane filing system, your notion of how to reorganize the bureaucracy, your preferred method of recording expenses, all must be accommodated. Redecorate if possible, order more furniture (even if it's only a desk lamp), or at least rearrange what you have. You've got special needs. If your demands are wasteful, so much the better. Richard Nixon kept a blazing fire in his office throughout the hottest part of the summer. The fire crackled away while the air-conditioner pumped full blast.

Expand the number of people working for you. You consume resources, and at the same time, you get the support needed to conjure the impression that you've got superhuman ability. You've got someone to write a persuasive editorial for your signature, to propose the first draft of your speech, to present memos with three action options for your consideration. Someone else keeps track of important dates so that you can send out thoughtful notes, crunches numbers so that you can make an instinctive judgment, researches the issues to keep you well-read and broad-minded. This kind of outsourcing is nothing new: Roman senators used *nomenclators,* whose function was to hiss into their ears the names of approaching VIPs.

TIP: Although a perennial favorite, tardiness is a tricky way to demonstrate power. On the one hand, it's a highly effective way to consume resources—other people's time and energy. Also, being late makes you seem busy, and therefore important. On the other hand, it's so well understood to be a power move, and so irritating, that you're often better off being prompt. So use tardiness cautiously.

TIP: Julius Caesar imbedded his mark in the calendar by altering the number of days and months in a year. You, too, should think big. The more grand, costly, and inconvenient the change you demand, the greater the power you command.

4. REWARDING FRIENDS AND PUNISHING ENEMIES

Rewarding friends keeps them loyal and grateful, and by improving their position, you help your own. FDR administration powerhouse

> **TIP:** Consume resources on the job even before you're hired. When offered a soft drink or coffee during a job interview, be sure to take it. Borrow a pad of paper. Ask to use the phone if you arrive early or when you're ready to leave.

and Supreme Court Justice Felix Frankfurter plucked out and promoted rising stars, the "hot dogs," and installed them throughout the Roosevelt administration at the time of the New Deal.

Punishing enemies weakens those who oppose you and, at the same time, discourages potential enemies from taking steps against you. FBI Director J. Edgar Hoover was ruthless in his punishment of his enemies—that is, anyone who crossed him—no matter how unimportant the issue or for whatever reason. But be careful: better to let an enemy go unpunished than to try to punish an enemy and fail. When you strike at a king, you must kill him.

5. STEAMROLLING THE COMPETITION

Because the exercise of power requires you to assert yourself over others, power demands hierarchy. You must work to move up the chain of command. Here are ten techniques to elbow competitors out of your way.

1. **Take command.** *Newsweek* editor Maynard Parker was known for his absolute assumption of authority. Once, after arriving late at a dinner party, he sat down, without a pause, at the head of the table. Later Parker realized he had taken the seat of his host, who had gotten up to carve the roast.

2. **Control the atmosphere.** Carefully plant spontaneous enthusiasm. Robert Moses stacked meetings with his claque, to drown out the voice of anyone who would oppose him.

3. **Create a bidding war for yourself.** Say you have job offers from several prestigious law firms. To distinguish yourself from the throngs of other first-year associates, pretend to be unable to decide between two rival firms. The dinners, lunches, and phone calls devoted to helping you make up your mind will raise your standing in both firms.

4. **Make thoughtful gestures.** Your thoughtfulness shows your interest in someone else—always a smart move—and implies intimacy. Former President George Bush and General Electric CEO Jack Welch were longtime masters of the handwritten note. Gift-giving is of paramount importance in Hollywood.

5. **Distinguish yourself by your command of your subject.** Never underestimate the power of being the best prepared and informed. Bill Clinton astonishes supporters and opponents alike with his command of details.

6. **Leverage a seemingly powerless organization into a power base.** In the early days of his career, Lyndon Johnson transformed the moribund "Little Congress" of congressional staffers into a true power center.

7. **Radiate energy.** Exceptional energy gives you an air of unceasing, brilliant dedication that distinguishes you from your colleagues. (Energy includes both frenetic activity and motionless concentration.) Consider the infamous junk-bond financier Michael Milken, who brooked ridicule to wear a miner's hat on the commuter train each morning, so he could use its light to read corporate reports and lose no opportunity for study. Furthermore, in the face of two equally good performances, the more energetic person captures more interest.

8. **Stake your claim.** As part of his campaign to succeed Robert Gottlieb as editor-in-chief of Simon and Schuster, executive editor Michael Korda argued that he was entitled to occupy Gottlieb's empty office until a successor was named. Before it was known who would get the job, Korda had moved into that office, painted it blue, ordered a blue office couch and carpeting to match, and

> **TIP:** Whether or not it's true, hint about how little sleep you need—it's believed that the most successful people get by on only three or four hours a night: Bill Clinton, Thomas Edison, Martha Stewart, Mel Karmazin (who, it is said, doesn't even need an alarm clock). Or apply the *principle of dis-expectation* (see Chapter 3) and boast—like Amazon.com founder Jeff Bezos or Netscape president Marc Andreessen—that you get more than eight hours of sleep each night.

even a blue typewriter, to enforce his claim. Soon he was given the title to accompany the office.

9. **Court controversy.** Set yourself apart, dramatize yourself, by picking a good fight. You may be unpopular, or branded a troublemaker, but who cares? As editor of the restrained *New Yorker,* Tina Brown shook up her readership with controversial covers: a cartoon of the Easter Bunny crucified on a 1040 long form; a drawing of a bearded Hasidic man kissing a black woman in dreadlocks. The buzz was tremendous.

10. **Thrust yourself in Fortune's path.** Even though most powerful people, if thoughtful, realize the enormous role that luck has played in their ascent, don't rely on Fortune. As Richard Nixon observed, "It is only when you take big risks that you are around to cash in on luck."

6. TRAVEL

Your method of travel is a sure indicator of your power. Flying by private or government jet—or, at the very least, first class—is a power statement. Jack Welch, CEO of General Electric, negotiated to guarantee lifetime access to the company jet. In New York City, the only way to get around is in a chauffeured car; in Los Angeles, you drive your own car (your contract provides you with a car allowance), but someone else parks it.

Demand that others come to you or, at the very least, meet you halfway—particularly important in cities with formidable in-town driving distances.

Sample power move: John Sununu, Bush's chief of staff, used his power to commandeer more than seventy-five flights on military planes, including trips to the dentist and ski slopes, and to use a White House limousine to travel to New York for a stamp auction. (However, Sununu made the mistake of overreaching, and these actions eventually contributed to his ejection from office.)

Sample power move: Hollywood stars like Madonna, Warren Beatty, Robert Redford, and Arnold Schwarzenegger appropriate a studio's private jet to demonstrate their Hollywood clout—and for the added convenience, of course.

7. TIME

Underscore the supreme value of *your* time. Someone else dials your phone, handles the contracts, books the flights, outlines options, drives your car, takes your dog to the vet, digests newspapers and memoranda to speed your review. The people around you dedicate a huge amount of *their* time on elaborate measures to conserve a snippet of *your* time.

Sample power move: James P. Rubin, as State Department spokesman under Madeleine Albright, made a habit of being the last person to join the conference call for the daily State Department briefing—keeping several high-level officials, including White House spokesman Michael McCurry, waiting for him.

Sample power move: Pete Peterson required his Lehman Brothers partners to ride uptown or out to the airport with him, only to ignore them as he talked on the phone or read memos.

Even if your time isn't in heavy demand, orchestrate that impression. Get interrupted by a phone call during a meeting. End the meeting in a rush to demonstrate your crush of pressing commitments.

As your power increases, your retinue expands to take over more of your functions; they liberate you to do nothing except think about problems at the highest level. Someone else worries about keeping track of your briefcase, your airplane tickets and passport, your keys. You never waste your time taking notes or reading an entire document.

TRUE RULE

The more power you accrue, the less you do.

<u>**Check your power status:**</u>
Your schedule is the written record of whom you see and how you
spend your time. Its physical appearance is a gauge of your power.
Where do you stand?

Low power:
You keep track of your own schedule.

Medium power:
Someone else types up your schedule and juggles conflicts.

Medium-high power:
Your schedule is elaborately produced for you, along with additional
information, such as every telephone number you might need,
description of destinations and events, packing tips, where to park,
and so on, so that you're prepared for any contingency.

High power:
The additional information drops off your schedule; it contains only
the simplest information (except that it might contain some
idiosyncratic information that you demand, such as hotel gym hours).
You don't have to move around much, because people come to you; if
you must travel, it's up to other people to worry about shepherding
you to the right place and making introductions.

Or else you don't bother with a written schedule at all. Someone is
always at hand to guide you through your day.

Super power:
Your schedule (same as above) is made available to the necessary
people, but distribution is tightly controlled so that the wrong people
can't get hold of it.

You're still in control. Your staff may be ordered to guard your
time to the minute, but *you're* free to disregard the schedule. Show
your power by chatting after a meeting, which makes you run late,
so the people scheduled for your next meeting must wait, patiently,
for their turn. Take time in the midst of a frantic day to make a long

personal call, while your staff sits and squirms. (Note that this particular power demonstration has its drawbacks. See Tip on tardiness earlier in this chapter.)

> Sample power move: During the stop in Xi'an on his 1998 state visit to China, President Clinton persisted in asking questions about the ancient terra-cotta soldiers even though his delay threatened to disrupt the day's carefully planned schedule.

8. SAFETY

You're too important to go unprotected, so take elaborate measures to guard your physical safety and privacy. The president and select cabinet members are under constant guard; CEOs pay $500,000 a year for round-the-clock protection; Hollywood celebrities get twenty-four-hour security. You need protection, too.

When picking a security force, decide whether you want the traditional conspicuous entourage or the almost-invisible defense team. Do you need a Kevlar bulletproof vest? A miniature Global Positioning System device?

> Sample power move: Even as a "nobody," businessman Ronald Perelman worried about security. Nowadays he's been known to send armed advance men to secure party sites and to protect his East Hampton property with submachine-gun-toting guards.

> Sample power move: While chief executive of Sunbeam, Al "Chainsaw" Dunlap deemed his personal safety important enough, and under threat enough, to charge the company for a bulletproof vest, a bodyguard, and a handgun for himself.

If you're not ready for an actual personal security force, use a symbolic one. Secretaries serve the protective function by controlling access to your person. Use several secretaries, if you can; you may also want to have a male secretary to suggest your need for virile protection (and also to show the extent of your dominance). Take elaborate measures to protect yourself from the elements— you're so important that neither a drop of rain nor a tiresome passerby should be allowed to disturb you.

<u>Sample power move:</u> Bush's secretary of commerce, Robert Mosbacher, set aside an entire building entrance for the exclusive use of him and his guests, and topped it with an expensive red awning running from door to curb. No risk of contact with weather or the common bureaucrat for the secretary or his visitors.

<u>Sample power move:</u> With an apparent similar reluctance to risk the rain, Ivana Trump installed a red awning from the door of her Upper East Side townhouse to the curb. Some of her neighbors—Pierre Cardin, David Geffen, and Laurance Rockefeller inhabited the same block—weren't pleased by the conspicuous innovation.

Not only do you need to be kept safe, but so do your ideas. You may want to consider the popular measure of making everyone with whom you come in contact—a person you're dating, interviewing for a job, asking for an investment, or paying to clean your house—sign a nondisclosure agreement. Your concept is *very* important and must be protected.

9. SPEECH

Adopt the confident conversational habits of power. Powerful people speak at length, set the agenda for discussion, resist interruptions, argue, joke, and laugh. They propose plans or solutions. Powerless people ask many questions, avoid argument, offer empathy, nod and smile, and above all, fail to finish their sentences.

That said, tailor your speaking style to your particular office culture. Microsoft employees mimic Bill Gates's verbal and physical idiosyncrasies, especially in his presence—they sit around the conference table leaning forward, elbows on their knees, looking ready to pounce, just as he does, and imitate his habit of nervous rocking. Does your office favor bold assertions? Careful, deliberate statements? Polite deference? Off-color jokes? Adopt the speaking style that suits your situation (usually, it's the style employed by the most powerful person).

Assert your power by what you say, as well as by the way you say it. Meetings are ripe ground for jockeying for position. Consider

---

A sampling of power statements:

- *"I don't need all the details. Let's just get to the bottom line."* (You imply that others are quibblers and small-minded technicians, while deflecting the possible need to master complicated details.)

- *"Well, these are the facts."* (You emphasize that *you* attend to hard facts, while others are distracted by prejudice, sentiment, and assumption.)

- *"You might be right."* (You seem open-minded while simultaneously undermining your interlocutor's authority and credibility.)

- *"I'm wondering about ———. Pat, please get back to me on this."* (You demonstrate your habit of reasoned decision-making, while making Pat—who may or may not actually report to you—do the necessary work and report back.)

- *"You did a great job on that, Pat!"* (You demonstrate a positive attitude, while showing that you're in the position to judge and condescend to Pat.)

- *"I think what Pat is trying to say is . . ."* (You show that you're a good listener and give credit to others, while demonstrating that you can take Pat's simple thought further than Pat could.)

- *"I can see why you might think that."* Variant: *"I used to think that too."* (You sound sympathetic, while indicating that you've moved far ahead in understanding.)

---

using the examples above to assert your power over your colleagues. But be subtle: if you're too heavy-handed, you'll arouse resentment.

You may also find that it helps to speak softly—you force others to listen with undivided attention. Richard Nixon observed that "talking loudly tends to make you much less impressive." Hollywood powerhouse Michael Ovitz is known for making people strain to hear his words. Or don't talk at all. New York real-estate mogul Jerry Speyer sometimes unnerves his interlocutors by remaining silent.

10. OFFICE

To gauge your power, people will examine your whole context—not only what responsibilities you shoulder and how other people treat you, but also the appearance and location of your office. How many power signs can you check off this list? Do you have:

- custom-built furniture?
- expensive art?
- your own conference room?
- your own dining room?
- your own bathroom, with shower, sauna?
- your own elevator?
- a prestigious position (often a corner office)?
- a breathtaking view?
- several arrangements of fresh flowers or plants?
- a phalanx of busy and protective secretaries who guard your door?
- photographs of yourself arm in arm with stars and dignitaries?
- trophies from earlier victories—Lucite deal-toys, congratulatory plaques, and the like?
- several phones scattered around the room, each with multiple phone lines?
- your Internet connection at the highest available speed?
- your dog, brought with you from home each day (or, if you want to underscore your unconventionality, your parrot or ferret)?
- ashtrays for the cigars or cigarettes you smoke (in blatant violation of the rules of your smoke-free building)?
- more privacy than others have: a buffer office between your door and the hall, or, if your floor is "newsroom" style, a closed office on the edge of the open space?
- a touch of whimsy that's unique, inventive, and expensive—like a bookshelf that spins around to reveal a full wet bar; a pinball machine; an antique dentist's chair?
- a low, squishy sofa or placement of your desk on a dais so you loom over visitors?
- *for Internet start-ups only:* a cubicle the same size as everyone else's, dominated by an expensive, ergonomically correct chair

and a flat-panel monitor and surrounded by colorful, zany art?
- *for presidential appointees only:* as many standing flags—the Stars and Stripes, the institution you serve, your home state, the different departments you oversee—as you can justify?

A power office is also remarkable for what it *lacks*. Use a desk with no drawers—or no desk at all. Put your Bloomberg terminal on your secretary's desk if you don't want it cluttering up your space; or keep it nearby, but hidden in a frame of fine wood that matches your desk. Refuse to house any filing cabinets—someone else, not you, shuffles paper. No bulletin board, no overflowing trash can, no disposable cups anywhere.

Strategic geography, of course, is always an office's most important aspect. Every institution has an area—a certain floor or corner or particular individual's office—that is the true heart of power. You must sit there, or as close as possible. Hillary Clinton understood this principle; that's why she claimed an office in the West Wing, where the president and his top staff have their offices, rather than the East Wing, which contains the social offices and is traditionally used by First Ladies.

Often a geographical description of this power center is used to

Geography Quiz
Match the institution to the location of its most powerful people.

a. President's top staff	1. 7th floor
b. Prime Minister of England	2. 8th floor
c. State Department powers	3. West Wing
d. Federal Communications Commission	4. Number 10
e. Top people at ABC *World News Tonight*	5. Building 8
f. Microsoft top brass	6. The rim

Answers: a.-3; b-4; c.-1; d.-2; e.-6; f.-5.

denote, in elegant metonymy, those who hold the power, as in: "We're going to have to run this by the Thirty-fourth Floor."

Sample power move: During the Nixon administration's first year, then-aide Daniel Patrick Moynihan passed up the opportunity to occupy a large suite of offices outside the White House to take a cramped basement office in the West Wing. "Why," he explained, "it meant I could piss standing next to Haldeman in the same toilet."

11. TELEPHONE

Exploit the telephone's power potential:

- have an assistant place your calls;
- refuse to come to the line until the other party is holding for you;
- call from car or plane to emphasize your hectic schedule;
- place calls from an impressive place, such as the White House (or better, Air Force One) or venture capitalist John Doerr's offices;
- flaunt your "golden" Rolodexes (you should have several);
- make sure you can get to a phone anywhere, including in the wilderness, by the pool, in an airplane, or on the toilet;
- have your assistant's voice, not yours, recorded on your voice-mail message;
- furnish your office with phones and have several lines;
- furnish your car with cell phones and have several lines;
- prevent others from hearing both sides of the conversation by refusing to use a speaker phone;
- don't answer a call yourself, but have your assistant respond;
- have your assistant feed you "rolling calls"—so that you don't waste a minute, several people are lined up on hold, waiting for you to pick up;
- show respect for a caller by returning a call immediately, or show disrespect by waiting or refusing to return a call;
- call at an ungodly hour;
- refuse to speak on the phone with a person of insufficient status; instead, have an assistant convey your message—even if that

means that you sit right next to your assistant in the car or at a desk and dictate what should be said into the handpiece.

> **TIP:** Keep up with the changing fashions in cell phones. You've done StarTAC and headset. Now what?

Be creative with phone use. For example, just before starting a meeting, you might tell your secretary (within earshot of your colleague): "Hold all my calls—except if George Lucas calls, put *him* through." To slight a person with whom you're meeting, take unrelated phone calls during the meeting.

<u>Sample power move:</u> The telephones at the $440-a-night Washington, D.C., power hotel, The Jefferson, have preprogrammed numbers for prosaic needs like front desk and room service, but also flatter hotel guests by including speed-dial buttons for the White House, State Department, and the Old Executive Office Building, to show that guests would naturally be expected to need those numbers at their fingertips.

Special note on the beeper

Using a beeper to demonstrate power requires some finesse, because a beeper can show either your power, or your lack of power, depending on your place in a hierarchy.

If you're still clambering to the top, by all means, use the beeper. A beeper shows that you play an essential role and that you're in constant demand. But as you move up, if you can, consider refusing to wear a beeper. That way you demonstrate that nothing can happen without you anyway, and you have innumerable people keeping track of your whereabouts.

If you're high-powered but *must* carry a beeper, or you choose to do so, leave the

> **TIP:** A way to underscore your power while using a cell phone is to say, "I don't want to discuss this over a cell phone. Call me back on a secure line when you get to the office." This emphasizes the importance of your conversation and suggests that outsiders might be interested enough to eavesdrop.

sound on. That way, you show that no matter where you are or what's going on, you're unconcerned about causing a disruption. The room is hushed while the crowd listens to the governor speak; you don't even show a flicker of dismay when a piercing beep begins to emanate from your pocket. You calmly reach in and retrieve it. (The same goes for cell phones.)

12. CASH

Never touch cash. Others must cope with the bother of money; for you, it's enough to sign your name, if that.

> Sample power move: Movie producer Robert Evans ran tabs at restaurants in Los Angeles, so a check never appeared at his table. He left without paying or leaving a tip and was billed later.

> Sample power move: Like the Queen of England, Nancy Reagan assigned an aide to carry her purse.

TIP: A common axiom of self-assertion is that you must have a firm handshake. But in some circles power-sensitive Los Angelenos violate this rule. There, the power handshake is a limp grip with a languid but rapid withdrawal. This handshake makes the person you're greeting seem overanxious and eager, and shows that you know the "secret handshake" of L.A.

> Sample power move: English empire-builder Robert Maxwell never carried money. Underlings scurried behind him to supply cash; he just reached out and took whatever he wanted. One director recalls that once, at a football match, he produced masses of change for Maxwell, who wanted to throw handfuls into the crowd.

13. POWER MASTERSTROKE

The most artful demonstration of power is the *masterstroke,* the ingenious gesture, perfectly suited to the situation, that allows you to assert yourself. Look out for opportunities to make a masterstroke—and to thwart a masterstroke made at your expense.

A masterstroke must be done right in order to succeed. For example, remembering names and faces is a popular but challenging masterstroke. "Hi, Pat!" you say to a faintly familiar face. "We met at the convention last July." Pat is sure to be impressed and pleased by this display of recognition and interest. And this feat becomes more impressive as you become more important, and presumably meet many more people. But *don't* take risks with names. In the receiving line at a White House reception honoring the nation's mayors, Ronald Reagan grasped the hand of Sam Pierce and said, "Good to see you, Mr. Mayor." Oops. Pierce had served in Reagan's cabinet as secretary for housing and urban development for more than a year.

TIP: You're talking to someone well known, or who should be known to you, but can't place the person. How can you fake your way? One safe question: "What project are you working on these days?" The word "project" covers many bases, and the use of "these days" suggests that you're familiar with a long history.

Sample power move: Writer Larry Ferguson had heard that movie producer Don Simpson could be quite intimidating— and indeed, at their first meeting, Simpson had a nine-millimeter automatic resting conspicuously on his desk. So Ferguson took the gun off the desk and field-stripped it, without a comment. Simpson got the message—a triumphant countermasterstroke by Ferguson.

Masterstrokes need not be conspicuous. Consider the detail of forgoing a coat: when landing at Orly, President Nixon noticed that French president Charles de Gaulle was coatless, so Nixon promptly shrugged off his topcoat. Nixon, perhaps, remembered the vigorous impact his rival Jack Kennedy had made with the simple gesture of delivering his inaugural address without a hat or coat despite the bitter cold (his secret: thermal underwear). President Bill Clinton copied Kennedy's masterstroke and went coatless at his own January swearing-in ceremony in 1992.

Sometimes the best masterstroke is one that softens the shock of your other power moves. Consider the star securities analyst who, after he was wooed to a new bank along with two less prominent figures, insisted that his announcement be made in its own separate press release. In order to avoid being perceived as pushy or self-aggrandizing by his future colleagues, he apologized, "Please permit me my one moment of vanity." Nicely said.

Those who have mastered power are able to exploit subtle, gracious techniques that seem counterintuitive to less sophisticated aspirants:

- **Share the credit.** Don't make the mistake of thinking you're better off claiming all the credit for a job well done; in fact, you should always share it. You create goodwill, you demonstrate a winning modesty, and you'll attract support for your next project. At the same time, you should . . .
- **Accept blame.** If you're willing to accept the blame for errors, people will eagerly cede you all manner of responsibility—that is, power. Plus, by accepting blame, you show that you're in a position of significance, you're honest, and that you recognize error. These qualities suit you for more power.
- **Ask for favors.** As Ben Franklin recommended, "If you want to make a friend, let someone do you a favor." Ask for help, for advice, for contributions. By doing so, you place yourself under obligation to your favor-givers—which makes them feel kindly toward you. And their help gives them a stake in your success.
- **Accentuate the negative.** When trying to persuade, first emphasize your argument's weak points. Then explain that, although you recognize these drawbacks, you nevertheless advocate your position. Your admission disarms your opponents, shows your appreciation for the pitfalls of your position, and highlights your reasonableness.
- **Self-deprecate.** Disarm others by showing that you recognize your faults. Make fun of yourself—at your advanced age, at your habit of losing your keys, at your dependence on coffee.
- **Turn the other cheek.** While suffering excessive abuse isn't a good idea, in general you should absorb criticism and slights with good humor. A person of strength and self-possession doesn't react to every sling and arrow.

- **Be impressed.** *Being impressed* is as important as being impressive. "You've got a good memory." "I think you've hit on the crucial point." Jot down a note of a fact that someone tells you. Your appreciative attitude make others feel esteemed and valued—by you.

APPLYING THE *PRINCIPLE OF DIS-EXPECTATION*

As long as others know that you could indulge in power demonstrations, you can flaunt your power, paradoxically, by refraining from exhibiting it. You apply the *principle of dis-expectation* to underscore your victory, by showing that you transcend ordinary expectations. Reverse custom. The absence of the conventional trappings of power only intensifies the aura of power.

How do you apply the principle of dis-expectation? Identify in your circle a customary method of displaying power. Then violate it. If your colleagues crowd their offices with fancy, expensive equipment, keep your office ostentatiously low-tech and simple. If the power herd eats a heavy, manly breakfast, you eat only dry wheat toast; if they eat sparingly, you gorge on grits, bacon, and eggs. While the people around you make a great show of their indispensability by flaunting beepers, juggling multiple cell phones, and calling the office with minute-by-minute updates on their whereabouts, you make yourself inaccessible.

Apply the principle of dis-expectation to your office. Entertainment mogul David Geffen and investment mastermind Warren Buffett refused to have power offices, despite their billions. Infamous White House Counsel John Dean recollected that

> The first time I heard the expression "baby" used by one cat to address another was up at Warwick in 1951. . . . It was like saying, "Man, look at me. I've got masculinity to spare." It was saying at the same time to the world, "I'm one of the hippest cats, one of the most uninhibited cats on the scene. I can say 'baby' to another cat, and he can say 'baby' to me, and we can say it with strength in our voices." If you could say it, this meant that you really had to be sure of yourself, sure of your masculinity.
>
> CLAUDE BROWN,
> *MANCHILD IN THE PROMISED LAND*

TIP: The more deeply held the expectation, the better. Take the presumably universal desire to be paid as much as possible for your work: Steve Jobs violated this expectation by accepting a salary of only $1 a year for serving as Apple Computer CEO. By doing so, he showed that the fortune forgone was insignificant to him.

although he decorated his office with photographs of himself with President Nixon, the supremely powerful H. R. Haldeman and John Ehrlichman didn't bother with these "ego-boosting badges of intimacy."

Or use your clothes to make your statement. Superlawyer David Boies favors suits from Sears in place of the powersuits of his counterparts. Leaders of Silicon Valley, like Andy Grove and Marc Andreessen, dress casually and walk around in bare feet, violating the expectation of traditional corporate dress. But billionaire software mogul Larry Ellison surpassed his peers; recognizing that casual Friday is, in fact, the daily expectation of Silicon Valley, he shows up wearing double-breasted suits, French cuffs, and knuckle-size cuff links. Dis-expectation could be seen at work at the announcement of the mega-merger of AOL and Time Warner in January 2000: new-media-mogul Steve Case of AOL wore a suit and tie, while old-media-mogul Gerald Levin of Time Warner wore chinos and an open shirt. The fact that several commentators scoffed at these ensembles as affectation is a good reminder of the importance of *sprezzatura*. Dis-expectation should never look like a pose.

The expectation breached should be one of style or appearance, not one whose violation will actually diminish your effectiveness—for example, refusing to use a computer would work in some situations, but would be deadly in others. Note that dis-expectation works at the level of symbol and is applied narrowly. If everyone, absolutely everyone, in L.A. is car-mad, you drive an old clunker—but that does *not* mean you must live in a modest house and dress cheaply.

Your subordinates make an impressive show of their jammed schedules and jangling phones; you transcend that. You're never harried, you're never interrupted, you give the impression that you have nothing more pressing than what you're doing at the moment.

Because it is not widely appreciated as a power strategy, the principle of disexpectation often yields a double bonus: the unsophisticated take its application as a sign of a modest, artless character whose self-possession obviates the need for glittering apparatus. They don't realize that contradicting the ordinary rules of power is, itself, an assertion of power. The wide-eyed journalist reports that the CEO pads around the office in his stocking feet—such a down-to-earth guy. The journalist never stopped to ask himself whether he or the secretaries or even the second in command would ever consider going without shoes. Well, they wouldn't. The humble gesture cloaks supreme assurance.

> Speed is not part of the true Way of strategy. Speed implies that things seem fast or slow, according to whether or not they are in rhythm. Whatever the Way, the master of strategy does not appear fast. . . . Of course, slowness is bad. Really skillful people never get out of time, and are always deliberate, and never appear busy.
>
> MIYAMOTO MUSASHI, *A BOOK OF FIVE RINGS*

T R U E   R U L E

Simplicity and modesty can be the most effective way to demonstrate complete triumph.

• • •

If you draw on as many sources of power as possible and then use your power base to generate more power, you'll find yourself in an increasingly solid position. The acquisition of power carries risk, so be on guard; if you let power intoxicate you, you may destroy the very power you've worked so hard to attain.

CHAPTER FOUR

CAUTIONARY NOTES ON POWER

Power changes those who possess it—some qualities enlarge, while others atrophy. If you're not careful, you may find your capacities undermined by the lapses that frequently accompany power. Susceptibility to flattery, arrogance, a sense of invulnerability, and pomposity grow out of your lofty sense of your place in the world. Your underlings begin to persuade you with their blandishments. "You were way ahead of everyone on that issue," they murmur in your ear. "You were the only one who could have gotten that project pushed through." "*You* deserve all the credit." "No one could replace you." *So true,* you reflect smugly. It's true that their praise strengthens you by fortifying your sense of yourself and your abilities, but swallowed whole, it threatens your position because it tempts you into error.

SUSCEPTIBILITY TO FLATTERY

You begin to believe all the compliments people pay you. Sharp-eyed underlings spot your vanities and turn them to their advantage; they work to win your heart by satisfying your acknowledged—and unacknowledged—desires.

Your claque finds (or pretends to find) significance and merit in your simplest actions, the way Michael Deaver gushed about Ronald Reagan's actually deigning to

> Augustus' eyes were clear and bright, and he liked to believe that they shone with a sort of divine radiance: it gave him profound pleasure if anyone at whom he glanced keenly dropped his head as though dazzled by looking into the sun.
>
> SUETONIUS, *THE TWELVE CAESARS*

dial a telephone himself at an important moment: "It was interesting that he dialed the number himself. No assistant. No operator. Just Ronald Reagan reaching out." Flatterers often have a perverse capacity to find (or at least pretend to find) even your unattractive traits praiseworthy. In his *Conversations with Kennedy* Ben Bradlee details how charmed he was with Jack Kennedy's coarse language: "Jackie's question, 'What is a Charlie-Uncle-Nan-Tare, for heaven's sake?' went unanswered. (Kennedy's earthy language was a direct result of his experience in the service, as it was for so many men of his generation, whose first serious job was war. Often it had direct Navy roots, as above when he used the signalman's alphabet. He used 'prick' and 'fuck' and 'nuts' and 'bastard' and 'son of a bitch' with an ease and comfort that belied his upbringing, and somehow it never seemed offensive, or at least it never seemed offensive to me.)" All this inspired by Kennedy's coded use of a vulgar word.

You make a fool of yourself by lapping up the praise that sycophants dish out. CBS founder and art collector William Paley noted in his memoir, "I had shown Matisse several series of photographs I had taken while in Paris and he advised me avuncularly at one point: 'Please, whatever you are doing (as a career), drop it, and take up photography seriously.'" Paley explained that, "I admired him enormously as an artist, but I declined to take his advice." It apparently never occurred to Paley that Matisse might have been other than absolutely sincere.

Maybe you're unaffected by excessive admiration. But if, like many, you're eventually persuaded by your flatterers, you may disregard your limitations and the risks you face.

ARROGANCE

You congratulate yourself on being smarter than other people, on having better instincts, a savvier political sense, superior business judgment. This arrogance is dangerous if unfounded; it blinds you to the facts. When someone counseled him to reject the offer of the ceremonial vice-presidency to keep his powerful Majority Leader's seat, Lyndon Johnson replied glibly: "Power is where power goes." But Johnson discovered, to his dismay, that even he couldn't take his power with him into the powerless VP's office.

GLENDOWER: "I can call spirits from the vasty deep."

HOTSPUR: "Why, so can I, or so can any man; But will they come when you do call for them?"

WILLIAM SHAKESPEARE, *HENRY IV, PART ONE*

Arrogance betrays you into overreaching. Director Steven Spielberg was so sure he'd be nominated for an Academy Award for directing *Jaws* that he invited a TV camera crew to film his reaction—then he didn't get the nod. The cameras whirred as he moaned, "I can't believe it. They went for Fellini instead of me!" with his face in his hands. At a press conference after President Reagan had been shot, Secretary of State Alexander Haig said, "Constitutionally, gentlemen, you have the president, the vice president, and the secretary of state in that order." He continued, "I am in control here in the White House pending the return of the vice president." But Haig had his facts wrong. He wasn't the next one in the line of responsibility. Haig's actions that day, and particularly those chilling words—*"I am in control here"*—marred Haig's reputation from then on.

Your hubris stirs up other people's desire to put you in your proper place. The missteps of Charles Wick, director of the U.S. Information Agency in the 1980s, blared from the front pages of the *Washington Post:* he was politely turned down when he asked to be met in Japan by an armored limousine and a police escort, and he was required to make repayments after charging the government $31,700 for an elaborate home-security system and two private telephones. The government, it seemed, estimated Wick slightly lower than he himself did.

You forget that proven ability in one area doesn't make you a universal expert. Ross Perot and Steve Forbes (has Forbes proven much ability in any area?) never doubted that they were qualified to be president—the voters weren't so sure. "Suits," or business executives, regularly crash TV program meetings to dispense their show-business wisdom, in apparent belief that the same skills that got them MBA degrees will make them successful TV programmers.

You forget that your acumen might not have been the sole factor responsible for your success. Maybe you were just lucky, or maybe you had one good idea and won't have another.

As Jonathan Swift observed, "The power of fortune is confessed only by the miserable: for the happy impute all their success to prudence and merit." It's painful to acknowledge the role of luck, the fact that events might well have followed a different path.

Be even more wary of arrogance if you harbor secret feelings of inferiority. The combination of insecurity and powerlust is combustible—you're enraged by criticism, you fire good people whom you fear will make you look bad, you bluster rather than seek counsel. You're afraid to take a vacation, for fear it will reflect on your importance. You're rude to those who serve you, because you think that's the way superior people behave.

> [Newspaper publisher] Julian was didactic and told the ambassador what an ambassador's life was like, told the banker all about banking, explained the refugee problem to the famous refugee, and informed the labor leader on labor problems and their solution. . . . Nor did any guests ever contradict his superior opinions, since this would have been not only rude but unpractical.
>
> DAWN POWELL, *A TIME TO BE BORN*

POMPOSITY

Impressed with your title, you adopt attitudes and airs. You forget that much of your power inheres in your position—as a political force, as a controller of wealth, as a celebrity—not in you personally.

Your sense of importance makes you self-conscious. Your gestures become histrionic, because you imagine that people are watching (and maybe they are). You can't help preening at any glimpse of your reflection. You strike an excessively familiar air with people you don't know—you make hearty conversation with your driver, or overwhelm strangers with jovial hellos, smug with certainty that they are delighted to be speaking to you. (I've got such a nice touch with the little guy, you congratulate yourself.)

Your swells of self-worth have people snickering. Upon arriving at their hotel rooms for Condé Nast's annual retreat, each participant found a silver frame engraved with his or her name and the words "Condé Nast All-Star Team 1998," and inside the frame, a

> "Washington was no politician at all, as we understand the word," replied Ratcliffe abruptly. "He stood outside of politics. The thing couldn't be done today. The people don't like that sort of royal airs."
>
> "I don't understand!" said Mrs. Lee. "Why could you not do it now?"
>
> "Because I should make a fool of myself," replied Ratcliffe, pleased to think that Mrs. Lee should put him on a level with Washington. She had only meant to ask why the thing could not be done, and this little touch of Ratcliffe's vanity was inimitable.
>
> HENRY ADAMS, *DEMOCRACY*

color publicity shot of their President and CEO, Steve Florio. Just what everyone had always wanted.

You're impatient with anyone who questions your wisdom or ignores your advice. According to a probably apocryphal story, Washington power-lawyer Clark Clifford once got a call from a lawyer asking what his company should do about a piece of tax legislation. After some weeks passed, Clifford provided a succinct answer: "Nothing." He also sent along a bill for $20,000. When pressed for a more lengthy explanation, Clifford responded with a curt, "Because I said so"—which cost an extra $5,000.

A SENSE OF INVULNERABILITY

You have more power than the people around you. You're constantly praised, accommodated, consulted. You begin to feel invulnerable—but you're not.

Dick Morris thought that he had unique ability that exempted him from common standards. He was wrong. Morris was kicked out of President Clinton's inner circle after prostitute Sherry Rowlands sold the story of her sordid $200-per-hour relationship with Morris—complete with role-playing, toe-sucking, and eavesdropping on presidential phone calls. As Raymond Chandler wrote, "There is no trap more deadly than the trap you set for yourself."

Feeling secure in your own power, you may think that it can't matter how badly you treat other people. So you insist that your office's travel agent book you a first-class seat, against official policy.

You jeer at your subordinate in a large meeting. You insult the guys in the mail room. Be careful. You never know when a seemingly powerless person will be in a position to cause your downfall—perhaps without you ever knowing it. (What would happen if, before hiring you, a potential employer called the secretaries at your previous job to get a reading on you?)

The wheel can turn, and someone you wronged can come into power. Take heed of Lord Chesterfield's warning to his son: "There are no persons so insignificant and inconsiderable but may, some time or other, have it in their power to be of use to you; which they certainly will not, if you have once shown them contempt."

• • •

And even once you've achieved considerable power, and even if you've managed to stave off its worst corrosive effects, you may nonetheless find that you're haunted by the *power blues*.

CHAPTER FIVE

FINAL NOTE: POWER BLUES

You've got power, more and more. You've reached the enviable state where one award, opportunity, and position tumbles after another. There is a momentum to prominence, as each new prize prepares you for the next. "One honor," La Rochefoucauld pointed out, "is a surety for more." You've become the beneficiary of the platinum rule: To whom much is given, more is given.

And now you've got the blues. You thought power would make you great, allow you to feel your own greatness, but in fact, you aren't transformed. You're shaped by your office, but you can't transcend it. Now—just when you've gotten what you worked so hard to achieve—you begin a lifetime of anticlimax.

You strove to arrive at the pinnacle, where you would keep company with giants. Now you realize that most of the crowd at that pinnacle is utterly ordinary. You're comforted, in a way, but also disappointed. You had wanted to consort with the best, but these are no better than yourself.

And, you realize with some disquiet, there is no assembly of excellence. You wish you could still trust that, somewhere, the unevenness of human ability and character disappeared, and the room filled with brilliant, hardworking, honest people. Now you know too well that personality quirks and selfish squabbles butt their way into even the highest meetings and decisions.

And, as anticlimactic as it may be finally to grasp power, the loss of that power can be devastating. You can fight it, but eventually you must admit—if only to yourself—that your power is coming to an end.

When the time comes, you must decide whether to struggle to oppose the forces that would drag power from your grasp (your age, the new administration, the technology that makes you obsolete, the up-and-comers impatient to replace you) or whether to surrender gracefully to time and change. Perhaps you try to preserve the illusion, at least, of your power, with a bustling, haughty staff, visitors wedged in every twenty minutes, a sumptuous office, a bodyguard and driver—measures calculated for an audience.

> The limits of happiness itself, Charles was thinking, were continually changing. You got somewhere and then you wanted to move somewhere else, to another, larger bar, to better, brighter company. Charles could still remember how pleased he had been when Mr. Forbush had asked him why he did not drop in sometimes and sit at the round table. It had meant that he had made good, that he was a part of a small group within a group. It had never occurred to him then that Mr. Forbush could be dull, or Mr. Swiss either.
>
> J. P. MARQUAND, *POINT OF NO RETURN*

Now you dial the phone yourself, and once placed, your phone calls aren't immediately returned. You flip through magazines in someone else's reception area, as the long minutes tick by. The small courtesies that were once heaped on you—that you took for granted, as your personal due—aren't tendered anymore.

Or maybe you suffer from the knowledge that you never quite attained the power you sought—you're an also-ran, a has-been. "Rhodes scholars are people with a great future behind them." Your dreams, your plans—somehow you never achieved your potential. What makes it worse is that you see others (not as smart, not as hardworking) ascend higher than yourself.

Sic transit gloria mundi.

ILLUSTRATION: HOW ANNE USED POWER

Anne was hired as the most junior of accountants at a major accounting firm, but she vowed she wouldn't stay at the bottom of the heap for long.

She finagled to get assigned the office closest to her boss, Stephen. After observing his habits for a week, Anne timed her day to arrive at the office five minutes before Stephen and to leave five minutes after him. She bought her lunch at Sam's Deli, where Stephen bought his lunch, and often ran into him there (like Stephen, Anne ate lunch at her desk).

While poking around in a supply closet, Anne discovered a chair abandoned behind some cartons. Early the next morning, she dragged the chair into her office, which gave her two visitors' chairs instead of the usual one. She managed to persuade Stephen that she needed a cell phone and a particular software program—and in fact she did make good use of both. (Why did *she* get a cell phone? her colleagues wondered. Because she'd asked for it.)

Over time, Anne made herself indispensable to Stephen: she volunteered to research and write periodic memos briefing their entire department on proposed accounting changes; she prepared short bios of people with whom he was scheduled to meet (well, actually, Anne had her secretary put together the bios); she worked during the Christmas holidays to help him prepare his presentation to the committee. Although Anne worked very hard, she never seemed rushed or anxious. Her automatic response to any request, "Sure, no problem," became an office joke.

Because Stephen was very shy (which made him seem aloof), he had little interaction with Anne's peers; but he was at ease with Anne and happy to give her advice and direction. Anne tried to show her appreciation with small gestures: she brought Stephen a box of his favorite cigars for his birthday; she sent a baby present when his second child was born.

Anne also spent time with her fellow junior accountants. She went out for drinks with her peers and spent part of every day drinking coffee and chatting with her coworkers. Because she worked so closely with Stephen, Anne was often able to pass along useful information she'd gleaned from him. Her coworkers, in turn, told her whatever they knew—which she passed up to Stephen.

Anne was fortunate to have Stephen, a real star in the firm, directing her career. His advice greatly improved her effectiveness. People began to look on Anne as Stephen's chief deputy; many assumed that she actually held some additional title. When Stephen was promoted, Anne was the logical person to take his place.

money

CHAPTER SIX

INTRODUCTION TO MONEY

Money. It offers infinite possibilities. Can money buy happiness? No—but it can buy things that contribute mightily to happiness. No need to be embarrassed by your car, your shoes, your haircut; no need to worry about paying the landlord or the doctor or the exterminator. You eat in a nice restaurant and order dessert. You quit that tiresome job. You watch the figures gleam on the pages of your monthly financial statements. You're safe at last.

And of course money—if you've got enough—wins you the deference and attention of the people around you. You're so much more interesting and engaging, now that you've made your fortune.

You strive to amass your store, and you want to make the best use of it. But what category of use suits you? Take this quiz, and as you read on, pay particular attention to the chapter that best describes you.

> For often Sir William would travel sixty miles or more down into the country to visit the rich, the afflicted, who could afford the very large fee which Sir William very properly charged for his advice. Her ladyship waited with the rugs about her knees an hour or more, leaning back, thinking sometimes of the patient, sometimes, excusably, of the wall of gold, mounting minute by minute while she waited; the wall of gold that was mounting between them and all shifts and anxieties (she had borne them bravely; they had had their struggles) until she felt wedged on a calm ocean, where only spice winds blow; respected, admired, envied, with scarcely anything left to wish for, though she regretted her stoutness.
>
> VIRGINIA WOOLF, *MRS. DALLOWAY*

Quiz: Why do you want money?

Assuming that you already possess whatever you consider your basic requirements, if you were suddenly handed $5 million to spend in any way you chose, what is the first thing you'd do?

A. Completely redecorate my house, then have a party to show it off to everyone.
B. Hire a servant so I could have my breakfast and newspapers brought to me in bed each morning.
C. Immediately buy several outstanding pieces for my collection of nineteenth-century clocks.
D. Deposit the money into various bank accounts and funds, wait a few hours, then repeatedly call to listen to the computer read me my new million-dollar statements.
E. Divvy up money among political candidates in the hope that I'd get appointed to an important government post.
F. Donate money to a museum for the construction of a new wing, on the condition that my name appear (in letters no smaller than twelve inches) on the wall.

If you answered A . . .
You want money to signal to others about your position and character. Pay particular attention to the chapter on "Signaling."

If you answered B . . .
You want money to enjoy the selfish pleasures it can provide. Pay particular attention to the chapter on "Self-Gratification."

If you answered C . . .
You want money to feed your object lust—that is, your love for objects themselves. Pay particular attention to the chapter on "Object Lust."

If you answered D . . .
You want money because you suffer from miser's hoard—the grasping love for the accumulation of money. Pay particular attention to the chapter on "Miser's Hoard."

If you answered E or F . . .
You want money to gain power or fame. Pay particular attention to the chapter on "Money for Power or Fame."

•   •   •

If you're like most people, you'll find that your use for money isn't contained entirely in one category, but includes elements of several.

> Everybody has to make up their mind if money is money or money isn't money and sooner or later they always do decide that money is money.
>
> GERTRUDE STEIN,
> *EVERYBODY'S AUTOBIOGRAPHY*

CHAPTER SEVEN

MONEY FOR SIGNALING

"I'd completely redecorate my house, then have a party to show it off to everyone."

If you want to use money for display, you crave the objects and activities that will make the right impression. Call this process *signaling*—you exhibit your possessions to reveal your sensibility, your status, your knowledge, and your fortune. Everyone signals to some degree (it's unavoidable), but for you, the ability to send the desired signals is the principal use for money.

Objects are loaded with specific, detailed significance, but don't be fooled into assuming that an object's signaling value depends merely on cost or appearance. Factors such as context, pedigree, authenticity, and fashion weigh heavily in determining an object's signal. Because the signaling system is complex, expect to spend some time and effort mastering it.

A culture based on possession and display can boast the virtue of fluidity: signaling allows anyone to change position, while a society that emphasizes breeding, race, or religion is more stagnant. At the same time, however, a culture organized around signaling breeds materialism and ostentation.

SEVEN PRINCIPLES FOR EFFECTIVE SIGNALING

To use money most effectively for signaling, follow these seven principles:

First Principle: **Signaling is relative.**
Second Principle: **Only visible objects send a signal.**

Third Principle:	**You are what you buy.**
Fourth Principle:	**Manipulate signals to change position.**
Fifth Principle:	**You can't refuse to signal.**
Sixth Principle:	**When in doubt about how to signal, use art.**
Seventh Principle:	**Distinctions matter, so . . .**

1. Always choose "the best."
2. Consider pedigree.
3. Choose only the authentic.
4. Buy bespoke.
5. Follow fashion.
6. Spend your *time* as carefully as your *money.*
7. Remember *sprezzatura,* and never let your effort show.
8. Apply subtlety and understatement.

FIRST PRINCIPLE

Signaling is relative: You only need to keep up with your particular Joneses

Remember, it's the opinion of your colleagues and social group that matters. At every level of fortune, the impulse is the same: to acquire the possessions and habits that signal others in your set that you're a person of significance. Subtle, relative distinctions among neighbors matter far more than dramatic distinctions between widely separated groups.

TRUE RULE

Comparison drives competition.

Your desires take shape relative to the people around you. The *principle of relativity* explains how the lawyer who owns a $2 million house can sincerely believe he lives modestly—he compares himself to the people he considers his peers, each of whom owns a house worth more than $3 million and keeps a place outside the city too. The principle of relativity also explains why information-age millionaires stir up so much anxious envy. Few people compare themselves to a sixty-five-year-old CEO who has spent a lifetime clambering up the company's ranks or to the investment

TIP: To strike it rich, you need a business plan. Try something like: "A Harvard Business School classmate [or McKinsey associate or high school friend] and I have founded south-sea.com. We're in stealth mode; all I can disclose is that we'll operate in the B-to-B space and combine knowledge-based content with direct-market sales. Our venture partners are extraordinarily bullish."

Or you could try: "A company for carrying on an undertaking of great advantage, but nobody to know what it is." That was also quite successful.

banker who's been working fifteen-hour days in front of a Bloomberg terminal for years; but when a twenty-four-year-old business-school dropout becomes a multimillionaire by selling a company he founded five months ago or when a program manager retires in luxury because, by pure chance, she was one of Microsoft's instantly rich "Class of 2000"—well, feelings of comparison and competition abound. "Why not me?" you grumble. "I'm just as smart." You're just as entitled to their money as they are.

Don't be surprised if, when you're settling into new surroundings, you want more. Now that you see what other people have, you want it too. The *snare of mounting expectations* is responsible for your chronic dissatisfaction: expectations, once fulfilled, give way to further desires, as you see what the world offers and others possess. Karl Marx observed, "Our wants and pleasures have their origin in society; we therefore measure them in relation; we do not measure them in relation to the objects which serve for their gratification. Since they are of a social nature, they are of a relative nature."

Signals take their meaning from context. A leather appointments calendar with "Concorde" stamped on it might provide an invaluable signal that showed you'd taken the astronomically expensive Concorde flight to Europe. But the executive who takes the Concorde frequently would never consider using such a thing.

SECOND PRINCIPLE

Only visible objects send a signal

If you must conserve, scrimp on objects that others won't see. Follow the example of the celebrated leader of fashion, the Duchess of Windsor, who bought the best, but only where it showed—clothes, food, and house. Because Hollywood celebrities rarely receive invitations to parties (that sort of thing is faxed to their assistants), no one giving a star-studded bash spends money on lavish invitations. Why bother? The guests who count would never see them.

By the same token, spend where you'll get a good signaling return—even if it means crossing your fingers each time you charge a purchase at Gucci, as you wonder whether your credit card will be accepted or rejected. If the price for the premier personal trainer is too much for you,

> She never could understand when it was worthwhile to spend money. Of course the main purpose of Chieftain Manor—or The Old Chief, as Willis came to call it affectionately—was to be expensive. It was a symbolic prize for industry and endeavor, a happy resting place only for those who had made good. . . . Somehow Sylvia never seemed to see that if you worked hard for what you got, it was a pleasure to show that you had money. It never hurt you at all, for example, to be able to say that you enjoyed April at Hot Springs or that you had found that the service at The Breakers at Palm Beach had improved from what you had known of it last.
>
> J. P. MARQUAND, *SINCERELY, WILLIS WAYDE*

cut down your appointments to once every two weeks, but mention your "relationship" often. Eat peanut butter at home so you can spend $14 for a drink at the hottest bar in the city.

THIRD PRINCIPLE

You are what you buy

The choices you make determine the signals you send. What you serve for dinner and what you wear to bed locate you in the world of jaded sophisticates, blue bloods, hipsters, ruthless businessmen, intellectuals, or the Net Set. As William James noted, "It is clear that between what a man calls me and what he simply calls mine, the line is difficult to draw."

After all, your tastes are unoriginal and predictable, and you imitate your neighbors in almost everything you buy and do. Your preferences may *feel* idiosyncratic and spontaneous, but that's because your long indoctrination has made your tastes feel natural. You've so internalized objects' signals that you can't recognize why you want what you want.

In fact, signaling patterns are consistent enough to form the basis of sophisticated marketing tools, such as the categories devised by the marketing group Claritas, in its "PRIZM" lifestyle clusters. Do you recognize yourself in any of these categories?

- "Kids and Cul-de-Sacs" spend money on Disney World, private school tuition, and groceries; they listen to adult contemporary radio, drink caffeine-free diet Coke, grill outdoors, drive Volvos or Buick station wagons, often in carpools.
- "Money and Brains" are dual-income couples who like to travel, buy classical music, have passports, play chess, and collect stamps.
- "Shotguns and Pickups" frequently use chain saws, snuff, canning jars, frozen potato products, and whipped toppings.
- "Furs and Station Wagons" are more likely to have a second mortgage, buy wine by the case, read *Architectural Digest,* drive a BMW, eat natural cold cereal and pumpernickel bread, and watch the *Tonight* show.

> Donny performed a sprightly minuet of acquisition: he could retire in Fiji or the Côte d'Azur if he chose, or spend a million on a Pissarro. Lasso koi from the Sargasso or bid on a *boulle* Louis XIV *bureau plat* at Sotheby's, three million for a piece of fucking furniture, thank you very much. Something to set the teeth of his colleagues on edge—they were always jockeying for rarefied outside investment interests that made them more than "just agents."
>
> BRUCE WAGNER, *I'M LOSING YOU*

You think you stake out your individuality in the choices you make among objects, but viewed on a broad scale, it's clear that your selections are made within an extremely narrow range. You think your pick of a diaper bag colored in electric green, aqua, and brown marks you as a free thinker, but you're still buying it from Pierre Deux like all the other mommies in your neighborhood.

You are what you buy. By acquiring the notebooks of Leonardo da Vinci, geeky Bill Gates signaled his identification with a vibrant icon of art, learning, and culture. (© Nubar Alexanian/ CORBIS)

Highlight specific personal qualities by acquiring a distinctive, precisely calibrated possession. Bill Gates spent $31 million to buy the Hammer Codex; by acquiring these notebooks of Leonardo da Vinci, Gates (dry, nerdy, monomaniacal) signaled his identification with a real Renaissance man, a towering genius of art and engineering.

FOURTH PRINCIPLE

Manipulate signals to change position

Because you are what you buy, signaling allows you to re-create yourself. Shrewd owners manipulate their identities and histories through their possessions—but first you must determine how to project the signal you're trying to achieve. Music mogul David Geffen bought the famous Warner estate to relocate his identity from Brooklyn to Hollywood. What's the right signal for you? a yacht, or a rare first-edition novel, or a Caribbean vacation? Maybe buying a basketball team will transform your short, pudgy, cautious self into a brazen, macho talent.

Model your signaling after that of people who are close enough to permit your easy comparison. You might even choose to signal in imitation of those who have less—like the children of wealth who deliberately forsake an atmosphere of power and fortune. These defectors live in fashionable dropout places like Boulder or Berkeley and often pursue amateur arts (pottery, cooking, drum-playing, paper or jewelry making, karate) that retain desirable associations of expression, refinement, and education. In either case, possessions allow you to pick the identity you exude. The boy from Greenwich, Groton, and Yale sports his beef jerky and shotgun with the same careful pride that the girl from south Jersey places in her pearls and *New Yorker* subscription. The painstaking process of redefinition-through-signaling follows predictable patterns (to be effective, signaling must be predictable), which are often used quite unconsciously. You're a rich young white guy from Massachusetts, transplanted to Colorado, and you suppose that wearing your red hair in dreadlocks is your own innovation. You don't realize that this signaling move is so typical that you and your ilk are called "trustafarians" by the amused townies.

If you're in a new position, you'll feel the strong

It was a time to be more careful than ever, to measure the new balance of power, and not to antagonize the crowd that you were leaving. One day, it seemed to Charles, though of course it was not one day, he was living in a two-family house in Larchmont that smelled of cauliflower in the evenings, stumbling over the children's rollerskates and tricycles, taking the eight-three in the morning, keeping the budget on a salary of six thousand a year. Then in a day, though of course it was not a day, they were building at Sycamore Park. The children were going to the Country Day School. They were seeing their old friends, but not so often. Instead they were spending Sundays with Arthur Slade. There was a maid to do the work. He was earning eleven thousand instead of six, and he was an executive with a future.

J. P. MARQUAND, *POINT OF NO RETURN*

urge to change your signals, to adapt. Let's say you're starting a new job. At first, you feel the anxiety of the new boy, wondering what the other kids bring for lunch. Do the guys at work wear suspenders or bow ties? After a week or so, though, another emotion creeps in. You feel that sweet ache for new things—for the French cuffs and trench coats and Palm Pilots you see around you. Now you want them, too. A new job requires a new tennis racket; newlyweds register for china; freshmen hide the compact discs they brought from home and buy new ones. You show that you belong by acquiring the appropriate possessions.

Old signaling habits and traditions die hard, even for those most determined to escape convention. That's one reason it's difficult to change your identity. After all, even maverick superstar Madonna registered for formal china when she got married—at Tiffany, in the Carnival and Monet patterns, no less. And it's almost impossible to be a signaling insurgent. It's hard not to smile when you walk past a girl whose hideous outfit proclaims her to be a rebel (pierced nose, tufted dyed hair, tattered jacket, heavy black boots) and you notice her best friend beside her, dressed meticulously in an only slightly different version of the same outfit.

The nouveau riche (by definition, "new") spend so ostentatiously because they're trying, as fast as possible, to establish themselves in a new set by means of objects they purchase. By an unfortunate misstep, they often mark themselves as outsiders by the very signals meant to demonstrate their belonging. If you're a newcomer who wants to flash some fortune without risking vulgarity, give a staggering sum to a hospital, university, or library instead of buying that jet or another country house. (The prosperity of the great charitable institutions stems, in large part, from their value as money launderers of vulgar new money.)

TRUE RULE

Signaling matters most when you arrive in a new position.

You're not born knowing how to manipulate your signals correctly, so study up. Don't be discouraged—signaling is complicated but not impenetrable. As countless examples prove, a person from any background can master signaling, and thus, change position. You can, too.

Take a class—on wine, cigars, gardening, golf, or Pilates. Look for expert guidance from Martha Stewart (from Jersey City, New Jersey), whose empire is built on providing lifestyle instruction, or from Ralph Lauren (born Ralph Lifschitz in the Bronx), who dresses and furnishes in the style of American aristocracy.

Newsstands and bookstores are heaped with aids. That "Daily Diary of the American Dream," the *Wall Street Journal,* regularly reports on how to spend money—the right kind of opulent vacations, the latest in fashionable purchases like grills or Jeeps, the most coveted neighborhoods. Although its circulation is tiny, the salmon-colored *New York Observer* is one of the best guides to money and signaling (as well as power, fame, and sex) available. Business magazines often feature guides to spending the money you've made. As one *Fortune* article put it, "We believe in life after business. . . . And so we celebrate The Business Life by giving you access to amazing people at home, alluring places to explore, and extraordinary things to own." Magazines from *Architectural Digest* to *Town and Country* to *New York* provide instruction, and books, too, can be invaluable. Authors such as Tom Wolfe, Judith Krantz, Terry McMillan, and Dominick Dunne lard their writing with helpful information for the attentive, right down to the brand names.

> [The gentleman] must also cultivate his tastes, for it now becomes incumbent on him to discriminate with some nicety between the noble and the ignoble in consumable goods. He becomes a connoisseur in creditable viands of various degrees of merit, in manly beverages and trinkets, in seemly apparel and architecture, in weapons, games, dancers, and the narcotics. . . . Closely related to the requirement that the gentleman must consume freely and of the right kinds of goods, there is the requirement that he must know how to consume them in a seemly manner.
>
> THORSTEIN VEBLEN,
> *THE THEORY OF THE LEISURE CLASS*

FIFTH PRINCIPLE

You can't refuse to signal

You might decide not to bother with signaling—you don't want to make the effort to learn the proper signals, or you're afraid of making a mistake, or you'd rather spend your money on other things. But you can't opt out of signaling. Every object you use expresses something about you. (Even something as innocuous as a telephone number is loaded with meaning; the establishment of new area codes is causing terrible distress where the triumphant acquisition of a prized number—212, 283, 324— is threatened by the introduction of inferior new area codes, like 646 or 329.)

> **TIP:** A popular signaling strategy for those who aren't much interested in signaling is to dress casually and cheaply, with just one item of expensive clothing—to show that your style is a matter of choice, not necessity.

Consider the paradox of countermaterialism: adherents take the trouble to purchase handmade candles or insist on beer from a microbrewery or shop for clothes at thrift shops, to show superiority to mainstream products peddled to the masses. Such possessions exhibit devotion to a nonmaterialistic, even antimaterialistic, way of life, but like everyone, countermaterialists are caught in the need to signal their identity through what they purchase (or don't purchase).

You can, however, apply the principle of dis-expectation. Even though you can afford new, beautifully tailored clothing, you wear ripped, worn jeans to show that you're not caught up in the need to signal with expensive clothes—for double effect, you might wear faded, beaded jeans that insiders will recognize as Gucci's $3,800 creation.

SIXTH PRINCIPLE

When in doubt about how to signal, use art

Want to make a statement, but aren't sure how? Possession is a rich medium for communication, but fraught with possible missteps. The nouveau riche are notorious because in their haste to flaunt their new money, they get their signals wrong. Art is safe and effective, so make a major gift to a museum or buy an expensive painting for yourself, or at the very least, associate yourself with the idea of art.

True, art's value is volatile, educated decision-making is difficult, insurance is expensive, and artwork can be difficult to work into your interior design. Nevertheless art operates extremely well as a signal. Art is the irreplaceable, unique product of genius, and you, the possessor, become distinguished by association. This procedure is even more pronounced if the artwork was previously owned by some celebrity. You can burnish your own personal pedigree by donating the artwork to a museum, where a plaque's grateful acknowledgment of your gift will tell the world both that you owned this museum-quality object and that you could afford to give it away.

TIP: Never give anonymously.

Art also offers a convenient way to signal on the proper scale—it's expensive, prestigious, and capable of being easily displayed. (The same considerations account for the late-nineties' popularity of the megabucks power wristwatch—you can't bring a Rolls-Royce into a meeting, but you can wear your Breguet or Patek Philippe. Or you can substitute the right sunglasses for the watch—consider the $1,500 gold-rimmed, rectangular Cartiers sported by rappers Bobby Brown and L.L. Cool J.)

If you can't afford expensive art, collect it in less expensive forms—contemporary photographs, vintage movie posters, African sculpture. If you can't afford even that, show your interest in art by conspicuously subscribing to magazines such as *Artforum* and mentioning that you're a frequent visitor to artnet.com.

SEVENTH PRINCIPLE

Distinctions matter

Don't make the common mistake of assuming that it's enough to spend a lot of money. Absolutely not. To use your money to impress others, you must understand critical distinctions. Signals must be conspicuous and correct—the right restaurant, the right sports, the right address, the right company, even the right bodily structure. Apply these key rules when making distinctions—once again:

1. Always choose "the best."
2. Consider pedigree.

3. Choose only the authentic.
4. Buy bespoke.
5. Follow fashion.
6. Spend your *time* as carefully as your *money.*
7. Remember *sprezzatura,* and never let your effort show.
8. Apply subtlety and understatement.

DISTINCTIONS MATTER—ALWAYS CHOOSE "THE BEST"

By choosing "the best," you show that you understand distinctions, and you're able to afford what you want. You want Aubusson carpets, or linens from Léron (you used to want pashmina scarves—now you take them for granted).

Some rules of thumb: Things that are "the best" are usually scarce, archaic, made of natural materials, hard to find, difficult to care for, handmade, and costly. An object's perceived beauty and worth depends on those qualities. Orchids are better than daisies; Afghan hounds are better than German shepherds. Those bedsheets must be ironed by hand or, failing that, sent out to a fine launderer. Even things that were inexpensive and common in their origins (tartan boxes, Victorian board games, carpet balls) become treasured once they become antique, scarce, and obscure.

Paradoxically, "the best" often contains slight imperfections to show that the object (silver, quilt, cigar, glassware) was wrought by hand, and therefore costly—but these imperfections can't be so crude as to show sloppy workmanship.

Find ways to associate yourself with "the best" even if you can't indulge to the degree you'd like. If you can't afford to get your hair cut at the premier salon, get your eyebrows waxed there—that allows you to say to your office mates, "I'll be back after my appointment at Bumble & Bumble." If you can't afford the most expensive suit, flash a Cohiba cigar. Even if you can't afford to shop at Tiffany, use that distinctive robin's-egg-blue Tiffany bag to carry your drugstore purchases.

TIP: Show your discernment by refusing to settle for anything less than exactly what you specify. You want a specific brand of bottled water or an obscure, imported brand of toothpaste.

> I personally find it offensive to think that the destiny of these intensely personal memorabilia will be as ego-affirming adornments on some mongrel hedge-fund player's side table in East Hampton or Bedford, or to patinate the decor of tricked-up commercial establishments peddling Anglo or WASP gentrification. There is, of course, some consolation in the awareness that what is purchased is not necessarily possessed, that buying is not the same as belonging, an awareness—satisfying to some of us but gut-churning to others—that lies upon this part of the world like ground fog now that summer is here.
>
> Michael Thomas, "Young Winston Churchill's Crass Harriman Auction," *New York Observer*, June 2, 1997

You demand "the best" in service, as well as in objects. That means that you're served by an actual person. When you stay at the best hotels, you expect your wake-up calls to be rung personally, by hotel staff, never by a recording. You use a courier service, not regular mail.

DISTINCTIONS MATTER— CONSIDER PEDIGREE

Some things—such as real estate, jewelry, antiques—come with a pedigree, a register of previous owners. By joining the chain of title, you buy yourself equal rank among the company of eminent owners.

Plus, if you're uncertain about a purchase, the right pedigree proves that a possession carries the proper signal. For example, new, wobbly socialite Julia Koch bought Jacqueline Onassis's apartment—which guaranteed that the Koch apartment would carry solid-gold signaling value.

The value of pedigree accounts for the astonishing successes of the auctions of the mediocre personal possessions of celebrities—the prices reflect the importance of the previous owner, not the object. Consider that in 1999, one bidder paid $1.15 million for the "skin and beads" dress Marilyn Monroe wore to sing "Happy birthday, Mr. President" to President Kennedy, and another paid $240,000 for her used makeup case. A few years earlier, a bidder had paid $29,900 for a tiny, beribboned, white box containing a morsel of the Duke and Duchess of Windsor's wedding cake, and when the Duchess's jewelry was auctioned by Sotheby's, it raised $50.3 million, far more than the $7 million estimate. These high prices reflect the value of the pedigree.

Canny celebrities profit from their own pedigree value. Barbra Streisand assured herself top prices for the sale of her possessions by placing her own (airbrushed) photo on the catalogue's cover, and Cher exploited her celebrity by methodically buying, fixing up, and selling her houses in Los Angeles—at a pedigreed premium, naturally.

Pedigree is important not only in objects, but also in people. Broadway producer Leland Hayward's daughter Brooke said that her father "loved the idea that he and all these very rich, powerful, and talented men were all sharing [his wife Pamela Harriman]. He loved the idea that they all had something in common . . . The Pamela Club." And when Pamela Harriman left Washington to become ambassador to France, and ambitious Arianna Huffington moved to Washington, Huffington hired Harriman's former cook and butler—their pedigree was irresistible to one who wanted to nominate herself as Harriman's proper successor.

The pedigree of new possessions matters just as much as old, so shop at the proper places. Objects must have acceptable origins. Don't buy at Perfumania or Filene's Basement or Loehmann's—or if you do, at least don't be seen with their shopping bags hanging off your arm. Signaling-stricken shoppers have been known to transfer purchases from the "wrong" bags into the "right" bags, for fear of being caught on the street with an offending brand name. What's inside doesn't matter if the outside is correct.

If you can't purchase pedigree, try to purchase associated pedigree. You buy an apartment—in the same building and in the same line as Woody Allen's. You buy a chair—the only other one like it is in the Queen of England's collection. The architect who designed your offices also designed CAA's.

DISTINCTIONS MATTER—CHOOSE ONLY THE AUTHENTIC

Authenticity matters, whether you're buying porcelain, Oriental rugs, or a Nantucket lightship basket. That's why cubic zirconia, though almost indistinguishable from real diamond, is worth only a fraction as much.

Even fakes must be the right kind of fakes—professional *trompe l'oeil;* the zaniest, most synthetic polyester; the *faux*-est fur, of the highest quality.

Distinctions Matter—Buy Bespoke

Whenever possible, order possessions made to your specifications (golf clubs, shirts, shoes, wallpaper, shotgun), even if that object is *almost* indistinguishable from one that was mass-produced, and even if customization doesn't improve its serviceableness.

These possessions announce your discrimination—you're willing to pay the price for additional quality. You want nothing but the best.

> **TIP:** If you're wearing a custom-made suit, *don't* leave the last buttonhole on the sleeve undone to signal your superiority. That shows you're trying too hard.

Apply this principle in a restaurant by demanding that a menu item be tailored to your peculiar taste—a move that is particularly effective when you take the most complex, sophisticated item and ask for it plain (you don't care if you *are* eating in the most expensive restaurant, with the finest chef; you want plain broiled fish with lemon).

Take the principle even further by ordering off the menu entirely— a move that also serves to signal your power, because not just anyone can persuade the chef to whip up that dish you've been craving.

Real buttonholes. That's it! A man can take his thumb and forefinger and unbutton his sleeve at the wrist because this kind of suit has real buttonholes there. Tom, boy, it's terrible. Once you know about it, you start seeing it. All the time! There are just two classes of men in the world, men with suits whose buttons are just sewn onto the sleeve, just some kind of cheapie decoration, or—yes!—men who can unbutton the sleeve at the wrist because they have real buttonholes and the sleeve really buttons up.

Tom Wolfe, "The Secret Vice," *The Kandy-Kolored Tangerine-Flake Streamline Baby*

Distinctions Matter— Follow Fashion

Fashion is the condition that allows you to believe you're expressing your individuality through objects sold to a mass market: thirty-somethings crowd into Pottery Barn looking for the latest things to distinguish them from their friends, who also shop at Pottery Barn.

You must stay in fashion, to demonstrate both that you

recognize the trends and that you can afford to keep up. You realize that it's not enough to have a taste for truffles; this year, you know, black truffles from France are *out,* and white truffles from Italy are *in.* This year, you've noticed, the focus of parties is on the cake—so you're looking for something splendid in a birthday cake, in the $2,000 to $3,000 range, from Sylvia Weinstock perhaps. The style of your possessions may show your sophistication, originality, erudition, boldness, or whatever you like, but you must pick precisely. Properly chosen, your possessions will vastly enhance the impression you make. (But wait . . . maybe it's black truffles from France that are *in,* and white truffles from Italy are *out?*)

Manufacturers exploit fashion's demand for novelty: the people are eager for new things. The need to stay abreast with the latest styles can reach ridiculous extremes. The *New York Times* explored the "The best of the fall styles" in *andirons*—implying that hordes of readers are expected to rush to the shops each fall to get the latest in hearth-ware.

TIP: Once something goes utterly out of fashion, it becomes fashionable.

Another approach, as always, is to apply the principle of dis-expectation, and flout fashion altogether. This will give you a far greater triumph than merely being fashionable; but to succeed it must be done with style. Violate convention, like the heiress who decorates her walls with paintings on black velvet or by Thomas Kinkade. Don't make the mistake of thinking that applying dis-expectation exempts you from signaling—it's just a different set of signals.

DISTINCTIONS MATTER—SPEND YOUR TIME AS CAREFULLY AS YOUR MONEY

You signal with time as well as with objects. What pastimes occupy your leisure? Choose carefully. Given a choice, select the pastime that demands more training and equipment, is more archaic, costs more, and is quieter and cleaner.

DO	DON'T
Go skiing	Go snowmobiling
Play squash (or better, court tennis)	Play racquetball
Fly fish	Spin-cast
Sail	Jet-ski
Ride horses	Ride motorcycles
Weed a flowerbed by hand	Cut grass on a riding mower

DISTINCTIONS MATTER—REMEMBER *SPREZZATURA,* AND NEVER LET YOUR EFFORT SHOW

Sprezzatura—ease, carelessness—is indispensable to signaling. Because people embrace the fiction that a person of natural refinement has an instinctive passion for excellence, never hint at the time and energy spent learning. Consider the opera scene in the movie *Pretty Woman,* where the uneducated prostitute played by Julia Roberts demonstrates an inborn appreciation of the music ("It was so good I almost peed in my pants!"). Her untutored response reveals her inner worth.

So disavow effort and expense. Let it slip that you've never taken a tennis lesson, you use the cheapest tailor, you wear so little makeup. Never admit to plastic surgery, regimens of Rogaine, or elocution classes to soften that once-grating accent. Pretend you don't watch your weight—order dessert after every meal, then eat just a few bites: you show that you can be free and easy with calories as well as cash.

TRUE RULE
Naturalness rarely comes naturally.

Your carelessness demonstrates your true mastery over objects and their meanings. Let's say you took a cooking class, and you've decided to have guests for dinner. Never admit, "I've worked for months on my knife techniques. And I had to go to three different gourmet stores to get these ingredients." Instead, you say with a laugh, "Oh, this? I just threw a few things together. Let's see how it turns out—I didn't even use a recipe." You still wear the button-down shirts you wore in high school, you explain.

Cultivate an offhand, nonchalant manner. You're desperate to be asked to join the ranks of the country club, but you know better than to let your desire show: seeming too eager will disqualify you. Impeccable taste

> **TIP:** Above all, avoid the appearance of affectation. Wondering whether to take the bold step of sporting an ascot? Remember the Ascot rule: If you haven't been, don't wear one.

indicates a deliberate effort, so cultivate some charming, spontaneous, jarring notes. Perhaps you love eating processed American cheese or reading Harlequin novels or listening to Gaelic music.

True *sprezzatura* can sometimes save a bumpkin or boor. Such people don't know enough to worry about the fact that they're wear-

In every aspect of your behavior, cultivate *sprezzatura;* emulate the master of ease and grace, John F. Kennedy. He seemed effortlessly rich, powerful, athletic, cultured, scholarly, glamorous, youthful, manly, playful, family-centered. (© Bettmann/CORBIS)

ing the wrong suit or don't know how to order in a restaurant. Their unconscious ease allows them to transcend their mistakes.

DISTINCTIONS MATTER—APPLY SUBTLETY AND UNDERSTATEMENT

Buy expensive things that don't openly signal their expense, but instead require sophistication to be appreciated. Instead of expensive clothes with a designer label (Donna Karan, Armani, Calvin Klein), buy the even more expensive items by the same designer—ones that lack a visible label. Buy the Gucci wallet without the *G* and the Ralph Lauren shirt without the polo player.

TIP: Cultivate a vocabulary of understatement—emulate the owners of the extravagant Newport "cottages."

Restrain your love for ostentation. In a description of the rivalry between the outstanding beauties of the demimonde in Monaco in 1895, Consuelo Vanderbilt wrote of La Belle Otero and Liane de Pougy: "It was not surprising therefore that Otero should challenge her rival [Pougy] by appearing at the Casino one night covered from head to foot with priceless jewels. It was a dazzling display, but in seeking to outdo her rival Otero had sacrificed good taste and had lent herself to ridicule." The crowd buzzed with speculation about how Pougy would respond to the challenge. Quite simple. "The next evening, appearing in a simple white gown without a single jewel, she was followed by her maid gorgeously arrayed in jewels that far outshone Otero's."

Apply the principle of dis-expectation and underscore your wealth by refusing to flaunt it in the usual ways. Make a point of relishing cheap wine or use objects—khakis, tablecloths, car—that are old and worn. Follow the Silicon Valley billionaires who compete to be ostentatiously unostentatious (of course, once this set of signals becomes prevalent, dis-expectation will require you to live opulently).

Special note on the trophy wife

Are you a man of means? If so, you may have considered acquiring a trophy wife. Trophy wives are usually thought of as sex trophies, but that's not their chief purpose. The principal function of a classic tro-phy wife is to supervise the couple's signaling.

The trophy-wife phenomenon reached its apex in the look-at-me, look-at-my-money 1980s. Breathless accounts of avatars such as Patricia Kluge, Gayfryd Steinberg, and Susan Gutfreund filled the soci-ety pages; Carolyne Roehm even made the cover of *Fortune* magazine.

While the husband's position and income set the raw standard, it's the wife who controls the fine distinctions of social place: house, entertaining, civic activities, vacations, clothing. (Women's very bodies offer more opportunity for display—through dress, jewelry, and general appearance—than men's do.) So when a man wants a more glamorous lifestyle, he needs a woman who knows what to do—generally, a person has time either to *make* money or to *spend* money, but not both.

The trophy wife's ambition is to conquer the new world of signal-ing—a challenge that her husband is too busy or uncertain to assume alone. What are you supposed to buy? Where are you supposed to go? The first wife was no help—she was preoccupied with the children, with vivid memories of humbler days; she was unskilled in the new parties, the right shops, the stylish activities that her husband's position now, he believes, merits.

TRUE RULE

A first wife marries *for better or for worse*. A trophy wife marries *for better*.

And so the trophy wife's greed for money and position is part of her allure. She lives up to her part of the bargain by exerting considerable effort to create the precisely correct signals.

Politicians don't need tro-phy wives. The trophy wife's function is to spend and sig-

Come spring, most everyone agrees, [Julia Koch] is going to have to do something about the resentful crouch she has adopted when it comes to her plans for the Fifth Avenue apartment. That does not mean allowing in every clamoring shelter magazine in America, but also not decreeing, as she did to *W,* that there would be no photographs at all because "I don't want people judging our taste." She lives, after all, in a world where taste is her business, her reason for being.

ELISABETH BUMILLER, "WOMAN ASCENDING A MARBLE STAIRCASE," *NEW YORK TIMES MAGAZINE,* JANUARY 11, 1998

nal, and because the position of even a rich politician is derived from his political power rather than wealth, he has little need for a trophy wife to help him achieve a desired social position through consumption. Furthermore, politicians must worry about appealing to the average voter, so a diamond- and fur-wearing wife could quickly become a liability.

Of course, fashions change in everything, including wives. Many of the most visible 1980s trophy wives were cast aside in the 1990s—as out of fashion as the first wives they once replaced. The new style for a new wife is more genteel, more educated, more professionally oriented, even if she quits working after the marriage. After his divorce from Anna, his wife of more than thirty years, media tycoon Rupert Murdoch, sixty-nine, married Wendi Deng, a thirty-two-year-old Star TV executive with an MBA; Murdoch commented that, "She could get a job anywhere, but the fact is she cannot do that and travel with me."

TIP: Apply the principle of dis-expectation to marriage. *The Wall Street Journal* reported that "a long first marriage has become a status symbol" because so many marriages have ended in divorce.

And the more recent trophy wives (they're still around) don't command the same attention such women once did. The ostentatious, "trophy" aspect is downplayed, in keeping with the more moderate, more professional post-eighties spirit. In some circles, people are so busy making money that they have no time for the demands of a marriage and signaling, and there the trophy-wife fashion has dissipated altogether.

While the fashion in trophy wives has changed—so much so that some even argue that trophy wives, themselves, are unfashionable—the practice still flourishes.

Here's the test to identify the classic, eighties-style trophy wife:

Trophy Wife Quiz

To qualify as a trophy wife, you must satisfy these six conditions. (It's often noted that trophy wives tend to be taller than their husbands, but this is *not* required.)

___ You must be a second or third wife. Not a first wife, because there is no "trophy" in a first wife; a first wife merely reflects the husband's position and attractiveness at the time of the first marriage, while a trophy wife takes her significance from the fact that her husband is triumphantly *trading up*. But a trophy wife is never a fourth, fifth, or sixth wife, because although having had three wives is excessive, having had more than three is tacky.

___ You must be at least eight years younger than your husband. Comparative youth is an essential element of the conquest of a "trophy." Draw attention to this disparity—he mentions some well-known figure or event (Tommy Dorsey, the Tet Offensive) from the past, and she demonstrates a delightful lack of recognition. "Well, John, remember that that happened way before I was even born!"

___ You must be deeply concerned with appearances—only proper, given that your principal occupation is to signal for yourself and your husband.

___ Your husband married you not *despite* your desire to spend his money, but at least in part *because* of it. A trophy wife's husband wants her to do everything necessary to establish a glittering profile.

___ You must be willing to give up having children if your husband doesn't want them. He's probably already satisfied his dynastic needs with his first wife, and he's had enough of young children around the house.

If you work—and it's quite suitable to work, as long as you don't let it interfere with your wifely responsibilities—you should pursue something feminine, preferably in a field that complements your signaling duties: a cosmetics-company executive, something in fashion design or interior decorating, philanthropic boards and committees, or light journalism.

• • •

Money for *signaling* is the most universal use; a close second in popularity is *self-gratification*. Money buys comforts that satisfy you, even if there's no audience to appreciate the expenditure (though having an audience often deepens your pleasure).

CHAPTER EIGHT

MONEY FOR SELF-GRATIFICATION

"I'd hire a servant so I could have my breakfast and newspapers brought to me in bed each morning."

If you want money to use for personal comfort and pleasure, you're chiefly interested in self-gratification. It takes three basic forms: *leisure, predictability,* and, most spectacular, *luxury.* A bonus is that the selfish pleasures also act as effective signals, because people recognize that the selfish pleasures are the privileges of money.

LEISURE

Why use your money for leisure? Leisure means that your work is done for you. No more frustrating hours spent waiting in line to get a passport renewed, no more spending the morning on the laundry, no more trips to the drugstore.

TRUE RULE

Let someone else sweat the small stuff—and it's all small stuff.

Leisure gives you more time for amusement—and more capacity. The world is more fun when someone else cleans up any mess. A blazing fire spontaneously combusts in the grate, and the ashes disappear a few hours later. Fresh flowers materialize every afternoon. The Duke and Duchess of Windsor arrived at their honeymoon destination in Austria with 266 pieces of luggage, including 186 trunks. Elizabeth Taylor and Richard Burton were similarly inclined—their travel required 156 suitcases, four children, one governess, three male secretaries in mink jackets, a hairdresser, a

One would like to give a party now and then, if one could be a billionaire.—"Antoine, I am going to have twenty people to dine to-day." *"Bien, Madame."* Not a word or thought more about it, but get home in season to dress, and come down to your own table, one of your own guests. "Giuseppe, we are to have a party a week from to-night,—five hundred invitations—there is the list." The day comes. "Madam, do you remember you have your party tonight?" "Why, so I have! Everything right? supper and all?" "All as it should be, Madame." "Send up Victorine." "Victorine, full toilet for this evening,—pink, diamonds, and emeralds. Coiffeur at seven. *Allez."*— Billionism, or even millionism, would be a blessed kind of state.

OLIVER WENDELL HOLMES, SR.,

ELSIE VENNER: A ROMANCE OF DESTINY

nurse, four dogs, and two Siamese cats with diamond collars. Why not just bring everything?

And money buys you relief from money. Someone else copes with its bothersome, dirty presence and the effort of spending. Jack Kennedy, Yoko Ono, and Eddie Murphy always let their aides take care of paying.

TRUE RULE

The more money you have, the less money you handle.

Soon, there's little left for you to do. You don't want to devote the time to cultivating artists, as the rich did in the old days, so you patronize a gallery owner who handles that for you. You pay a personal assistant to answer invitations and pay bills, and a shopping consultant to handle gift-buying. You have an audiovisual consultant to install your VCR and stereo and to keep those pesky remote controls working. Servants handle even the intimate gestures of friendship. One socialite said of another: "She was an incredible friend. She knows I love homemade chips, so she would have her cook send them over." Truly, it was the thought that counted.

Your servants can handle anything. Novelist Edith Wharton described Mrs. Beaufort, a character who "always gave her ball on an Opera night in order to emphasise her complete superiority to household cares, and her possession of a staff of servants competent to organise every detail of the entertainment in her absence." After you have a maid, a secretary, a cook, a driver, a nanny, and a handyman, you have complete leisure; at which point, freed from necessity, you *choose* to wash the car, chop firewood, set the table, or bake bread. The leisured ladies of Greenwich, Connecticut, leave their fully staffed houses, where gardeners labor over boxwoods, to spend the afternoon at Hortulus—the garden club. Tasks seem onerous until they're voluntary.

A pleasant offshoot of leisure is convenience. Tasks you can't delegate are arranged to accommodate you. Manicurist and masseur pay a visit. Barber and shoeshine man labor along your office hallway. Your personal trainer bounces into your at-home gym in the mornings.

Your most valuable convenience is good transportation. In fact, because everyone wants quick, comfortable transportation, it's a common target for excess and abuse. David Watkins, the former Clinton White House director of administration, was forced out in 1994 after he commandeered a Marine One helicopter to "check out" a golf course for the president. William Aramony was ejected as United Way president when it was discovered among other things that he was spending the charity's money on private car service and first-class airfare.

TIP: If you throw in a showy transportation benefit, you can pay people less salary. The comparatively low-paying federal government supplies important officials with ostentatious transportation perks: VIP reserved parking, portal-to-portal service in distinctive dark sedans, police escorts with sirens and flags to cut through traffic, direct flights on military aircraft.

As part of convenient transportation, insist on freedom from the hassle of luggage. Use an overnight shipping service, like Federal Express, to deliver your luggage to your door. You carry just what you need during the flight. In fact, a status symbol among Concorde-regulars is to travel with the most minimal luggage. (One traveler was known to take the Concorde himself, to save time, and send his bags back on his private plane.)

Money also buys you the delightful convenience of spontaneity. No need to make reservations twenty-one days in advance or to scissor out coupons or to wait until the after-Christmas sales. You can afford to be impulsive. When you get a phone call at work, "Let's get away for the weekend," you answer, "Great idea. You pick the place, and we'll go." A secretary and travel agent handle the plans. "Hurry up," you complain when it's time to leave for the airport. "Aren't you ready yet? If we forget something, we can just buy it when we get there." You quietly congratulate yourself on your zest for life. Spontaneity is often loftily claimed as a virtue, but it's quite an expensive virtue.

You have the convenience of immediate gratification and refuse to wait for what you want. One Bridgehamptonite was irritated by his driveway's narrow width; he wanted more room to turn his Ferrari around. So he called the contractor to ask the cost of having the driveway widened ten feet. And, oh, yes, he wanted it done by the end of the day. No problem. The right amount of money gets anything done.

THE DOWNSIDE OF LEISURE

Leisure comes at the cost of privacy. Your assistants monitor your habits and itineraries, they shake out the trash, they overhear conversations. You've lost count of the number of people who have keys to your house and who know your security code. You don't realize it, but everyone in your office smirks when you telephone your mistress—they know what you're up to because it's the only time you dial the phone yourself. Your secretary, her face a discreet, expressionless mask, sorts through your receipts, vouchers, and pink "While You Were Out" slips. Your partners all use the same car service, and they listen to your comings and goings blared over the dispatch radio, just as you listen to theirs. *Hmmm,* you wonder, why would your cohead of merchant banking need to be picked up at the Ritz-Carlton at three P.M.? Doormen know who goes in and out. The washerwoman sees the stains.

TRUE RULE

Lack of bother means lack of privacy.

PREDICTABILITY

Why use your money for predictability? Surprisingly, of the comforts money can buy, this drab pleasure turns out to be one of the most treasured. You get uniformly good hotels, safe neighborhoods, immaculate bathrooms, prompt attention.

A friend visits from out of town, and you arrange for dinner at your favorite restaurant. The maître d' greets you by name and leads you to your usual table. (Predictability includes the pleasure of being known.) You don't need to see the menu. After dinner you suggest, "Let's call a car." "Let's just grab a taxi outside," your friend replies. You shake your head. Why not? The pleasure of *convenience* explains why a taxi is so much nicer than a bus or subway, but the pleasure of *predictability* explains why car service is so much nicer than a taxi. Although both give you a ride door to door, car service also offers the predictability of cleanliness, competence, and comfort. (Also, no cash changes hands.)

Predictability is worth the high price you pay for private security guards, private schools, private trash services, and private libraries, for comfortable airport waiting rooms and special wings in hospitals, where every thought is to the comfort of the "guests."

Predictability—and its cousins, *belonging* and *exclusivity*—are nursed by institutions like schools, clubs, and firms. Money shrinks the world to the "right" crowd, where people are of uniform quality: no need to wonder about the other children at school, the other people on the tennis courts, the other customers in the grocery store. Because your favorite restaurant, Le Bilboquet, disdains to list its telephone number or display its name, you know that the wrong people will have an impossible time finding it. Pity the poor corporate raider: he's got a zillion dollars, but the co-op board wouldn't approve him. Why not? Some of the current residents might feel uncomfortable riding in the elevator with him. The residents' money allows them to safeguard their environment.

TIP: Avoid public-sector services.

TRUE RULE

Insulate, insulate, insulate.

The prize of predictability doesn't come cheap. When Julian Davies died in 1922, a group of robber barons feared that undesirables might buy his estate or, worse, subdivide it. Together they turned the estate into their private club, the Timber Point Club, open to just one hundred people. They hired the world's most famous golf-course designer, a famous professional to give golf lessons, the best chefs for the kitchen, and added a large boat basin. When an adjoining estate came on the market, the Timber Pointers bought it. They hired caretakers and stocked the place with deer and wild pheasant—all this for less than ten days of hunting a year, and the knowledge that they'd never have to face a stranger. They paid a staggering sum for the simple, common comfort of knowing their neighbors.

Predictability requires exclusivity. The chief allure of such establishments—say, Florida's Jupiter Island—isn't the facility, but the exclusivity. In fact, some institutions exist for no other reason than to define an exclusive crowd. Although most clubs offer some comforts to justify their existence—library, bar, gym, golf course—the most fastidious needn't bother with such pretense. Washington, D.C.'s Alfalfa Club swings into activity only briefly during the year, and the chief reason to belong is to revel in your membership. The atmosphere seems ebullient and self-congratulatory (after a few years the thrill wears off, and you realize you are among others just like yourself).

A tantalizing feature of exclusive institutions is that often money can't buy admission. Telling someone "who has everything" that something is out of reach is a sure way to fire desire. Some clever promoters have taken to sending invitations to a select list of people for an event that's actually open to the public. The fact that an exclusive few were expressly invited sets everyone else scrambling.

Institutions boost their cachet by exclusion. Sororities and fraternities have elaborate screening processes to choose the "right" candidates for admission. Nightclubs turn up their heat by waving only certain people past the velvet rope. Restaurants hand out a secret VIP telephone number, used by only their Very Important Diners. Social events such as galas, charity balls, art openings, or fund-raising dinners often include both an enormous event to which everyone is invited and a more intimate and exclusive event that precedes or follows the main show. Make sure you're invited to both (if not, skip the event altogether).

Exploit exclusivity's value. A recent fashion-house innovation:

While the average customer is merely buzzed inside, the celebrity shopper is whisked away beyond view into an enormous fitting room stocked with every indulgence. By barring ordinary shoppers, guaranteeing an extraordinary level of service, and adding a delicious garnish of exclusivity, the boutiques feed their best customers' craving for predictability and exclusivity (and freebies).

Of course, the ultimate exclusivity is to limit membership to yourself. Billionaire entrepreneur Wayne Huizenga belongs to the world's most private golf club—an 18-hole golf course in his backyard, complete with a 55,000-square-foot clubhouse and 46 golf carts. No more worries about getting a good tee time or having to play with someone you don't like.

Predictability takes the stress out of making decisions. You know what you're supposed to do. Where does your crowd go? Aspen, Palm Beach, Hobe Sound, Hilton Head, Martha's Vineyard, Fire Island, Sun Valley . . . Take care to stay current. Is your ranch in Montana or Wyoming?

THE DOWNSIDE OF PREDICTABILITY

Predictability has its price. You sometimes flag beneath the weight of expected standards—the obligatory social schedule, the need to wear black tie or the latest in sunglasses. From time to time, your set feels cramped and inbred; but you're too far gone to step into the mongrel world. You must hold up certain standards, even at personal cost.

And being known is no pleasure when you're trying to pass anonymously. The top-rated Four Seasons Hotel prides itself on addressing its guests by name, never by a generic "sir" or "ma'am." But maybe you don't want the hotel staff to know your name.

LUXURY

Why use your money for luxury? Luxury is the ability to satisfy every desire, large or small, without counting the cost. Price is no object, and nothing is out of reach. When Candy Spelling, wife of television producer Aaron Spelling, discovered during construction that the view from the bedroom of her unbuilt house would include a neon sign, she reportedly ordered that a new foundation be dug to lower the house ten feet. James Gordon Bennett, Jr., the inheritor of the old *New York Herald,* was once unable to get a table at his favorite Monte Carlo restaurant. So he bought the restaurant on the spot, had another customer ejected, ate his meal, then handed the deed to his waiter. He'd gotten what he wanted.

Those who can't afford true luxury must count every nickel. They worry about appearances, and so they lavish money on things in view while neglecting things out of sight. The expansiveness of luxury, however, allows you to extend beauty, comfort, and order into every forgotten corner. No more putting up with hidden junk closets or chipped china. You prefer a computer mousepad made of leather. You keep beautiful lingerie, carefully arranged, out of sight in a dresser drawer. You wear cashmere-lined gloves. All members of your household get their own copies of the daily newspaper. There's no hoarding of hotel shampoo, no waiting to buy the book in paperback. Jacqueline Kennedy had the sheets changed not only each morning, but each afternoon after her nap as well. According to her private secretary, her maid explained, "Mees Kennedy likes nice fresh sheets."

You luxuriate in the fulfillment of even your most casual desires. Fashion designer Calvin Klein once dispatched a limousine to his mother's Riverdale apartment to pick up a Tupperware bowl of soup, which then traveled back to East Hampton in style, nestled in the back as the sole passenger. Terri Holladay married Cecil Chao, a notorious Hong Kong playboy more than twice her age. She craved the Dunkin' Donuts of her suburban Miami childhood, but they weren't available in Hong

> Winsett himself had a savage abhorrence of social observances: Archer, who dressed in the evening because he thought it cleaner and more comfortable to do so, and who had never stopped to consider that cleanliness and comfort are two of the costliest items in a modest budget, regarded Winsett's attitude as part of the boring "Bohemian" pose that always made fashionable people, who changed their clothes without talking about it, and were not forever harping on the number of servants one kept, seem so much simpler and less self-conscious than the others.
>
> EDITH WHARTON, *THE AGE OF INNOCENCE*

Kong. She solved the problem by having packages of chocolate honey-glazed doughnuts couriered to Hong Kong by Express Mail. Christina Onassis also had trouble finding American delicacies overseas. When diet Coke wasn't available in France, she sent her tenseater jet each week to New York, to bring back one hundred bottles. When Yves, the head waiter at her Avenue Foch apartment in Paris, inquired of Helene, the chief housekeeper, why a thousand bottles were not brought back, Helene explained, "Because Madame doesn't want old diet Coke." The bottles were handled gingerly; each one ended up costing $300. Why give up life's simple pleasures?

T R U E   R U L E

No desire is too large, *or too small,* to satisfy.

THE SUPREME LUXURY: EXCESS

As more pleasures come within reach, your appetites change. The old desires and goals have long been satisfied, but larger, obscure longings rise to take their place. You must exaggerate your indulgences to feel gratified. Because most people's tastes are limited by their resources, their secret aptitude for excess is never roused. But once you're freed from constraint, you can use money to satisfy the taste for the luxury of excess—a delicious, illicit pleasure.

You dream of making an unprecedented, extreme gesture. But how? The mere size of a price tag isn't enough to slake your urge for excess. Don't do something sensible—your gesture should be glorious, not necessary. Lila Acheson Wallace had the right idea. She gave a $4 million endowment for fresh flowers in the Great Hall of the Metropolitan Museum, a pure grace note.

Your excess celebrates your release from the *principle of balanced accounts*—that is, you consume money, time, and effort without any need to calculate or offset the cost. You accumulate things you don't particularly want and can't possibly use. Most people must balance their checkbooks, consider cheaper alternatives, pace their purchases—but not you. You ignore necessity.

TRUE RULE

The bigger the private plane, the fewer the passengers.

Your disregard for the principle of balanced accounts arouses mixed feelings in others—for the same reasons it fascinates, it threatens, with its overtones of wanton indulgence, dissipation, and loss of control. And without some polite disguise, an expression of excess reveals *waste,* too shocking, too thrilling, to be widely tolerated. So be sure to indulge your taste for excess in ways that will allow you—perhaps—to spend without risking societal disapproval.

So how, exactly, do you help to make your excess acceptable? Here are seven common methods to force the luxury of excess into socially palatable forms. Although expenditures in these categories may nevertheless appear outrageously *extravagant,* they are at least arguably defensible as justified by some goal—practical or aesthetic—other than sheer indulgence of excess. (As you'll see in some of the following examples, if your excess is great enough, these disguises won't be successful.)

SEVEN WAYS TO DISGUISE EXCESS IN AN ACCEPTABLE FORM

1. Simplicity

2. Scope

3. Suitability

4. Order

5. Displacement

6. Fastidiousness

7. Party- and gift-giving

1. *Disguise excess—Simplicity.* Explain that you prefer simple, spare arrangements. (Your rooms are so simple and spare, in fact, that now you need a full-time maid to fight off the encroachments of mail, magazines, and loose change.) Examples:

   • For the house he planned outside San Francisco, Oracle founder and billionaire Larry Ellison aimed to create an authentic Japanese structure—hand-crafted, wooden, with hand-fitted joints, few nails, hand-planed wood, and mud-plastered walls. Ellison explained that he wanted to give his guests "a taste of a disciplined, uncluttered lifestyle." The estimated cost of such discipline and lack of clutter? Forty million dollars.

- In pursuit of a simple elegance, designer Calvin Klein wanted dark, old, wide planks for his house's floors. When he couldn't find any that passed muster, he sent scouts out to scour the Northeast for three-hundred-year-old wood. After the right wood was discovered in an old Vermont farmhouse, the planks were sent to a warehouse where they were individually numbered and photographed, and each plank personally approved by Klein. The planks then had to be hand-stained individually to get the eggplant color Calvin wanted, and finally, after the planks were done, wooden toilet seats were dyed to match.

- "Think Shaker" was society paragon Annette de la Renta's instruction to event planner Robert Isabell for her daughter's wedding at the family farm in Kent, Connecticut. The Shaker aesthetic flowered into a wedding attended by more than five hundred guests, with three tents, Federal blue sisal carpeting on the ground, catering by Glorious Food, *Vogue* photographers capturing the event for its readership, and, of course, fashions from Oscar de la Renta. "Simple is hard," proclaimed Isabell.

2. *Disguise excess—Scope.* Lavish money and attention on commonplace things, or buy a vast number of an ordinary possession. Examples:

- To use an invitation as a means of excessive display, don't merely get it printed up or handwrite it; hire a professional calligrapher as well as a messenger to deliver it by hand. But sometimes using regular mail is unavoidable. Social swan Babe Paley directed her secretaries to snip off the edges of stamps when they addressed envelopes for invitations.

- Building a house is a normal aspiration. Amplified by excess, billionaire Ira Rennert planned a controversial 66,000 square-foot house in the Hamptons, with 29 bedrooms, 30 bathrooms, 11 sitting rooms, two libraries, an art gallery, a perhaps 100-car garage, and a 10,000-square-foot "playhouse" holding two bowling alleys, squash courts, tennis courts, a basketball court, a game room, a billiards room, a playroom, an exercise room, and four full bathrooms.

- Just buying a private DC-9 airliner like other business bigwigs wasn't enough for Hugh Hefner. His *Big Bunny,* the only black jet in the world (black except for the white Bunny logo on the tail), was equipped with a dance floor, a sunken Roman bath, and an elliptical bed upholstered in black Himalayan goatskin and white silk sheets. "Jet Bunnies" dressed in miniskirts and thigh-length boots serviced travelers' needs. Hefner liked to refer to his jet as "just a convenience."

Always cloak your excesses in some justification. *Playboy* founder Hugh Hefner argued that just like many businessmen, he needed the convenience of a private plane— reasonable enough. Then he used that reasonable possession as an opportunity for excessive display. (AP/Wide World Photos)

- In his favorite house (one of four), Elton John packed every room with fresh flowers—more than one hundred arrangements in a single week, enough to keep two florists busy working only for him.

3. *Disguise excess—Suitability.* Hyperspecialize your possessions to fulfill your peculiar taste or a highly refined purpose, or go to enormous lengths to arrange things to suit yourself. Examples:

- Socialite Susan Gutfreund was so particular that she kept a refrigerator in her bathroom to chill her perfumes.
- Silicon Valley supermogul and billionaire Jim Clark dug up his swimming pool and moved it to a place he liked better—not once, but twice.
- People, like possessions, can be hyperspecialized. William Randolph Hearst's estate included a staff member with the job of dusting table legs; someone else dusted the tops of the tables. One Lake Forest, Illinois, millionaire hired a servant just to place sugar water in his hummingbird feeders.

Enhance the thrill of excess by violating the laws of nature as you arrange things to suit yourself. Examples:

- Candy Spelling, wife of TV producer Aaron Spelling, decided to give her children a white Christmas in Southern California. She arranged to have tons of snow manufactured, trucked to their house, and spread over the lawn just before the children woke up.
- One New York hostess transformed her gardens overnight. A guest would go to sleep in room with a view of an all-white garden, and wake to see only pink flowers. (The secret? Gardeners worked through the night to replace the former garden with thousands of water-filled glass vials holding cut flowers.)

TIP: Keep two households in the same city. You're at a party in SoHo, and it's late—you spend the night at your TriBeCa loft rather than return uptown. Or you stay over at your Malibu beach house instead of making the long trip back to the Hollywood Hills.

- Entertainment mogul David Geffen, clothes designer Ralph Lauren, and press magnate William Randolph Hearst all moved full-grown trees onto their property.

4. *Disguise excess—Order.* Demand a design of extravagant order or cleanliness. Examples:

- The exacting standards of Buckingham Palace and ducal establishments required "matching" footmen, of the same height and build. The taller the footmen, the more impressive the household, because footmen were paid extra for every inch they cleared above six feet.
- Legendary gardener Adele Herter's house in East Hampton (later known as The Creeks) featured a brick walkway covered by a trellised arbor of Concord grapes. Because she didn't like ugly purple marks smeared on the path, she kept a servant whose sole job was to sweep the brick of grapes three times a day.
- The Duchess of Windsor ordered napkins changed twice during dinner, had her hair done three times a day, and ordered the soles of her shoes polished daily.

5. *Disguise excess—Displacement.* Spend huge sums on unlikely subjects, such as children, servants, or pets. Examples:

Children
- Boxing promoter William MacDonald built his daughter a tree house with curtains and carpeting to match the main house, and for her eighth birthday, added a jukebox.
- Toy store F.A.O. Schwarz offers the "Ultimate Sleepover Adventure," more than $17,000 for an in-store slumber party for fifteen kids. Each child receives a backpack crammed with goodies before being turned loose in the three-floor megastore, and a midnight treasure hunt, DVD movie, and $100 gift certificate add further diversion. (However, cell phone reception, the children often complain, is poor.)

Servants
- The Sultan of Brunei once left a $170,000 cash tip at the Four Seasons Hotel.
- One L.A. fashion is to leave a restaurant tip of one hundred percent—or more—to show that you have the money to do so (on top of the hefty bill) and also assure yourself royal treatment, and discretion, each time you come in.

Pets
- When fashion designer Oscar de la Renta's Norfolk terrier ate rat poison at a Dominican Republic estate, a veterinarian was rushed by chartered jet to arrive within hours to save the dog.
- The Four Seasons Hotel, one of the country's best, offers room service for pets, featuring the "Tail Wagger" of shredded braised beef and steamed rice and the "Claw Cleaner" of albacore tuna, chopped egg, and sour cream—all served on appropriate petware.

6. *Disguise excess—Fastidiousness.* Add a touch of refinement to even the lowest objects. Examples:
   - At director George Lucas's July Fourth potluck for his Skywalker Ranch's eighteen hundred employees, the portable toilets were wood paneled.
   - In addition to other prosaic items, like her feather pillows, her hot-water bottles, and her favorite china tea set, Queen Elizabeth travels with a white leather lavatory seat.

7. *Disguise excess—Party- and gift-giving.* Lavish your excess on others. Because such expenditures are directed elsewhere, they don't appear self-indulgent. Examples:
   - One notorious 1980s birthday party, given by socially ambitious Gayfryd Steinberg for her husband, Saul, cost about $1 million, and Saul Steinberg's daughter's Metropolitan Museum wedding reception was so expensive that caterers, florists, and other workers were asked to sign confidentiality

agreements about the party's cost. (They didn't have a chance of keeping the secret. Details, like the fact that the flower bill alone approached $1 million, leaked out.)

- At the 1990s version of the big wedding, Kerry Packer, the richest man in Australia, threw a $6.5 million wedding for his son. Guests were told not to bring gifts, but instead received them— $5 million worth of golf clubs, designer handbags, chess sets, cuff-links and pendants wrought of pure gold, and more.

Incidentally, giving sumptuous gifts serves another important purpose: it reinforces or creates social ties, by creating social debt. You can create the appearance, and perhaps the reality, of intimacy by giving a gift—particularly if you pick a gift that shows you know the recipient's tastes. Example:

- Barbra Streisand told a story about the late media mogul Steve Ross. After Streisand decided that a sculpture she loved was too expensive to buy, Ross invited her to dinner and presented it as a gift for finishing work on her movie *Yentl.* "How he found it, how he traced it!" Streisand exclaimed. With a single—expensive but economical—gift, Ross showed the world his intimacy with a star and reinforced a social bond.

TIP: While lavish gift-giving is usually acceptable, if your gift is *too* excessive, you risk ridicule. One New Yorker handed out Bulgari jewelry to acquaintances who had done nothing more than serve on a committee with her. Recipients (even those only too pleased to get the jewelry) scoffed at her gift.

Remember, the thrill of excess comes from its immoderacy. You don't need to spend thousands or millions of dollars to indulge in excess; you need merely violate the principle of balanced accounts *at your level.* That violation could mean indulging in the purchase of a Boeing Business Jet (for those for whom the Gulfstream V just isn't enough); deciding that you hate the new kitchen cabinets, tearing them out, and ordering a new set to match the floors; hiring a neighborhood kid to walk your dog instead of doing it yourself; or ordering dessert and coffee after splurging by eating in a restaurant.

But maybe you don't care about disguising your excess. You choose to flout public censure and indulge in the luxury of excess in its most deeply satisfying, and repugnant, form: *destruction*.

In its less extreme, more palatable guise, the excess of destruction appears as *waste*. On a yachting trip during his 325 days as King Edward VIII, the King (soon to be Duke of Windsor) drove three thousand golf balls off the deck to keep in practice—exclaiming, "I love a splash!" Deranged tycoon Howard Hughes squandered both possessions and people. He leased expensive houses he never occupied, staffed them with round-the-clock guards to keep out intruders, and allowed the lawns, pools, and gardens to disintegrate. Hughes maintained at least five young starlets, tucked away in his mansions, with cars, drivers, and restaurant charge accounts. Hughes never visited his starlets, but he hired private detectives to make sure no one else did, either.

> **TIP:** The simplest way to waste is continuously to pay for something you never use. Keep up with the monthly fees for that swanky gym, even though you haven't gone for a year. Board a horse at a stable without ever going riding (a popular technique in L.A.).

Because waste shows you need not observe the convention of conservation, it's an effective signal of wealth. In Dominick Dunne's novel *People Like Us,* social upstart Ruby anxiously instructs her husband on the proper behavior for their new set. "Elias, you're not supposed to wipe the plate clean with your dinner roll. . . . You're supposed to waste some of the food." When, like Scarlett O'Hara, her husband protests, saying he gets hungry, she decides, "I tell you what we're going to do. I'm going to have the cook feed you before we go out to these functions, and then you can pick at your food, like all these people do, when we sit down to dinner." Movie producer Don Simpson wore his Levi's once and then threw them away. He kept a stack at home—with the tags on them to ensure they were new when he put them on for the first and only time. Infamous arbitrageur Ivan Boesky was known to order every entree on a restaurant's menu, taste each one, and then send all but one dish back to the kitchen.

Need some suggestions about how and what to waste? Try ordering an expensive wine in a restaurant, then leaving it opened and untouched when you leave. Buy the latest copy of your favorite magazine from a newsstand to read on the plane, even though you've got one waiting in your mailbox at home. Spend a huge amount dressing your baby—she outgrows that $250 Clements Ribeiro baby cashmere sweater before the weather turns cold enough for her to wear it.

But at a certain point, mere waste becomes too slow and cumbersome, and only a spectacular, outright destruction of wealth can satisfy you. Getting anything you want breeds the desire to demolish everything you see. Others watch, enthralled, as you sink into devastation. Rock stars take the trouble to trash their hotel rooms because they're too inured to a hotel's pleasures to seek enjoyment in mere possession of the presidential suite.

Everyone feels the thrill, the taboo, of destruction. The ninth Duchess of Marlborough (Consuelo Vanderbilt) recalls a dinner where the guests were startled by the tremendous crash of shattered china when a footman dropped a tray. It turned out that their host, Lord de Grey, had specially bought the china for the purpose of being dropped, to provoke the boisterous pleasure that such destruction elicits. Frank Sinatra felt the same impulse. Once, in Las Vegas, he offered a waiter $100 to drop a tray full of glasses. (The waiter refused to do it.) Actress Mia Farrow recalls the time she deposited two of her children with her then-lover Woody Allen. "When I returned less than an hour later, he was throwing his hats and gloves into the fire. The kids were ecstatic. 'I ran out of things to do,' he shrugged."

Destruction thrills because it is taboo—and sometimes the violation is so shocking that it's not permitted. In 1991, Japan's Ryoei Saito bought a Van Gogh and a Renoir for a total of $185 million. He announced that his paintings would be cremated along with him, at the appropriate time—but the pressure of international disapproval was so strong that he was forced to change his plans.

Your destruction need not be quite so blatant. Follow the latest millionaires' trend of the "tear-down": buy a perfectly good house, or a couple of houses, then tear them down to make way for an enormous new mansion. Bill Gates sold his house for more than $8 million; the new owner razed it to build an Irish-country-style house out of imported stone. It's far more thrilling to destroy and replace an existing house than to build on an empty lot. (And to destroy a house with a Bill Gates pedigree! Even better.)

The *Marie-Antoinepisode*

Never forget that people regard—or at least pretend to regard—excessive expenditure with resentment and disapproval. That's why it generally must be disguised. Avoid *Marie-Antoinepisodes* (so called after French Queen Marie Antoinette's famous remark, upon hearing that the people were starving for lack of bread, "Then let them eat cake"). You have a Marie-Antoinepisode if you make a remark or gesture that demonstrates an offensive disregard for cost, value, and proportion.

Be on particular guard against Marie-Antoinepisodes when you're holding yourself out as a moral example. Consider the blunder by the Environmental Media Association, a group of entertainment bigwigs formed to guide Americans to be more environmentally conscientious. It didn't look good when these supposedly energy-conscious Hollywood heavyweights turned up at the first meeting in gas-guzzling luxury cars and stretch limousines.

The Reagan administration had particular problems with Marie-Antoinepisodes—the press had a field day with each one. First Lady Nancy Reagan wanted her White House legacy to feature a set of state china in her name. Unfazed by a quote of $1,000 per place setting, she designed place settings for 220, with seven styles of plates, plus finger bowls, cereal bowls, berry bowls, ramekins, and cocktail cups for holding shrimp sauce. Each handcrafted plate bore wide scarlet borders and double rings of gold etching, and was capped with a raised 24-karat gold presidential seal. The Marie-Antoinepisode came when, with unfortunate juxtaposition, Nancy Reagan announced the acquisition of this state china on the same day that her husband, President Reagan, announced cutbacks in the federally subsidized school-lunch program—with a declaration that thereafter *ketchup* would be categorized as a vegetable. The coincidence of timing did not pass unnoticed. Charles Wick, one of the Reagans' longtime friends, had an infamous Marie-Antoinepisode when he explained his view that penny-pinching Americans enjoyed watching the luxurious lifestyle of Reagan administration members, much as Americans during the Depression enjoyed watching movies with glamorous Hollywood stars. "They loved those glamour pictures . . . showing that people were living the glamorous good life." So that glamorous lifestyle was actually a real public service?

A Marie-Antoinepisode can also take the reverse form, of claiming to be constrained by a thrift that's obviously unnecessary. In its coverage of corporate raider Ronald Perelman and Patricia Duff's custody battle over their daughter, Caleigh, the media pounced on Perelman's claim that he could feed his daughter on $3 a day. This, from a man worth billions.

Beware of the temptation to put on airs foreign to your age or background. You offend people, and you look ridiculous. During her notorious marriage to Donald Trump, twenty-something Marla Maples of Dalton, Georgia, required her staff to stand in uniform behind their charges during dinner.

If the rich are fortunate in being able to travel to Dresden as soon as the desire to do so arises, or to buy a dress just after they have seen it in a catalog, they are cursed because of the speed with which their wealth fulfills their desires. No sooner have they thought of Dresden than they can be on a train there; no sooner have they seen a dress than it can be in their wardrobe. They therefore have no opportunity to suffer the interval between desire and gratification which the less privileged endure, and which, for all its apparent unpleasantness, has the incalculable benefit of allowing people to know and fall deeply in love with paintings in Dresden, hats, dressing gowns, and someone who isn't free this evening.

ALAIN DE BOTTON, *HOW PROUST CAN CHANGE YOUR LIFE: NOT A NOVEL*

THE DOWNSIDE OF LUXURY

Constant sensual indulgence paradoxically leads to loss of pleasure; deprivation is an indispensable part of gratification. As Nietzsche observed, "Possessions are generally diminished by possession."

Gratification depends on a measure of delay, denial, and anticipation—on having been tantalized with pleasure before being satisfied. Indulgence cuts this process short.

TRUE RULE

Satisfaction
breeds dissatisfaction.

You've been to that island resort so many times now that

it hardly feels like a vacation. You don't particularly look forward anymore to going. Yes, the weather's perfect, the rooms are large, the food and the facilities are good. But there's nothing special about the place, and you wonder why those honeymooners seem so pleased. You complain to the manager about the air-conditioning and the weak coffee. The monotony of delight has robbed you of the ability to feel pleasure. Now, what will you do to spice up the weekend?

> We felt very nice and snug, the more so since it was so chilly out of doors; indeed out of bedclothes too, seeing that there was no fire in the room. The more so, I say, because truly to enjoy bodily warmth, some small part of you must be cold, for there is no quality in this world that is not what it is merely by contrast. Nothing exists in itself. If you flatter yourself that you are all over comfortable, and have been so a long time, then you cannot be said to be comfortable any more.
>
> HERMAN MELVILLE, *MOBY DICK*

Instant satisfaction diminishes enjoyment. So, if you find that ceaseless indulgence has begun to cloy, try one of two cures:

Indulgence in the highest pleasures: *Rarefaction*

To counter overindulgence, educate your tastes to rarefied extremes. High perception consigns you to a narrow range of enjoyment, and soon you can appreciate only the highest delectations. You'll search in vain for the wine, dry cleaner, furniture, to meet your high standards. A single pea disturbed the sleep of the true princess, because her cultivation kept her from resting on a dozen mattresses.

Indulgence in the lowest pleasures: *Nostalgie de la boue*

If you're tired of being rich, play at being poor. Cultivate the perverse, the wrong people, dirty things. The monotony of wealth stimulates *nostalgie de la boue* ("yearning for mud")—a search for novelty in the trappings of indigence or depravity, a romantic attraction to poverty and "primitives," the impulse to capture the vitality of the lower orders by imitating them.

One hundred years ago, the "Poverty Social" was in fashion. Guests dressed in rags and tatters, sat on broken soapboxes and coal hods, used newspapers as napkins, and ate scraps of food off wooden plates and drank beer from rusty cans. Around the same time, the famous hostess Mrs. Stuyvesant Fish gave a Servants' Ball at Newport, where everyone dressed up as ladies' maids, valets, cooks, chauffeurs, and footmen. It's fun to look ordinary, or even poor, when it's clear that you're playing a part. A whole industry has sprung up to make new denim appear old and dirty, because consumers will pay for that worn look. A $20 pair of pristine Calvin Klein jeans is worth four times as much if it can be purchased prestained—what jean-maker Diesel calls "the luxury of dirt." And if you've got the money, you can afford to vacation poor. Nowadays some people are escaping their restaurant-quality kitchens at home to travel to places with no heat, electricity, or indoor plumbing. They will pay handsomely to vacation simply.

TRUE RULE

Money can buy anything, even poverty.

Be careful, however—these days, admitting to this taste isn't always politically correct. After the late media head Steve Ross and his wife, Courtney, bought a castle in Todi, Italy, along with its peasant village and 240 surrounding acres, Courtney Ross gushed, "What my husband and I found so charming about it is that, as [our architect] put it, it's so poor." Apparently someone thought to regret her choice of words—but although the Ross lawyer tried to explain that she'd really meant not "poor" but "rustic," it seems more likely she'd meant exactly what she said.

• • •

Signaling and *self-gratification* are the two most common uses for money. If neither describes your use for money, you may be one of the rare people who uses money to feed object lust. *Object lust* is a stern, demanding passion; it is an aesthetic, inborn love of beautiful objects.

CHAPTER NINE

MONEY FOR OBJECT LUST

"I'd immediately buy several outstanding pieces for my collection of nineteenth-century clocks."

If you want to use money to feed your craving for beautiful objects, you suffer from *object lust*—that sensual passion for things, not for signaling or for gratification, but just in themselves. A man like George Way has a powerful case of object lust. This New York deli counterman spent all the time and money he could spare collecting early English and Dutch furniture and sixteenth- and seventeenth-century portraits, treasures that he crammed into his tiny three-room apartment.

Before you proclaim that yes, you feel object lust, consider that it's difficult to distinguish true object lust from the desire for an object's signaling value. You love your sleek Prada shoes with their distinctive red vertical stripe. But do you have object lust? Or do you just crave the signal that the shoes make? Take this quiz to determine whether you experience true object lust:

> "One gets the greatest joy of all out of really lovely stockings," said Ursula.
>
> "One does," said Gudrun, "the greatest joy of all."
>
> D. H. LAWRENCE,
> *WOMEN IN LOVE*

Object Lust Quiz

____ Would it bother you to buy an unlabeled knockoff of a Mont Blanc pen, even if the quality of the pen were *exactly* the same as the Mont Blanc?

Do you feel a passionate attraction toward expensive objects of the highest quality, but indifferent to common objects like brooms, pencils, or teakettles?

Are the objects of your desire—a sports car, fur coat, watch— commonly held among your peers?

Is carrying a handsome umbrella more satisfying to you than using a fine hairbrush?

If you answered "yes" to these questions, you don't have real object lust. What's the test? *Object lust needs no audience; signaling requires an audience.* With object lust, there's no premium on grandeur or labels, and no need to impress other people. Object lust is an aesthetic, overwhelming passion for objects.

Of course, even if you don't have true object lust, you can learn to admire objects. A decorator points out the marvelous construction of a sofa, a gallery owner explains the beauty of brushstrokes, the sales clerk expounds on fabric, cut, and detail, and you learn to appreciate things. But although you can train your tastes, true object lust is more visceral and passionate, even when educated, than acquired appreciation. Virginia Woolf mused, "But I must remember

He took out a pile of shirts and began throwing them, one by one, before us, shirts of sheer linen and thick silk and fine flannel, which lost their folds as they fell and covered the table in many-colored disarray. While we admired he brought more and the soft rich heap mounted higher—shirts with stripes and scrolls and plaids in coral and apple-green and lavender and faint orange, with monograms of Indian blue. Suddenly, with a strained sound, Daisy bent her head into the shirts and began to cry stormily. "They're such beautiful shirts," she sobbed, her voice muffled in the thick folds. "It makes me sad because I've never seen such—such beautiful shirts before."

F. Scott Fitzgerald, *The Great Gatsby*

to write about my *clothes* next time I have an impulse to write. My love of clothes interests me profoundly; only it is not love; and what it is I must discover."

Object lust can bring exquisite pleasure, when satisfied—but object lust is also melancholy, sickening, when the feeling of love for beautiful things is wrapped up in the yearning for things out of reach.

> Strike had no real love of things for themselves, but he loved the idea of things, the concept of possession. Sometimes he was crazed with wanting, blind with visions of things he was too cagey to buy, and at moments like this he felt tortured, tantalized, sensing in some joyless way that he was outsmarting someone, but he wasn't sure who.
>
> RICHARD PRICE, *CLOCKERS*

Unattainable objects taunt and tempt you, and can entice you to take reckless measures. One man's devotion to antique clocks led him to embezzle more than $12.4 million from the corporation where he was a senior vice president, to feed his lust for eighteenth- and nineteenth-century European timepieces.

Each lost opportunity brings pain and regret. Should you feed your desire by looking, knowing that you can't own? So few have the money to slake their lust. Perhaps it's better not to look, and not to give shape to longings that are sure to arise. Just walking the city streets awakens the passion for *things* with an unbearable intensity: the multiplicity of offerings crowded into the shop windows, the sense of infinite variety behind closed doors.

And even when you acquire an object, you're infu-

> Who has not, on passing some large public masterpiece of architecture, or glimpsing an exquisitely ordered and human domestic interior through a ground-floor window (the sheet music open on the piano, the steepling bookcases and expectant hearth) felt an uncomplicated urge to set fire to them? Of all the Emperor Nero's amusing and instructive misdeeds— the collapsing bedroom with which he attempted to murder his mother, the forcing of audiences to hear his execrable singing—it is the burning of Rome which has the satisfying quality of an archetypal act.
>
> JOHN LANCHESTER, *THE DEBT TO PLEASURE*

riated by the ultimate unattainability of *things*. Although ownership of perfect objects has the aspect of a triumph, objects can't truly be possessed, except through destruction. And so the longing to possess gives rise to the urge to smash, to shred, to set things to burning.

To love objects is to resent them.

COMMON VARIATIONS OF OBJECT LUST

Pure object lust is very rare. Far more common are its two variations: the love for *the grab,* and for *the collection.*

THE GRAB

This first variation, the love for *the grab,* is an indiscriminate, childish variant of object lust. The grab is the greediness you feel when you know you can get *something for nothing.* It explains the surprising persistence of the free gifts no one really wants, but everyone takes: the dreary repetition of baseball caps, key chains, mugs, tote bags.

To exploit the power of the grab, add a *lagniappe,* a free bonus. The lagniappe has extraordinary appeal—from the Cracker Jack prize, to the thirteenth doughnut, to the gifts lavished on first-class airline passengers. Use the lure of the freebie to guarantee attention for your charity event, press release, or store opening.

The delight of the grab lies in its violation of the principle of balanced accounts. (The intellectual admission that the price paid incorporates this cost doesn't diminish the pleasure.) Its siren call is practically irresistible. You can't resist nibbling at the complimentary cookies brought to the table, even though you've already had dessert. You're delighted when the car-parking valet brings you a single rose when she returns your car—even if you throw away the flower the minute you get home.

Once your expectations for the grab are aroused, you respond violently to any inter-

TIP: To keep people feeling good, load them up with free goodies. Staff-starved Internet companies shower their workers with everything from $750 status-symbol Aeron desk chairs, to free in-house yoga instruction, to "Beer Fridays."

ference—no matter how petty the freebie. One of Lew Glucksman's first, ill-advised decisions as the new CEO of Lehman Brothers Kuhn Loeb was to stop the practice of having a tuxedoed waiter pass around a box stocked with expensive cigars. Even though Glucksman wasn't proposing to end the practice of giving out free cigars, but merely to require partners to ask for them, the partners were so outraged by the decision that it was reversed within a day.

No matter how much they have, people want something for nothing. Nancy Reagan was astounded to learn that she and her husband were expected to pay for their own food, dry cleaning, and toiletries while in the White House. The rich are just as susceptible to the grab, or perhaps more so, because they're so accustomed to the platinum rule: To whom much is given, more is given. Rich people get for free things for which others must pay (complimentary newspapers, free checking, charity gift-bags). And consider: When you select a gift for a wedding, birthday, or baby, are you likely to spend more on the person who has more money, or less?

Are you particularly susceptible to the grab? Does it jolt you with an erotic charge? Some become addicted to the intoxication of acquisition (the possessions themselves aren't important). You find yourself snatching up object after object, thrilled at the clattering of the credit-card reader and the overflow of shopping bags. Ten winter coats, a hundred pairs of shoes, dozens of swimsuits, piles of robes—you accumulate redundant objects, each almost untouched, many with the tags still attached. You're exhilarated by your violation of the principle of balanced accounts. By permitting your purchases, money allows you to keep yourself in a constant state of erotic, greedy excitement.

> There was something which almost relieved her constant tension in prowling daily through the boutiques and department stores of Beverly Hills, buying, always buying—what did it matter if she needed the clothes or not? . . . [She felt] a sexual buzz as she searched the windows for new merchandise. The thrill was in the trying on, in the buying. The moment after she had acquired something new it became meaningless to her.
>
> JUDITH KRANTZ, SCRUPLES

The grab accounts for the irrational, enduring popularity of lotteries—both in pure, line-up-for-tickets-at-the-convenience-store form, or in variations like *Antiques Roadshow,* eBay, or *Who Wants to Be a Millionaire.* The lottery is the modern fairy tale of spontaneous money: the pot of gold at the rainbow's end, the goose laying golden eggs, straw spun into gold.

At the same time, lotteries also raise powerful feelings of resentment in the nonwinners, because of the popular conviction that money properly accrues only to those who earn it. "Envy," observed English essayist William Hazlitt, "has a mixture of the love of justice in it. We are more angry at undeserved than at deserved good-fortune." One jackpot winner bought two radio stations. When word got out that he had won the lottery, station employees walked out, demanding hugely inflated paychecks and charging exploitation. Because he suddenly had come into money, they felt that they too, by the transmigration of capital, *deserved* a windfall. Another winner, a woman who won $2.8 million, was sued by her son's teenage friend, whom she had asked to pray for her. The prayers, the friend felt, entitled the supplicant to a portion of the profits. (Imagine that your best friend hit the jackpot on *Who Wants to Be a Millionaire*—and you provided the phone-a-friend winning answer. Would you feel entitled to some of that money? How much?)

Like lottery winners, Internet-age millionaires inspire resentful envy in those who haven't won their own IPO fortune. The newspapers are full of stories of young, untrained entrepreneurs getting rich off their half-baked, money-losing ideas. If *they* deserve to be rich, don't *you?*

The Collection

The other variation of object lust is the common urge to collect. Collections draw power from the strange pleasure that inheres in large masses of similar things, in accumulation. You revel in the profusion of your chosen object—whether humble, like salt and pepper shakers, or imposing, like Jerry Seinfeld's collection of sixty classic cars.

Some collectors enjoy the common pleasure of collecting; others possess true object lust. Because those with object lust convey

intense knowledge and passion (giving them the attraction of prowess), you might
decide to pose as a person
with true object lust. If so,
don't blow your cover by one
day announcing that you've
completed a collection. A
great collector is never finished, wants never to finish.

Or you might take that
collecting impulse in the
opposite direction: rather
than amass many similar
things, you strip them all

In the old days, sex was amusing as
much for possibilities never acted on
as for fulfillment. At any moment an
encounter might turn erotic, a man's
eyes would light up or mine would.
There were many drawbacks to that
life and I vastly prefer being married,
but one thing I regret is the loss of
universal eroticization—the world
charged with possibility. This I now
find in collecting.

PHYLLIS ROSE, *THE YEAR OF READING PROUST*

away, to contemplate one perfect object. Your possession, set off by
itself and perfectly lit, embodies the ultimate achievement of an ike-
bana basket; a Greek head; an arrangement of lilies. Instead of the
delight of profusion and repetition, you enjoy the definitive expression of an object. The collection is inherent in the ideal you possess.

• • •

Object lust is a rare and sometimes uncomfortable passion. *Miser's
hoard* is less rare—most of us have a mild case of miser's hoard and
take joy in accumulation and pure money. A serious passion for
miser's hoard, however, can be choking.

CHAPTER TEN

MONEY FOR MISER'S HOARD

"I'd deposit the money into various bank accounts and funds, wait a few hours, then repeatedly call to listen to the computer read me my new million-dollar statements."

Miser's hoard is the terrible longing for and love of money. You've got it if your favorite use for money is to stockpile it, to heap it up, to calculate compound interest and accrual. Most people have a strain of miser's hoard, but for some this passion overpowers all other uses for their money.

Miser's hoard can take the form of gloating over accounts, watching the swelling of numbers on paper ledgers or computer screens, or it can take the form of rapture over physical wealth, such as gold and silver, jewels, bills, coins, treasure trove. Although miser's hoard is most conspicuous in the extraordinarily rich—they have no need to save, so their refusal to spend is more obvious—it affects people at every level of wealth.

Of all the forms wealth can take, gold is supreme. Gold is the stuff of fairy tales, histories of ancient princes and their kingdoms,

> There was an opulent sunset. I was standing under an acacia in bloom and the words "shower of gold" came into my mind, followed by a surge of feeling. I call it greed, but it was more a feeling of wanting a surplus in my life, wanting to have too much of something, for a change. I didn't want to be a candidate anymore, not for a doctorate or anything else: I wanted to be at the next level, where things would come to me, accrue to me. It was acute.
>
> NORMAN RUSH, *MATING*

the lives of the gods. It retains a unique power to store and to demonstrate your fortune.

Because of the instinct for its accumulation, gold is lavishly used, in unexpected ways. Brioni, the men's clothier, sells made-to-measure suits constructed of cloth that looks almost ordinary, but in fact has a gold thread running through it. Cost: about $14,000. Don't want to spend quite so much to indulge your fetish for gold? Buy a tie from Paris shirt-maker Charvet—$185 buys a tie with 24-karat gold threads.

Jewels, too, seduce. They inspire a reverence and compulsive desire disproportionate to their value. One canny restaurateur promised a free diamond with each dinner purchased, and kept that bargain by giving away one thousand toothpicks topped with a diamond-studded crown. In the ten days it took to award the toothpicks, the restaurant sold ten times the average number of dinners. The customers weren't disappointed with their .5 point diamond jewel—the satisfaction came from the idea of getting a *diamond* for *free* (the tiny gems cost the restaurant only $500).

Currency entices, at all times and in all denominations. In his account of the Caesars of ancient Rome, Suetonius recounts the scene of Caligula "grabbing the handfuls and capfuls of coin which a mixed crowd of all classes pressed on him. At last he developed a passion for the feel of money and, spilling heaps of gold pieces on an open space, would walk over them barefoot, or else lie down and wallow." Nothing changes. Centuries later, friends showered Andy Warhol with thousands of dollar bills at his birthday party. Steve Rubell, founder of the legendary Manhattan nightclub Studio 54, was so aroused by the sight of money that one night he spread $80,000 of cash across his bed and masturbated on it. There's some provocative and irresistible essence in material money.

TIP: To encourage people to abandon their usual reluctance to relinquish money, remove the sting of spending by replacing familiar currency with make-believe money: chips, plastic cards, tickets, vouchers to sign.

Because of the reverence people feel for physical money, a powerful and impressive way to use money is to destroy it. Decades ago, the rich owners of Long Island estates handed out cigarettes wrapped, and designed to be smoked, in $100 bills. Heir Stuart Holzman was spotted tossing $100 bills off a speedboat after he fulfilled the requirements of his uncle's will that he could inherit the $50 million family fortune only if he held a steady job until he was thirty-five (Holzman spent ten years driving a bus in New Jersey.)

Artist Salvador Dalí would fling fistfuls of bills out hotel room windows, announcing: "Very important! Everything coming back one million times!"

> **TIP:** The best way to dazzle others with your wealth is to destroy some in an essential form.

But while it's common to suffer a touch of miser's hoard, true miser's hoard is marked by regular, extraordinary efforts to save proportionately paltry amounts of money, or by refusal to spend money in obviously appropriate, affordable ways. Many years ago, when *Washington Post* publisher Katharine Graham was walking through an airport with tycoon Warren Buffett, she asked him for a dime to make a phone call. He started to walk to get change for a quarter, until she pointed out that for her purposes the quarter would serve just as well. The children of John D. Rockefeller, then the richest man in the world, shared a single bicycle, and his son John Jr. wore only dresses until he was eight years old—hand-me-downs from three older sisters. And what about the guy who stooped to pick up a dime from the bottom of the urinal? He couldn't bear to walk away from money.

Miser's hoard can be an exceedingly painful condition; you may want to feel the pleasure of money, but you just can't let it leave your hands. Your wealth is sealed away from you by your own economy, as effectively as if it were behind locks and bars.

• • •

> In order that gold may be held as money, and made to form a hoard, it must be prevented from circulating, or from transforming into a means of enjoyment. The hoarder, therefore, makes a sacrifice of the lusts of the flesh to his gold fetish.
>
> Karl Marx, *Capital*

Money can also be traded to buy the other worldly passions: your money makes it possible for you to achieve power or fame that would otherwise be out of your reach.

CHAPTER ELEVEN

MONEY FOR POWER OR FAME

For guidance on how to use money to gain power and fame, read below. Turn to the "Power" and "Fame" sections for the complete treatment of power and fame.

POWER

"I'd divvy up money among political candidates in the hope that I'd get appointed to an important government post."

If your use for money is for the power it will give you, then it's power you really want. The money is incidental, except as a source of power.

First, money gives you power over your own circumstances. You triumph over necessity: no more worries about paying for food, clothing, shelter, doctors, education for your children, indulgences. Business schools teach their students to save up their "go-to-hell money" as soon as possible, to guarantee that they can always walk away from an unfavorable situation. Only having money allows you to disregard it.

Money also gives you power over others. Most obviously, money bestows power through your ability to choose where you spend. You decide to finance a start-up company, or to foot the bill for a lawsuit, and your decision alters the world. Billionaire currency speculator George Soros uses his fortune to affect the policies of world governments by funding projects to promote democracy.

To assert your power over your family line, use money to "guide" your heirs. The latest estate-planning trend is to immunize your children against *affluenza* (a hereditary condition, passed down

from the rich to their children, marked by an aimless and/or hedo-
nistic lifestyle) by setting up a trust so that your descendants get
your money only if they play by your rules. Maybe you deny pay-
ments unless beneficiaries take periodic drug tests; or you provide a
bonus for being a stay-at-home mother; or you provide extra money
for starting a business. You can't take it with you, that's true, but you
can decide who inherits it and how they spend it.

You can purchase power directly. Buy political power by using
your own millions to fund your campaign—consider how many of
today's candidates spend their own money to finance their efforts.
Steven Forbes seemed willing to spend his entire personal fortune to
win the presidency. Would former Goldman Sachs CEO Jon
Corzine have made a credible candidate for the Senate without his
$350 million? If you don't want to run for office, buy political
power and influence by giving money to candidates. In 1996, big
Democratic fund-raisers were rewarded with social events; exposure
was calibrated according to dollar amounts. Those who raised
$10,000 to $25,000 were asked to large dinners with the president,
those who raised $50,000 to $100,000 were invited to smaller dinners or coffees, and those who produced $500,000+ were asked to
ride on Air Force One, to play a round of golf with Clinton, or to
stay overnight at the White House. The more you raised, the more
presidential face-time you bought—and the greater opportunity to
put a friendly face on the sugar industry and to gather impressive
anecdotes to tell your friends.

TIP: When contributing during an election, give money to both candidates so you secure influence no matter who wins.

Buy power in society by making strategic
philanthropic contributions. Giving the
right amount to the right institutions gets
you a seat on the board, where you contribute to important decisions, hobnob with
important people, enjoy royal treatment, and
get your photograph in the papers.
(Charitable giving can also give your battered reputation an important boost—Bill Gates's generosity blossomed during his bitter
antitrust battle with the government. What a kind, public-minded
man, the news reports gushed, look at how much good he's doing
with his fortune. And he *was* doing good with his fortune.)
Membership on the influential governing boards of museums, ballet

companies, symphonies, and opera houses now requires the giving of a definite sum. As of 1999, board members of the Metropolitan Opera were expected to give $75,000 a year; the Los Angeles County Museum of Art, $50,000. Amounts are lower in smaller cities. The Houston Ballet is a bargain at $5,000.

Buy yourself a seat on the opinion-maker exchange by acquiring or creating an editorial platform, as Rupert Murdoch did with the *New York Post* and Fox News Channel, or as Larry Tisch did with CBS, or as Mort Zuckerman did with *U.S. News and World Report, New York Daily News,* and *Fast Company,* or as Jim Cramer did with *TheStreet.com,* or as Steve Brill did with *Brill's Content* (note the magazine's name, see "Fame," Chapter 14). This kind of power, with its buzz and prestige, is so thrilling that otherwise practical-minded businessmen have tolerated losing money for the privilege of having a place in the marketplace of ideas—as Si Newhouse did with the *New Yorker.*

Don't assume that you must be *personally* rich to use money as a power source: you need merely control its flow. Rich or poor, government officials are powerful because they wield the twin hammers of government funding and taxation. (The power of government officials is bolstered by their access, for free, to expensive resources like lawyers and PR support for which their private-sector adversaries must pay.) Even a very indirect influence over money is a potent source of power. College guidance counselors are flattered and feared because they influence which students get into the best schools, and presumably, therefore, who will have the brightest, highest-earning future.

A second note on *foot-washing*

Although they usually mask it in smiles, jokes, and friendliness, people harbor an extravagant reverence for money and grandeur, apart from the actual power money bestows. And so wealth gives rise to the foot-washing impulse, just as power does.

So, although it's true that the rich are often pursued by people who want access to their money, they also have tremendous influence over foot-washers who have no interest in siphoning off any money for themselves, but only want to pay their respects to the personification of

> People in Vanity Fair fasten on to rich folks quite naturally. If the simplest people are disposed to look not a little kindly on great Prosperity (for I defy any member of the British public to say that the notion of Wealth has not something awful and pleasing to him; and you, if you are told that the man next you at dinner has got a half a million, not to look at him with a certain interest); if the simple look benevolently on money, how much more do your old worldlings regard it! Their affections rush out to meet and welcome money.
>
> WILLIAM MAKEPEACE THACKERAY, *VANITY FAIR*

such riches. Anthony Powell described that his character Stringham "was, in fact, not substantially richer than most undergraduates of his sort, and, being decidedly free with his money, was usually hard-up, but from the foothills of his background was, now and then, wafted the disturbing, aromatic perfume of gold, the scent which, even at this early state in our lives, could sometimes be observed to act intoxicatingly on chance acquaintances; whose unexpected perseverance, and determination not to take offence, were a reminder that Stringham's mother was what Widmerpool had described as 'immensely wealthy.'"

FAME

"I'd donate money to a museum for the construction of a new wing, on the condition that my name appear (in letters no smaller than twelve inches) on the wall."

If your use for money is for the fame it can buy, then it's fame you really want—and if you're fortunate enough to have the money, you can, indeed, buy yourself fame.

Associate with something famous by buying a celebrity object. As owner of the Hope Diamond, the Mar-a-Lago estate, or Van Gogh's *Sunflowers,* you'll glean at least brief fame. But it will cost you. Contact with fame is so precious that the prices become astronomical: Mark McGwire's seventieth home-run ball was auctioned for an astounding amount—with commission, $3,005,000.

Or simply buy your fame by purchasing coverage. Most of the tens of millions that Steve Forbes spent in his runs for the presidency went to buying media space—the presidential power forever eluded him, but he did succeed in becoming famous. Place your photograph on a billboard at a popular intersection, and soon every driver in town will recognize your name and face.

If you can't afford to buy your coverage outright, hire fame consultants who specialize in thrusting you into the spotlight while keeping tight control of the image that's created. Want renown as the boy-wonder of your industry? Your public relations agent can make sure that your achievements are noted, that the word "wunderkind" appears before your name, and that your departure from your last job is described in your terms, not your former employer's. Want fame as a socialite? (A "socialite" is a person famous for being social.) Your PR agent can tell you what shops to patronize, what benefits and parties to attend, where to buy your summer house and when to visit it; then the agent makes sure you're reported doing these things.

But remember: Play down the fact that you've hired a public relations agent. You don't want people to know that you're working hard to raise your profile. *Sprezzatura*—effortless, natural accomplishment—is as important in the field of fame as it is in the fields of power, money, and sex. Because fame reflects best on you when it's the spontaneous result of your distinction, deny taking steps to fan the fame flames. Most celebrities pretend that their fame visited them accidentally, that they were lifted from obscurity by the intensity of other people's interest.

You can also buy fame by giving money away. Make sure, of course, that your philanthropic gift is large enough to generate media attention, to inspire a dinner in your honor, to guarantee a plaque emblazoned with your name. The most effective—but expensive—way to use charity as a platform for fame is to endow an enduring, eminent institution. Do you crave to see your name emblazoned over the door of a public monument? Indulge your edifice complex and sear your name into the public domain, just as Guggenheim, Getty, or Carnegie did. Consider Joseph Hirshhorn: He bequeathed his art collection to the Smithsonian *provided* that the government build a suitable structure to house it. And so he got himself the Hirshhorn Museum, which, when it took its place on the Washington Mall, inserted the Hirshhorn name into the pantheon of Washington, Lincoln, and Jefferson.

NOTE: You can also use money, of course, to buy sex, but that straightforward commercial transaction does not require fuller treatment here. For a discussion of the more complex interaction between sex and money, see the section "Sex."

•   •   •

Although money buys tremendous satisfaction, it also carries the money blues. Once you have the money to satisfy (in some measure) your particular desires, you realize the cost of that pleasure— and you realize what pleasures remain out of reach. You're not transformed.

CHAPTER TWELVE

FINAL NOTE: MONEY BLUES

When you're just beginning to accumulate money, its effect is vast and wonderful. No more worries about the rent, the dentist bills, schools for your children. You can take a vacation or buy a new shirt without counting every penny. But you soon find that you don't have enough.

The dissatisfaction of money kicks in; you're caught in the *snare of mounting expectations.* You need more, not all that much more, just enough to take you to the next level. But as soon as you've managed to scramble your way up to that next level and you pause to look around with self-congratulatory pride, you see clearly, for the first time, the next set of possessions you need. Someone else has something bigger, finer, more rare. Money brings with it a profound anticlimax, as you realize that you're really not quite *there* yet. What is left for Microsoft chairman Bill Gates, one of the richest and most powerful men in the world, to wish for? He longs for the distinction of admission to the exclusive three-hundred-member Augusta National Golf Club. Will he get in?

You realize, too, the cost of the freedom that money buys. Sometimes it's harder to manage your staff than it would be to do the work yourself. You're never alone, never out of view. Someone's always listening, watching.

When you're paying so much, you expect perfection—and your life isn't perfect. As your standards rise, you find yourself increasingly irritated with the things and people around you. The curtains are slightly askew, the driver's running late, your eggs are underboiled. You're constantly upgrading, repainting, replacing. And you're haunted by the suspicion that people are overcharging you. It's harder to be comfortable. Now that you're accustomed to linen sheets and fresh-squeezed orange juice, you feel comfortable only in your own impeccable bedroom or in the most expensive hotels.

You've lost something quite important: the ballast of *necessity.* You worked so hard to free yourself from necessity that you don't realize how much it steadied you. Perhaps you still imagine that you can feel its weight, but your children don't.

Even if you weary of the cycle of spending and signaling, you find that you can't escape it. There is no way to opt out of signaling, and you feel trapped by the demands of the visible, material world.

You're not transformed. You thought that money could buy you a jet-setter's brilliance, a connoisseur's exquisite judgment, the right conversation to move in the right circles. But you've never learned to speak French or skipper a sailboat; you've got an uncultivated palate and an undiscerning eye. You still need to lose that fifteen pounds. You discover, to your dismay, that while money buys close substitutes, it can't quite supply these things. It can promote but cannot buy accomplishment; it can't buy unworldly success such as family happiness or a sense of purpose.

Prepare yourself for the blues. Once you've reached the height of your worldly ambition, you realize that you're not transformed. Jerry Seinfeld has it all—and here he is in his limo, just a guy in jeans and running shoes taking a nap. (© David Turnley/CORBIS)

ILLUSTRATION: HOW TOM USED MONEY

Over the last several years, Tom has risen through the ranks at a chain of expensive sporting-goods stores. Now he's the indispensable supervisor of the entire chain.

Not long after his latest promotion, Tom moved out of the tiny house he'd shared with two roommates and bought his own house in a better neighborhood. Seeing his neighbors' manicured lawns prompted Tom to spend a few thousand dollars on his yard. He could've done the work himself, but, he reflected, it had been worth the money to be able to sit inside, watching ESPN with a beer in his hand, while three guys slaved outside in the hot sun.

Tom loved watching the dogs in the neighborhood play, and now that he had a big fenced backyard, he decided to get the dog he'd always wanted. He wasn't going to adopt some stray from the pound but wanted the smartest, healthiest, best-natured dog possible. In the end, he opted for a golden retriever, the same breed his boss had. Tom bought his dog from Ellen Jones, who had a national reputation as a breeder and trainer—she'd provided dogs for the president, Madonna, and Will Smith. Ellen refused to give Tom an appointment, however, until he'd provided a character reference from a previous client. That done, Tom picked out a playful female puppy who was descended from a line of prize-winning show dogs. Tom loved his dog, Happy, and bought her a fancy leather leash and extravagant dog house (but then always let Happy sleep on the floor next to his bed). Tom took Happy to the groomer as often as necessary to keep her coat in impeccable shape.

Tom had always been a snappy dresser, but after his last promotion he allowed himself to buy in shops where before he'd only browsed. His weakness was outerwear, and over the course of several months he bought himself a light raincoat, a heavy raincoat, a fleece jacket, a winter coat, a parka, and, to top it off, ordered a jacket made for him.

The house, the landscaping, the dog, and those coats absorbed all Tom's available cash. He didn't have the money to go furniture shopping, so his house was going to have to stay shabbily and sparsely furnished until next year. Thrilled with his lawn, his pet, and his wardrobe, Tom hardly noticed the state of his house. After all, he asked himself, how often do you really need a dining room table or a guest bed?

fame

CHAPTER THIRTEEN

INTRODUCTION TO FAME

Fame. Don't you feel that hunger for recognition?—to know that strangers recognize your name, to watch them startle and stare when you walk into the room. That's what fame is: the recognition of strangers. *Have they noticed me yet?*

Don't you want the spoils of fame: the extra courtesies, that delicious, satisfying attention? "[T]here is a natural desire in the mind of man," William Hazlitt observed, "to sit for one's picture, to be the object of continued attention, to have one's likeness multiplied." You dream about it, how you'd behave—how graciously you'd sign autographs, how wisely you'd ruminate on the Sunday morning talk shows, how your audience would listen, spellbound, as you thundered from the stage.

But winning fame—even your paltry allotment of fifteen minutes—isn't easy. Just look at the lengths to which people will go to get it. Hundreds of people stand outside the *Today* show studio, glad to put up with the weather for a chance to wave into the camera and to talk to Katie, Matt, Al, and Ann. More than a thousand hopefuls rushed to audition for MTV's VJ search; some showed up at noon the day before the tryouts and slept outside in the rain. The hosts of tell-all talk shows, like Jenny Jones and Mother Love, never lack for guests who are willing to trade the most intimate, humiliating details from their lives for a segment on national TV.

Maybe you've had a taste of fame. Do you find yourself adopting the extravagant manner affected by those who know they are the object of attention?—the toothy smile; the oversized gestures; the heartiness or the insouciance, depending on your style. You plot out how your biographer would describe your divorce.

Fame makes all accomplishments sweeter, and often, only fame

> It was a very big deal of a kiss, as if they knew they were being watched, or had always hoped to be. Everybody wanted to be a star, even a childless banker weekending in the boonies with his childless photographer wife. Sam used to say that publicity has taken the place of grace. Now His eye wasn't on the sparrow, but a camcorder lens was.
>
> SCOTT SPENCER, *MEN IN BLACK*

can make those accomplishments *real*. Fame's imprimatur stamps your achievements as genuine; then you receive the attention and recognition you deserve. Power and fame gets you glory; money and fame gets you moguldom; sex and fame gets you glamour.

Your fame is dependent on others; it is a condition that exists only in *other people's minds*. You're the creation of your fans. But what kind of fame is right for you?

Quiz: What type of fame do you want?

Select the statement that best describes your attitude toward fame:

A.
"I don't care about seeing my name or picture in the papers, but I do want the respect and attention of my colleagues."

B.
"I want the public to recognize my name and appreciate what I do, but I wouldn't want to be stopped on the sidewalk by strangers."

C.
"I want strangers to call me by name and heads to turn when I walk past."

D.
"I want glory and renown so that people will study me and my work for years to come."

If you answered *A*, you want the fame of being a *big fish in a small pond*.
If you answered *B*, you want the fame of being a *household name*.
If you answered *C*, you want the fame of being a *star*.
If you answered *D*, you want the fame of being an *icon*.

BIG FISH, SMALL POND

If you're a *big fish in a small pond,* you have renown among your colleagues and acquaintances but no national recognition. The gas-station attendant in Delaware doesn't recognize your face, and the maître d' doesn't jump at the sound of your name, but when you introduce yourself at a conference or walk the halls of certain buildings, people fall over themselves to be near you.

The *principle of relativity* accounts for the fact that, although limited, big-fish-small-pond fame is enormously satisfying. Your own narrow setting is where fame matters most; that's where you meet the people you want to impress. So do what you can within your circle—be social and get involved in local charities, politics, and schools; get named to professional organizations and get involved in current issues. Your fame need not extend beyond your city limits or your professional colleagues. In any event, many big fish care only about earning the esteem of those who matter to them—the cognoscenti of chess, chemistry, Cleveland—and so a more widespread, less-informed fame holds little attraction.

Because big fish garner tremendous attention within their particular field but are unknown outside it, the names of big fish aren't generally familiar. In absolute terms, how many people have heard of Richard Posner (federal judge and legal scholar), Mary J. Blige (hip-hop soul singer), Seiji Ozawa (musical director of the Boston Symphony Orchestra), Alex Kuczynski (*New York Times* reporter), or Ian Schrager (hotelier)? And yet they're each famous.

As a big fish, don't make the mistake of overestimating the extent of your fame. Your small eminence might lull you into supposing that you're a celebrity outside your own pond. You aren't. Don't expect the same courtesy and deference from the public that you take for granted on your own turf. And keep in mind that comments that reveal an overestimation of your fame are likely to make your colleagues snicker. Consider one judge who remarked: "I love the anonymity of New York. Here I am, a federal judge, and I can walk into Fairway Market on the Upper West Side and no one recognizes me." As if. Or the partner at the white-shoe law firm who explained to a young associate, "I was in a semiprivate room at the hospital right after my baby was born, but when they found out who I was, they moved me to a private room." The associate made the innocent mistake of asking, "Why, who *are* you?"

HOUSEHOLD NAME

A household name possesses a widespread fame, but one that is attached more strongly to name than to face. There are several categories of the household name: the *faceless name,* the society scion, the fallen star.

If you're a faceless name, people know your name and the reason for your fame, but they wouldn't recognize you if they saw you. Household names include the author J. K. Rowling, the director James Cameron, or the late pediatrician Dr. Benjamin Spock. Being a household name gives you the thrill of widespread fame, and perhaps occasional recognition, but doesn't spark the intense public reaction that a familiar face ignites.

Another category of the household name is the *society scion.* Although they may not recognize you, when they hear your name, people understand that you're part of a prominent family. They thrill at the thought of meeting you—a real Rockefeller or Astor or Cabot or the equivalent families in other cities. You may be an established society scion, with your social fame ratified by unimpeachable references like the *Social Register* (familiarly known as the S.R.) or the *Social List of Washington, D.C.* (affectionately nicknamed the Green Book), or you may be a new society scion, with your social fame propagated by your newspaper's society pages or society magazines like *Quest* or *W.* ("Hey, isn't that one of the Miller sisters?" you hear someone ask.)

The final category within household-name fame is the *fallen star*—you've dropped from a stardom to mere household-name status. Your name and face are recognized, but only dimly. People ask, "Where is she now? Is he even still alive?" about fallen stars such as Troy Donahue, John Lindsay, Art Garfunkel, or Lee Iacocca. This poignant type of fame is the most difficult type to bear; a fallen star lacks the comforts of anonymity and must constantly confront the remnants of past glories. You wonder whether you'll ever be able to make a comeback.

TRUE RULE

It's more distressing to be a has-been than a never-was.

THE STAR

If you're a star, you're a person "who needs no introduction." Strangers know exactly who you are and what you do. They recognize you instantly and, indeed, can't take their eyes off you. Seeing you in person mesmerizes them. Because you qualify as a star only if people stare at you when you go out, you must do something that thrusts your name and face before the public eye. Position or accomplishment without exposure isn't enough to achieve stardom. Stars include Barbara Walters, Harrison Ford, Madeleine Albright, Spike Lee, Martha Stewart, and Alan Greenspan (Greenspan's stardom illustrates how the spotlight now provided by cable TV allows someone like a Federal Reserve chairman to become a star; Paul Volcker was a big fish, but he didn't get the exposure necessary to be a star).

Stardom feeds on itself. Shrewd marketers rush to take advantage of the public's fascination with your appearance and your actions. They plaster your face on merchandise, beg for your presence at events, pay you handsomely for your endorsement, and publish your life story, your poetry, your recipes. Exploit their greed to make yourself ubiquitous, and therefore even more famous. Soon your name is the answer to a *Jeopardy!* question; it appears in the crossword puzzle; it becomes the name of a deli sandwich. A scientist names a strain of bacteria after you (Michael Jordan was honored by *Salmonella mjordan*), and Madame Tussaud memorializes you in her wax museum. Remember that stardom often operates with little regard to the distinction of the underlying goods. Think Spice Girls.

A subcategory of the star is the *flash in the pan,* the overnight supercelebrity who blazes up everywhere and then vanishes. Already the names and faces of Joey Buttafuoco, Louise Woodward, and Mia Hamm are growing dim, although there was a time when they appeared on every talk show, editorial page, and magazine cover.

Like the fallen star, as a flash you enjoy your fame very briefly, but you probably didn't expect to keep your fame status for long. At the sixteenth minute you'll slide easily (or perhaps not so easily) back into an ordinary life, with a bit of glamour, a bigger bank account, and a bulging scrapbook.

The Icon

If you're an *icon,* you've achieved glory and renown on a historic scale. Only very few achieve icon status: Louis Armstrong, Anne Frank, Princess Diana, Eleanor Roosevelt, and Jackie Robinson are twentieth-century icons.

It's not always easy to tell why a star becomes an icon. The rare ascent seems more likely if history marks you for an unlikely fate, or if your accomplishment far exceeds anyone else's, or if you somehow capture and express the mood of an age or movement. You're also more likely to become an icon if your role in history is easy to understand, or at least to articulate. A general is more likely to become an icon than a diplomat. Even though very few people can understand the accomplishments of Albert Einstein (*Time* magazine's Man of the Century), everyone can repeat his catchy $E = mc^2$.

The most tragic way to be exalted from star to icon is through an untimely death—whether through assassination, like Abraham Lincoln, John Kennedy, Martin Luther King, Jr., or John Lennon, through recklessness or accident, like James Dean or Amelia Earhart, or by your own hand, like Marilyn Monroe. Death secures your accomplishments, silences your critics, and freezes you forever at the height of fame. You're saved from a decline into obscurity. In one morbid, apocryphal Hollywood legend, one agent says to another, "Elvis Presley just died." The other nods approvingly. "Great career move."

Your public expects its icons to be larger than life, and they call on you to perform superhuman acts. Martin Luther King, Jr., described the execution of a prisoner by poison gas, where a microphone was placed inside the death chamber. "The first victim was a young Negro. As the pellet dropped into the container, and gas curled upward, through the microphone came these words: 'Save me, Joe Louis. Save me, Joe Louis. Save me, Joe Louis . . .'" The dying man's last thought was a supplication to that legendary boxer, the heavyweight champion of the world.

As an icon, you inspire the collection and worship of relics. People want to touch you or, failing that, touch something that you've touched. Winston Churchill recalled that when he toured a bombed London neighborhood during the blitz, the people "crowded round us, cheering and manifesting every sign of lively affection, wanting to touch and stroke my clothes." A president uses several pens to sign a piece of legislation or important document, so each important guest can take home a historic implement, touched by the majestic hand. (A president acquires automatic icon status during his term, because of the stature of the office, but a president must earn icon status if it's to persist over time. FDR managed this; Gerald Ford didn't.) Legendary aviator Charles Lindbergh couldn't cash a check or send his shirts to the laundry; people revered these relics of his body too much.

Your public creates shrines in your memory—making pilgrimages to Graceland, laying flowers and mementos at the homes of Princess Diana and John F. Kennedy, Jr. (or at constructive "homes," such as the British Embassy).

Verifying true icon status requires some passage of time, to determine whether the public's frenzy springs from a temporary surge of interest or indicates a level of fascination that will endure for decades. Although it's not yet clear whether these icons will endure, today's technology bolsters the creation of icons, because the masses feel an intimacy with luminaries that feeds the creation of icon worship. Take the example of George Washington. Surely no greater man exists in the United States' history, but because he didn't leave behind film footage or extensive writings or a fascinating scandal, his image is dim and undefined. Wooden teeth, a cherry tree, a historic crossing of the Delaware, are all that stand out in the public imagination. Washington certainly *ought* to be an icon, but *is* he?

● ● ●

Okay, you think, now I know what kind of fame I want. That's an easy question to answer. The hard question to answer is—how can I become famous? Read on.

CHAPTER FOURTEEN

FAME—AND HOW TO GET IT

You're famous if strangers know who you are. You exist in the public eye only if you're photographed, interviewing or being interviewed, writing or being written about. So, if you want widespread fame, your paramount goal must be to put your name and face in front of the largest possible public.

The obvious method to increase your fame? Appear on television. In fact, today it's impossible to become truly famous without making a TV appearance at least occasionally; television has become the critical arbiter of who and what are important. Strive, too, to get your name and picture into print.

To appreciate television's remarkable power, consider how regular TV appearances further boosted the fame of superstar radio personalities Howard Stern and Don Imus. Scientist Carl Sagan owed his celebrity more to his twenty-six appearances on Johnny Carson's *Tonight* show and to his TV series, seen by more than half a billion viewers, than to his contributions to science. Any print journalist fortunate enough to participate in the Sunday morning shouting matches commands much greater attention (and speaking fees) than those who merely publish. "You could write your fingers off for twenty-five years," observed journalist and former *McLaughlin Group* member Jack Germond, "and never get the kind of hearing you could get from shooting off your mouth on television for a half hour every week." Nonstop Lewinsky-related television boosted the profiles of Monicanalysts *Newsweek's* Michael Isikoff and Howard Fineman and the *National Journal's* Stuart Taylor, Jr.—these writers had been covering prominent beats in national magazines, but it took television to make them celebrities.

Television is such a star-maker that you need only a brief flash across the screen to lift your profile. Vanna White is famous for nothing more than clapping and revealing hidden letters on the TV game show *Wheel of Fortune*. Even thirty-second exposures are enough to catapult you into celebrity—commercials have made Wendy's Dave Thomas known throughout the country.

Television works a strange influence; ordinary people burst into a frenzy of indiscriminate enthusiasm at any glimpse of a familiar TV face. Perhaps it's the shock of seeing a breakfast-table image appear in person. If *Early Show* host Bryant Gumbel appears on the sidewalk, waiting for the light to change, we're witnessing him in life—by connecting with him, we place ourselves within his famous existence. While in the past, few people had the opportunity to see a celebrity (princess, president, diva) for themselves, today we *know* Rosie O'Donnell and David Letterman, because we see and hear from them every day.

And so such figures are surrounded by eager followers. Sally Quinn was well known as the *Washington Post's* Style reporter, but television catapulted her to new heights. She recalled that during her brief stint in the 1970s as a national TV news anchor, "people followed, pointed at me, asked for my autograph and told me in worshipful tones that they had actually seen me on television." But, she added dryly, "I also knew that they would have mobbed Charles Manson or Cinque or anybody else they had seen on television." The public is adoring, but undiscriminating. It's the leap from image to reality, rather than the brush with greatness, that sparks their fascination.

The TV audience watching at home grows more demanding each year. They want the *real* story. What's she going to wear to the awards ceremony? How's his relationship with his wife? The audience has a recognized right to demand insider information about their TV companions, as illustrated by President Clinton in April 1994 when, to fulfill a campaign promise, he appeared in front of an MTV studio audience. One student asked, "Mr. President, the world's dying to know: Is it boxers or briefs?" Clinton didn't hesitate: "Usually briefs."

Surprisingly, fame's power is undiluted by proliferation. Largely because of television, many more people are famous today than ever before. The explosive propagation of channels engenders more celebrity lifestyle programs, more biographies, more once-anonymous commentators opining. More fame is created, and yet the fame effect doesn't wear off. Your cocktail party buzzes after the MSNBC anchor walks in, despite the fact that the ranks of TV personages have swelled and that the anchor was a Texas sportscaster until a few months ago.

TRUE RULE

Fame is not zero-sum.

Because print can never match TV's "see it for yourself" intimacy, it doesn't generate the same degree of fanatic enthusiasm. Nevertheless, print propels you into the public arena, and of course it's a terrific springboard to television. If you can't manage to appear on TV, demonstrate that you're noteworthy by getting your name in print; if no one wants to write about you, publish letters to the editor or op-ed pieces. As a last resort, buy a newspaper ad trumpeting your views.

Although the raw impact of television dwarfs that of print, you may prefer the dignity of print-fame to the frenzy of screen-fame. Sally Quinn didn't enjoy the intensity of the interest she aroused as a TV news face. "It's awful to have your privacy invaded. Not to be able to look like a slob if you want to. One wants to be known and admired among one's peers, but I have decided that the ideal kind of fame is to have everyone know and admire your name and no one recognize your face. A writer can have that kind of fame; a television personality cannot." Also, if you're struggling for fame as a serious intellectual, TV's mass-market, lowest-common-denominator, crowd-pleasing attitude will detract from your highbrow, high-culture image. (Nevertheless, stars from the intelligentsia—a Harold Bloom or a Catharine MacKinnon—might be pleased to stoop to a television audience, if anyone asked them to appear. Think Arthur Miller.)

If you can think of a method other than television or print to boost your exposure, by all means use it. Consider the Sultan of Brunei, who was asked to show identification when he wanted to charge some purchases while shopping in New York. He didn't carry any ID, but one of his ten bodyguards waved a stack of Brunei's currency graced with a picture of His Majesty's face. Of course, not everyone has access to alternative methods of exposure like that.

Now that you're convinced that you need media exposure, you

face the challenge of capturing the coverage you crave. Apply as many methods as possible. One shortcut is to associate with someone or something famous. More difficult, but also effective, is to attain a prominent position or to work a notable achievement in your field. If all else fails, do something scandalous. To take another route, if you've got a

> **TIP:** Apply the four-four rule: The public must hear your name four times a day for four weeks before you're recognized.

lot of money, buy your fame. Whatever method you pursue, you must make yourself a colorful subject, worthy of coverage.

1. Practice *fame frottage* (rub up against someone or something famous).
2. Attain a prominent position.
3. Accomplish a notable achievement in your field.
4. Achieve *ubiniquity.*
5. Buy your fame.
6. Cultivate your colorfulness.

1. PRACTICE *FAME FROTTAGE*

"Frottage" is the practice of *rubbing,* either to create a visual effect or to get sexual satisfaction. *Fame frottage,* then, is the practice of rubbing up against someone or something famous, to be seen with fame so that fame rubs off on you. How do you do accomplish fame frottage?

The most potent method of fame frottage is to interview celebrities on television—consider the examples of the celebrated interviewers Barbara Walters, Larry King, and Charlie Rose. Their ability to attract the most famous guests to their television programs reinforces their own fame.

Another surefire way is to establish a roster of famous clientele. Whether you're a plastic surgeon, divorce lawyer, hairdresser, money manager, interior designer, or prostitute, exploit the fame of those you serve. Your fame frottage will make you famous yourself, because the famous are so venerated that the public celebrates their habits, preferences, and gurus. Tiger Woods's caddy, Fluff Cowan, became famous—of course. Celebrity breeds celebrity. Just consider

A base service performed for a person of very high degree may become a very honorific office; as for instance the office of a Maid of Honour or of a Lady in Waiting to the Queen, or the King's Master of the Horse or his Keeper of the Hounds.

THORSTEIN VEBLEN,
THE THEORY OF THE LEISURE CLASS

how your fame would soar if you succeeded in winning Oprah Winfrey as a client. Every person who rubs up against Oprah becomes famous: her personal trainer, Bob Greene; her cook, Rosie Daley; her longtime companion, Stedman Graham; her advice man, Phillip McGraw; every author she features in her book club.

Link yourself with names more famous than yours. Consider how an ambitious, unknown academic is delighted to allow a famous colleague to share the credit on an important article—and even to list his or her name first as author—despite the colleague's having contributed little to the thought or writing (the contribution is the fame of the name). Write the biography of the celebrated politician or tycoon or movie producer, and you'll find yourself interviewed on all the talk shows. Cochair a committee with a well-known community leader—great access, great association, lots of work for you.

For a lucky few, fame is part of an inheritance. All Kennedys are famous. Henry Fonda's fame led the way for Jane, Peter, and Bridget, just as Martin Sheen led the way for Charlie and Emilio Estevez. Texas governor George W. Bush easily became the Republican front-runner when he announced he was running for president in 2000, in large part because of his famous ex-President father, George Bush.

If you're not lucky enough to have a famous family, marry into one. That's how Diana Spencer and Carolyn Bessette rocketed to stardom. After her last of three marriages, Pamela Digby Churchill Hayward Harriman dropped "Hayward," and even her ancestral name, "Digby." But she never relinquished "Churchill," even though she had not only divorced Winston's son Randolph, but had had the marriage annulled. Donald Trump commented on his female companions' fame frottage: "I create stars. . . . I mean, I have really given a lot of women great opportunity. Unfortunately, after they are a star, the fun is over for me. It's like a creation process. It's like creating a beautiful building. It's sad."

Fame frottage also works with attention-grabbing events involving famous people. Emulate those dozens of members of Congress, journalists, and lawyers who used the Monica Lewinsky scandal to elbow their way onto the television screen and into the papers. An obscure Belgian anarchist got himself written up in all the papers when he threw a pie in Bill Gates's face. Decades ago, Jesse Jackson lifted himself to prominence—not without controversy—by appearing on the *Today* show as a commentator the day after Martin Luther King, Jr., was killed, while still wearing a shirt stained with King's blood.

An organization can practice fame frottage by appointing itself the judge of famous people or things. The American Film Institute drummed up attention for itself by announcing its list of the top one hundred films of the century. *Fortune's* list of top companies has helped plant the magazine's name in the public mind. The obscure *Silicon Alley Reporter* put itself on the map by publishing its Silicon Alley 100, a list of the most influential people in New York's Internet business. (Such lists, of course, generate tremendous jockeying and controversy—which is part of why they're so effective.)

2. ATTAIN A PROMINENT POSITION

A more difficult and time-consuming way to become famous is to achieve a conspicuous position. Note that you need not reach an *eminent* position, but merely a *prominent* one.

TRUE RULE

Visibility justifies celebrity.

Identify a famous office and do what you must to attain it. Former Dallas Cowboys cheerleader Stephanie Scholz observed, "When I put on the uniform of a Dallas Cowboys Cheerleader, I was transformed into something royal. There was a mystique surrounding the Cheerleaders that created a frenzy wherever we went. People stood in the hot sun for three or four hours to get an autograph from an eighteen-year-old girl who led cheers for a football team; a girl who the day before might have been a waitress who they growled at, 'Hey, make it snappy with those French fries, will you, honey!'"

Invent a prominent position for yourself, if necessary. Several sets of parents arranged for their twins to be born straddling the millennium—on either side of midnight, December 31, 1999—and so guaranteed themselves coverage. Nancy and Donald Featherstone of Fitchburg, Massachusetts, won fame by wearing matching outfits, sewn by Nancy, every day for more than fifteen years; they've been featured on dozens of television shows and magazines in the U.S. and abroad. And you? You could become known as the "pigeon lover" who daily feeds hundreds of pigeons in a popular city park, or as the world's only parents whose children are named after the dwarfs in *Snow White and the Seven Dwarfs*. Run onto the field during a football game or streak across the stage during the Oscar Awards. With a little luck, you'll become one of your city's beloved local celebrities.

But remember: Don't fall into the trap of believing that you're *personally* famous if it's really your office that conveys fame. Fame based on position rarely survives the loss of that position. *Commentary* editor Norman Podhoretz noticed he was cultivated by people who weren't interested in him but simply "wanted to meet or associate with the editor of *Commentary*, whoever the present incumbent of that office might be, because it was an office that carried its own esteem in their eyes." If you've become accustomed to people paying court, you may forget that they're showing their reverence for your office, not for you as a brilliant strategist, wit, or performer.

3. ACCOMPLISH A NOTABLE ACHIEVEMENT IN YOUR FIELD

Even more difficult than achieving a prominent position is achieving a notable accomplishment in your field—although, happily, such a triumph often wins you a prominent position as well. But what must you do? Make a scientific discovery. Break an Olympic record for swimming—or a *Guinness Book of World Records* record for biggest hot dog ever grilled. Throw the most expensive birthday party ever. Write a best-selling novel. Organize the first girls' wrestling team at the high school. The achievement is more likely to make you famous if you're the first, the last, the oldest, the youngest, or the fastest.

Note that fame does *not* depend on achievement—achievement is just one way to become famous. In fact, as English essayist William

Hazlitt observed, "The way to fame through merit alone, is the narrowest, the steepest, the longest, the hardest of all others." Nevertheless, fame through notable achievement is probably the most satisfying form of fame, because it is largely self-generated. You didn't depend on someone else's imprimatur to elevate you into the public eye, and your accomplishment can't be taken from you. You've achieved the kind of fame that can't be bought or bargained for.

And even if you've won a significant achievement, you'll better your fame if you combine it with some other fame-fostering action. Muhammad Ali recognized that his celebrity was built not only on his extraordinary boxing ability, but also on his quick wit. He had an exceptional flair for attention-grabbing performances. "Where do you think I'd be next week if I didn't know how to shout and holler and make the public take notice?" he once said. "I'd be poor and I'd probably be down in my hometown, washing windows or running an elevator and saying 'yassuh' and 'nawsuh' and knowing my place."

Achievement alone may not make you famous, so take steps to secure your celebrity. Here Muhammad Ali enters the ring with the Beatles to create an extraordinary photo-op of superstar with superstars. (© Bettmann/CORBIS)

4. ACHIEVE *UBINIQUITY*

Maybe you don't have the money, the access, the connections, or the skills to get fame, but you're nevertheless determined to transform yourself into a celebrity. If you prefer infamy to anonymity, you can apply the questionable method of doing something scandalous and advertising your scandalous acts to achieve fame. Your misdeeds catapult you to notorious omnipresence: ubiniquity.

TRUE RULE

Succès de scandale is better than no *succès* at all.

Sell the story of how you took revenge for being left at the altar to the *National Enquirer.* Confide the shocking secrets of your double life to Jerry Springer or Ricki Lake. Write a tell-all detailing the sordid sins from your past sex addiction or shopping addiction or carbo addiction.

Then, once you've achieved a foothold in notoriety, promote yourself as much as possible. Follow the example of scandalebrities like Donna Rice, Paula Jones, and Marla Maples, who joined the advertising campaign for No Excuses jeans as a way to use their newfound fame to promote themselves. John Wayne Bobbitt's angry wife made him a celebrity when she cut off his penis; he capitalized on his fame by releasing a video, *John Wayne Bobbitt Uncut,* that was snapped up by eager crowds.

It is reprehensible to commit a crime to achieve fame, but fame is a surprisingly common motive. Some criminals eagerly await the media fury that their acts will ignite. Dreams of fame preoccupied Columbine High School students Dylan Klebold, seventeen, and Eric Harris, eighteen, who in 1999 mowed down thirteen people before killing themselves. In home videos the two left behind, they detailed their wish to have the school massacre immortalized in a big-budget Hollywood picture. "Directors will be fighting over this story," crowed Klebold. The pair debated the choice of director for the movie—Quentin Tarantino or Steven Spielberg? Harris added a suggestion: The film should have "a lot of foreshadowing and dramatic irony." Gian Luigi Ferri, who in 1993 shot eight people in a law office and then committed suicide, left behind notes showing he expected to have the opportunity to air his complaints with Oprah Winfrey, Phil Donahue, and Geraldo Rivera. A serial killer in Kansas wrote a letter to the police complaining, "How many times do I have to kill before I get a name in the paper or some national attention?"

To attain large fame, a criminal must commit a telegenic crime: one that is sexually sordid, exceptionally dramatic or gruesome or poignant, or involves a famous person. That kind of newsworthy criminal receives star treatment—the police motorcade and heavy guard, the sale of the criminal memoir for top dollar. Maybe his story will be told by a celebrated figure, as Norman Mailer, Truman Capote, Joe McGinniss, and Errol Morris have done.

In fact, for those who attack a politician or celebrity, the thirst for fame is the *most* common motive given. They recognize that the more important the target, the more recognition given to them as assailant. By targeting President Ronald Reagan, twenty-five-year-old John W. Hinckley, Jr., guaranteed the maximum possible coverage for the crime he committed in a bid to win actress Jodie Foster's respect. Hinckley reveled in the fame that he knew would follow his assassination attempt. Five hours after the shooting, he asked the Secret Service agents interrogating him, "Is it on TV?"

Obviously, however, while such methods may be effective, they are indefensible.

Note that if you're already famous, ubiniquity will only add to your fame—especially if you're cultivating an outlaw image. Rapper and Bad Boy Entertainment executive Sean "Puffy" Combs has had his brushes with scandal—beating up a record executive and fleeing the scene of a Manhattan nightclub shooting—but these "bad boy" incidents didn't seem to bother his fans. And they certainly kept his name and picture in the spotlight.

5. BUY YOUR FAME

If you don't want to use any of the above methods, and if you have the money, you can use money to buy your fame. See "Money," Chapter 11.

6. CULTIVATE YOUR COLORFULNESS

No matter which method you use to pursue fame, you need maximum visibility. But how do you encourage effective coverage of yourself? Present yourself as a colorful subject. Feed the media what it craves: good pictures, fighting words, rapid response, and witty sound bites.

TRUE RULE

Whether on TV or in print, it's survival of the briefest.

Exploit the media's constraints: accommodate their deadlines, encourage their competitive anxieties, cater to their areas of expertise and ignorance. Joseph McCarthy, the Communist-hunting senator, was a master of press manipulation. He was a fount of riveting copy and exciting allegations, and shrewdly, he timed his press releases so reporters had time to meet their deadlines but didn't have time to check with his opponents for rebuttal.

Nowadays, because more people sniff after the media, getting that kind of edge is harder. Media manipulation is big business, involving spin-meisters, pollsters, speechwriters, and consultants of every stripe. Ronald Reagan's publicity mastermind Michael Deaver revolutionized presidential spin with his insight that sympathetic news *pictures* make a far greater impression than critical news *stories*, but today every small-town politician labors to apply Deaver's principles. Even mediocre academics know enough to pepper their statements with one-liners and controversial proclamations if they want to be booked for the weekend show. Commentators may decry the triumph of the sound bite, the staged photo-op, the maudlin human-interest story, but that's what works.

TIP: If you're issuing a statement, how can you ensure that the press quotes the crucial passage? Don't prepare a page-long release that offers several choices for quotation; limit yourself to a few sentences. Then the press will have to quote what you want.

Work to keep the media spotlight trained on you. Once you've achieved some fame, take advantage of the *cynosure effect*—that is, the mere fact of being in the spotlight makes you interesting to an audience. Attention generates more attention; build this momentum as best you can. The more effectively you can attract and keep the world's attention, the greater your fame. Of course, you acknowledge—but *how?* Consider the following techniques:

Coin phrases that will lodge in listeners' minds, like Johnnie Cochran's "If the glove doesn't fit, you must acquit," Ross Perot's "giant sucking sound" of U.S. jobs going to Mexico, and Lloyd Bentsen's "I knew Jack Kennedy, Jack Kennedy was a friend of mine. Senator, you are no Jack Kennedy." If you lack creativity, co-opt familiar advertising copy or a memorable line from a movie, like Walter Mondale's use of fast-food-chain Wendy's slogan, "Where's the beef?"

Use romance (or a lack of it) to promote yourself. Have an on-and-off-again romance, like Gwyneth Paltrow and Ben Affleck. Get married, whether after agonizing suspense like Barbra Streisand, or in an impetuous rush, like Julia Roberts and Lyle Lovett. Madonna and Sean Penn, both canny fame-mongers, issued a press release to announce their engagement; Senator Alfonse D'Amato and gossip columnist Claudia Cohen held a giddy press conference to declare their love (an announcement made a bit awkward by the fact that the senator already had a wife). If news of your marriage wouldn't be newsworthy, win coverage by getting married in a colorful way—underwater, at half-time in a sports arena, in the space shuttle. Once married, give your fame another boost by getting divorced. Join the *split-erati,* those people whose divorces have boosted their fame: the ex-Mrs. Trumps, Ronald Perelman, Larry Fortensky.

TIP: To draw attention to a body part (your spectacular derrière or legs, your piano-playing hands), insure it for a million dollars.

Try debauchery or **titillation** if romance isn't the right platform for you, like Frank Sinatra or Richard Pryor or Madonna. **Flash bare skin** to capture people's attention, as exploited by rapper Lil' Kim, whose outfits leave nothing to the imagination.

Use activism as a way to expand your fame, the way Richard Gere uses Tibet or Warren Beatty used his flirtation with running for president. Get involved in politics, develop opinions on every issue. Extreme views attract the most attention, so stake your position on the edge.

Ignite controversy. Espousing unpopular or contrarian opinions, exposing secrets, reporting previously unreportable gossip will attract the public's eye. Exaggerate, startle, disturb. To attract attention to his father's sleepy trade newspaper, John Fairchild agitated the fashion establishment with the edgy, insider's gossip he incorporated into *Women's Wear Daily.* Do the opposite of what's expected of you. If you're known for railing against the patriarchy, write a book in defense of men. If you're a prominent banker, write a letter to the paper decrying the moral failings of the rich.

Establish a rivalry. From major-league baseball (Mark McGwire versus Sammy Sosa) to major-league fashion (Anna Wintour versus Kate Betts), people love to follow a rivalry and root for their favorite. Loudmouthed Speaker of the House Newt Gingrich gave a tremendous boost to House Democrats by being such a colorful and outspoken spokesman for the opposing side. There's only so much to write about pop music Britney Spears and Christina Aguilera, but their supposedly bitter competition provides another angle. And a fierce rivalry will etch your name in the public's mind for decades—think of Nicklaus and Palmer, Mantle and Mays, Evert and Navratilova.

Exploit humor to make yourself memorable, quotable, and likable. Yogi Berra became a baseball legend not for his successes as a player, coach, and manager, but for the things he said (about which he remarked, "I really didn't say everything I said."). When asked about his life philosophy, he answered, "When you get to a fork in the road, take it," when asked for the time, he asked, "You mean now?"

Plan a "spontaneous" event that can be easily reported, with photographs of you in the thick of the action. Chain yourself to a fence, refuse to leave an official's office, offer yourself as spokesperson for some unjustly accused figure. Tennis bad-boy John McEnroe revealed that his famous on-court rudeness—giving "the finger" to spectators, throwing his racquet, cursing at referees—was all just a show to generate excitement and interest in his game.

Paradoxically, one way to boost your fame is to **remain anonymous.** By hiding your identity, you create curiosity and controversy—the all-important buzz. Joe Klein cleverly whipped up huge amounts of attention (and sales) for his political novel, *Primary Colors,* by cloaking his identity. Many people who wouldn't have picked up the book otherwise read it to join the fun of the author-ship debate. The *Vanity Fair* article "My First Gulfstream" described the joys of joining the fraternity of private jet owners. The author, "Anonymous," was described only as "a top information age entre-preneur." The article would have excited less interest if Microsoft chief technology officer Nathan Myhrvold had signed his name to his piece so that no one had to speculate. The *New York Times* restaurant critic Ruth Reichl wore disguises whenever she was pho-tographed, so that restaurateurs wouldn't be able to spot her; of course, the fact that she was always masked aroused interest in her. But if you don't want to remain anonymous . . .

Use your name to boost your fame. Malcolm X's name is unfor-gettable. Journalist Jennifer Lee (saddled with the most popular girl's name of her birth year, 1976, and the second most common Chinese surname) adopted the middle name "8." So—"Jennifer 8. Lee." And not only is her name memorable and eye-catching—as an added bonus, its novelty also guarantees her an explanatory profile every time her byline appears in a new publication. Whenever possi-ble, advertise your name on your product, your theorem, your invention, or your service. Financier Michael Bloomberg turned himself into a household name when he named his investor infor-mation terminal "the Bloomberg." By naming their top restaurants after themselves, New York City restaurateurs like B. Smith (B. Smith's), Daniel Boulud (Daniel; Café Boulud), Elaine Kaufman (Elaine's), Jean-Georges Vongerichten (Jean Georges; Vong), Sylvia Woods (Sylvia's), and David Bouley (Bouley; Bouley Bakery) branded their identities into the public mind.

At the most basic level, **change your appearance**—Hillary Clinton, Princess Diana, and Gwyneth Paltrow generated a flurry of press coverage with every new hairstyle and color. You might consider getting an outra-geous, conspicuous tattoo.

Encounters with danger and tragedy, although unsought, are surefire ways to keep your star burning bright. The suicide of rock star Kurt Cobain dra-matically increased the public's interest in his widow, Courtney Love.

> **TIP:** Apply the principle of dis-expectation to your looks. If every other starlet in Hollywood or every woman in your social set is blonde, you go brunette.

Band together with a conspicuous pack of fame-seekers. You'll attract more attention as a group than you would separately. Baptize your group with an evocative name (something like "Young Turks" works well) and indulge in high jinks that make good copy—tales of your pack's reckless carousing, of your tangled sexual lives, of the bitter feuds and competitive struggles that agitate your relationships. The pack strategy worked best, perhaps, for the notorious Rat Pack of Frank Sinatra, Dean Martin, Sammy Davis, Jr., Peter Lawford, and Joey Bishop—an example emulated in the mid-1980s by the Brat Pack of Sean Penn, Rob Lowe, and others. By forming the brilliant and unconventional Bloomsbury Group, luminaries such as Virginia Woolf, Lytton Strachey, E. M. Forster, and John Maynard Keynes added to each other's considerable glory, as did members of the hard-drinking and acid-witted Algonquin Round Table, like Harpo Marx, Dorothy Parker, and George S. Kaufman. The public followed the friendships, rivalries, and social lives of the "supermodels"—Naomi Campbell, Christy Turlington, and Linda Evangelista, to name a few—with more interest than the models individually would have compelled. A recent application of this rule is Leonardo DiCaprio's Pussy Posse (with Leo, rapper Q-Tip, director Harmony Korine, actor Tobey Maguire, and others).

To distinguish yourself from the common herd, **fix your image with an eye-tag.** This flourish will help onlookers recognize you in person, and when your name appears in that dishiest of all gossip columns, "Page Six," your trademark touch will help identify you even in print, like a Homeric epithet (rosy-fingered Dawn, gray-eyed Athena). Cyber-tabloidist and self-promoter Matt Drudge adopted his signature fedora, writer Tom Wolfe wears white suits, *Playboy's* Hugh Hefner rarely changes out of pajamas, trial lawyer Gerry Spence sports a fringed buckskin jacket, and the late Payne Stewart played golf wearing traditional knickers and tam-o'-shanter. If you don't want to change your way of dressing, consider signature spectacles. Such disparate figures as architect Philip Johnson, the Hollywood superagent Irving Lazar, singer Elton John, and Hollywood mogul Lew Wasserman are known for their bold, eye-catching frames. Hair makes a great eye-tag: boxing promoter Don King's hair stands preternaturally on end, Dennis Rodman dyes his hair in a rainbow of colors, singer Sinéad O'Connor shaved her head, tennis-star sisters Venus and Serena Williams's beaded braids make them instantly recognizable. Artist Salvador Dalí's thin, upturned mustache made him instantly recognizable, even to the uncultured.

If you're a woman, you'll find it harder to concoct an eye-tag. Because women's fashions change swiftly, today's distinctive look might appear frumpy in a few years. Jocelyn Wildenstein ("Bride of Wildenstein" or "Lion Queen") conceived a dramatic solution to this problem. Instead of clothing, she used plastic surgery to give herself a singular, feline appearance, with jutting cheekbones, tight skin, and slanting, almond-shaped eyes. First Lady Nancy Reagan was at once more subtle and more extreme. Rather than adopt characteristic apparel—an oversized eagle brooch or American-flag scarf—she claimed the entire color red. She made it clear to other officials' wives sharing a platform with her that only she could wear that color.

When considering an eye-tag, avoid affectation. Lamar Alexander wisely decided to abandon his plaid shirts for the 2000 presidential election. He'd worn plaid for the 1996 race as a way to suggest his down-to-earth, rugged character, but the gimmick seemed contrived.

Having attracted coverage, try to **get an accompanying photograph**, to impress your face as well as your name into public consciousness. Magazines and newspapers use portraits to rank their subjects: a *Wall Street Journal* story might cover a team of ten, but it's the two most important people whose (unfailingly unflattering) sketches will enliven the page. If you're seeking social fame, being pho-

TIP: Use an eye-tag to promote your business as well as yourself. Red Hat CEO Bob Young wears (what else?) a red hat when he appears in public.

TIP: Think of yourself as a brand. Everything you do—hobbies, conversation, appearance—should enforce your distinctive identity. To show that you're brainy, yet wacky, play high-speed, high-stakes chess in the park. To highlight your analytical style, brandish a yellow legal pad.

TIP: Trying to see your photo published? When your picture is being snapped with someone famous, make a gesture that points your finger at that person's chest. You'll appear energetic, and you'll thwart any photo editor who might want to crop you out.

tographed is not merely preferable—it's essential. Cultivate society photographers, like the all-powerful Patrick McMullan, who can anoint you as a socialite or playboy by taking your picture for magazines like *New York, Harper's Bazaar,* and *Quest.*

Fame—Do	Fame—Don't
DO elope to a distant island where you say your wedding vows, then both bungee-jump off a bridge.	DON'T elope to City Hall where you're married by a harried judge in a room crowded with strangers.
DO hire a media coach.	DON'T admit you hired a media coach.
DO storm the stage at the awards ceremony to protest environmental crimes.	DON'T boycott the awards ceremony to protest environmental crimes.
DO, as a woman, hint that you might be bisexual.	DON'T, as a woman, suggest that you enjoy a ménage à trois.
DO, as a man, suggest that you enjoy a ménage à trois.	DON'T, as a man, hint that you might be bisexual.

If, despite your best efforts, you're unable to procure the fame you crave, slake your thirst by indulging in artificial fame. Movie producer Don Simpson instructed his personal publicist, Peggy Siegal, that he wanted to be rushed by a mob of screaming fans when he arrived at French customs for the Deauville Film Festival. If you don't have a publicist to give you a fame fix, pay $45 to visit the Anaheim theme park Tinseltown Studios. You enter by red carpet and klieg lights and are immediately surrounded by a crowd of teenagers begging for autographs, paparazzi popping flashbulbs, and reporters pleading for an interview. For one night, you're a celebrity. Closer to home, you can try taking the stage in a karaoke bar—that most obtainable form of fake fame.

The Internet provides a new way to imitate the delicious sensation of fame. Start your own website to experience the thrill of seeing your name in print, published for everyone to see—and it is a thrill, even if you put your name there yourself and you've only gotten five hits. Include photographs, video and audio clips, screeds on every topic. And while your website will give you the sensation of fame, it's not impossible that it could actually make you famous. Eccentric film enthusiast Harry Knowles started his own website far from Hollywood, in Austin, Texas, but his boisterous aint-it-cool-news.com, featuring "all that is cool within the film industry," won him features in newspapers, magazines, and television, and his site is widely read—despite his idiosyncratic and exclamatory (!!!) style. The lesson? Don't hesitate to use every tool you can find to promote yourself.

Consider the following suggestions for applying the techniques discussed above to achieve fame:

Type of fame	Suggestion
Fame frottage: associate with someone or something famous	• Offer free lawn care to a celebrity in order to leverage one famous client into other prominent customers. Soon you'll be "the" yardman, with everyone vying for your services.
	• Throw fashionable dinner parties that only the most prominent people attend. You'll be known all over town for the exclusive company you keep.
Attain a prominent position	• Establish yourself as the person with the most extravagant Christmas-light display. Everyone in town will drive by to gape, and you and your house will be on the front pages.
	• Start a petition or introduce a ballot initiative on some highly controversial subject. You'll find yourself regularly interviewed as a key player in the debate.

Type of fame	Suggestion
Accomplish a notable achievement	• Turn your hobby into an expertise; transform yourself from an amateur genealogist to your town's foremost authority on local history, to be consulted and quoted.
Participate in a scandal	• Indulge in heavy drinking and dirty dancing at your firm's annual party. Soon all five hundred employees will be talking about you.
Buy your fame	• Tip the maitre d' of the hippest restaurant so handsomely that he fawningly gives you the best seat in the house, night after night; people see you in the prime position, and soon tongues are wagging.

CASE STUDY IN FAME: MARCIA CLARK.
CLAIM TO FAME: LEAD PROSECUTOR IN THE
O. J. SIMPSON MURDER TRIAL.

Marcia Clark saw her chance at fame, and she exploited it for all it was worth.

Her celebrity sprang from her ubiquitous media presence during the almost nine months of the O. J. Simpson trial. The firestorm surrounding the trial, which included gavel-to-gavel coverage on Court TV, was ignited by the celebrity of the accused, O. J. Simpson—football star, sportscaster, actor, Hertz pitchman. His fame would have made anyone who served as his prosecutor a star by frottage; the prosecutor happened to be Marcia Clark. Once the public fixed on her, they demanded to know more. Any change in her hair or dress was big news (one successful makeover landed her hairdresser an *Oprah* appearance—celebrity breeds celebrity). Minor scandals buttressed Clark's fame by generating media coverage unrelated to the trial:

her child-care arrangements made headlines and spurred debate about working mothers, and the rumor that she was dating Christopher Darden provoked controversy both because he was her fellow prosecutor and because he was black and she, white. The public couldn't get enough. Although in the end Clark's notable achievement was her loss of the case, the controversy surrounding the "not guilty" verdict only won her more media coverage.

But while fate singled out Clark for the spotlight, it was her careful management of her opportunities that kept her there for so long. After the trial, she traveled around the country giving speeches. She started work on a book, for which she received an eye-popping advance of more than $4 million. She made frequent TV appearances and even got her own show.

In the end, however, Marcia Clark's success story illustrates the difficulty of maintaining fame. Although she has done everything possible to promote herself, her star is flickering out, and unless she manages a resurgence, she'll find herself in the category of fallen star. Where *is* Marcia Clark now?

FAME MYTHS

Whether you're already a big fish in a small pond, a household name, a star, or an icon, or if you're still trying to break into one of those categories, don't be misled by fame myths.

Myth: *You must tell the truth about yourself and how you rose to prominence.*

Reality: Don't be afraid to embroider your story. For example, the harder your childhood, the more spectacular your success. Publishing executive Steve Florio gave many false "impressions" about his past including that he'd spent a year counseling "kids with backgrounds similar to mine to stay in school." Demonstrably untrue. Top cable executive Leo Hindery, Jr., said that he left home to fend for himself at age thirteen and joined the merchant marine at age sixteen. No one else remembers it that way. Another executive, Jeffrey Papows, drew upon his exciting military career to motivate workers and win business; Marine Corps records show that Papows served as a humdrum air-traffic controller. One coworker recalled that Papows once arrived at work distraught from a terrible accident he'd been in while flying in the Marine reserves; curiously, the accident described bore a startling similarity to an incident in the Tom Cruise movie *Top Gun*. Oracle founder Larry Ellison for many years led people to believe that he had a degree in physics, but in fact, he'd never graduated from college.

Feel free to work the same transformation on your family's history. Marilyn Monroe portrayed herself as a little orphan girl, even though her mother was still alive. (Papows also claimed he was an orphan—nope.) Truman Capote's mother had been one of many regional winners of a beauty contest sponsored by Lux—Capote spun the truth into his mother's triumph at the contest for Miss Alabama. His version sounded better.

Given the world's love of prodigies, does anyone need to know exactly how old you are? Thirty-two-year-old TV actress and writer Riley Weston (born Kimberlee Kramer) almost succeeded in gulling Hollywood into believing her to be a precocious nineteen. Movie director Steven Spielberg, born in 1946, shaved off a few years to boost his carefully cultivated wunderkind image. Nancy Reagan fought with the writer who worked on her autobiography to keep out her birth date, July 6, 1923. (He managed to sneak it into his foreword.)

Myth: *You should exhibit modesty about your fame.*
Reality: Magnify any moment of fame. If you're a deal-maker who made the cover of *Fortune,* frame the cover for your wall. If you're a salesman who got profiled in an obscure trade magazine, send copies to all your colleagues and clients. Even criminals on death row work to get the proper renown due them—they write the national

death-watch newsletter to correct their middle initials and nicknames.

Modesty may once have been in vogue, but now you must promote yourself if you want to grab the spotlight. Just contrast two military heroes: Confederate Army commander in chief Robert E. Lee refused to write his memoirs, because to do so would be "trading on the blood of my men"; General Norman Schwarzkopf, field commander for allied forces in the Persian Gulf War, gave lectures for more than $50,000 an appearance and sold his autobiography for almost $6 million.

Of course, as always, the principle of dis-expectation applies. One executive plots to get listed in the Fortune 500 or to earn a bold-faced mention by Liz Smith; another pulls every string to keep his name out of the papers.

Myth: *You should let your story of fame speak for itself.*

Reality: You must tell—or invent—a compelling, archetypal story to explain your rise to prominence. Were you an *ugly duckling* who blossomed into a swan? A *persevering tortoise* whose years of anonymous toil finally paid off? Maybe you want to present yourself as a *discovery,* spotted by a talent scout who pulled you from coffee-shop obscurity, or a *comeback kid* who made a hard-won return to glory from scandal, divorce, addiction. Perhaps the most popular fame myths are the *American dream* in which you escape from the old country to freedom and riches, the *natural,* in which you possess inborn genius that flowered from your birth, or *David and Goliath,* in which you triumph over vastly superior forces.

> **TIP:** Steady success can be dull; success shot with failings is fascinating. The mix of brilliance and recklessness (boozing, gambling, womanizing, profligacy, temper) can transform a boring superachiever into a mesmerizing idol. So, if you have some unruly appetites, get them to work in your favor.

Myth: *If you're a person of substance, you shouldn't waste your time worrying about whether you're well-known.*

Reality: Wrong. You need the vindication of fame to be considered truly successful, because most people recognize ability only when they see it widely acclaimed. Also, fame itself translates into power and influence, and so the fact of your fame will significantly boost your effectiveness. Copy the efforts of people like U.N. ambassador Richard Holbrooke or Silicon Valley mogul Jim Clark, and take the time to cultivate the spotlight and the press.

While you're still working on building your profile, thrust yourself forward as much as you can within your own circle. Are you a self-promoter? Do you find yourself:

- handing out business cards many times each day?
- finding ways to meet prominent people, and whenever possible, to have your photograph taken with them?
- switching placecards to improve your placement at a seated lunch or dinner?
- giving a picture of yourself to a person who is neither your sweetheart nor a family member? (If you were given a disposable camera at a wedding, would you take photos of other people, or ask people to take photos of you?)
- cultivating people who could write letters of recommendation for you?
- offering to take someone to lunch so you can update him or her on what *you've* been doing lately?
- giving gifts to people you hardly know (particularly if you can give a gift that bears your personal stamp: a product you designed, an article or book you wrote, a compact disc you produced)?
- looking for ways to introduce two people who would benefit from meeting each other and who'll be grateful to you for making the connection?

TIP: A self-promotion gift need not be expensive. Even sending a holiday card is effective.

- shouldering your way onto panels and advisory groups?
- maintaining a personal web page to keep people abreast of your latest move, new job, what you've read lately, and so on?
- inviting prominent strangers or near-strangers to your house for a dinner or party?
- dressing to stand out in a group—dressing more formally than an occasion demands, or sporting some whimsical eye-catching details?
- encouraging others to call you by a nickname that reflects the qualities you're trying to promote, like "Gatsby" or "Blondie" or "Bull"? Or trying to get yourself associated with a particular trait? "She's such a workaholic." "He knows *everyone.*"
- angling, even lobbying, to be invited to the right weddings and funerals?
- making a point of asking valuable acquaintances for favors, like advice or recommendations, or even something as insignificant as a few aspirin?
- circling a party until you've met or talked to every bigwig in attendance?
- tirelessly pursuing people who've grabbed your attention, until you wear down any reluctance on their part to meet or to become friends?

If you answer "yes" to more than three questions, you're a natural self-promoter.

Note that while these tactics aren't necessarily disagreeable, onlookers find aggressive

> **TIP:** To self-promote, start an organization that, under the guise of promoting some cause, actually promotes you. Consider the composer of serious new music who founded a nonprofit to create a forum for new music. As he pulls together the organization's programs, he's able to meet prestigious composers, is in a position to grant them performance opportunities, and most important, can insert his own work into a night's program to take advantage of their audiences and the exposure.

> Any man who wants strongly enough to become the friend of another will succeed if there are no unbridgeable . . . gaps and if he wastes no time in worrying about his own inferior attainments.
>
> Louis Auchincloss, *The Rector of Justin*

self-promotion obnoxious—particularly if they think you're interested in show but not substance. Up to a point, your self-promotion can be effective even if annoying, but if too flagrant, your efforts may become counterproductive.

Myth: *You should become recognized for your unique personality—"yourself."*

Reality: As you become more famous, it becomes increasingly important to control and reinforce the image you want. That image need not reflect your true personality, and it can change over time. Remember, as Joseph Kennedy said, "it's not what you are that counts, but what people think you are."

Demand that only your approved head shot be used in the magazine article, corporate report, or brochure.

Re-create yourself. Celebrities like Oprah Winfrey and the Beatles reinvented themselves many times. Madonna went from the Boy Toy with smeared mascara, fingerless gloves, and giant crucifixes, to the platinum, Marilyn-esque Material Girl, to the fresh-scrubbed, innocent True Blue gamine, to the angelic, ethereal Ray of Light, to the eerie, spiritual "Frozen." It's true that, once extremely famous, you need only avoid a negative image, but for everyone of lesser fame, it's preferable to create a distinctive personality, your own brand.

As your fame grows, you'll find yourself surrounded by foot-washers scurrying to serve you, hanging on your every word, clawing for your attention. They worship the glow of your star and bask in your presence, but don't expect them to "know" you

TIP: Shape your name to suit your image. Copy CBS Chairman and CEO Mel Karmazin: any reporter who dares refer to him by his full name, "Melvin Alan," is instructed to use "Mel." After all, it's explained, "Walt Disney is not Walter Disney."

(although they may feel as if they do know you). They pay homage to a vision of celebrity. Sue Erikson Bloland, daughter of eminent psychoanalyst Erik Erikson, described the foot-washing that her father inspired: "I witnessed a dramatic transformation in how people related to him. . . . He became the luminous center of attention at most social and professional gatherings, where people milled around him, obviously excited, doing their best to make conversation with one another while awaiting their turn to engage with him. In his presence they became mysteriously childlike: animated, deferential, anxious to gain his interest and approval." There's no way for the foot-washers to know you, yourself, despite the clamoring tributes they demand to pay and their eagerness to draw close.

• • •

Once you've achieved a measure of fame, you must build on it by acting the part. Reflect on your ultimate goal and copy the manners of those who have already attained it. Keep in mind the following characteristics of celebrity-hood as you assume your role.

CHAPTER FIFTEEN

ASSUMING THE ROLE

If you're working to promote your fame or if you're still struggling to establish it, it helps to act the part—even if a bit prematurely. Fame brings privileges and attitudes, and by staking out your claim, you signal that you believe you belong in the category of the famous.

Shep Gordon, manager of superstar rock musicians, explained of one group: "I determined as soon as I began to manage them that they would be treated like stars at all times. They would be waited on, catered to, made to feel like they were the most famous performers who ever lived. And so, even before the public knew who they were, the band was being treated like millionaires. That way, when anyone from the outside came in contact with our organization, they felt like they were dealing with stars. The band really did believe they were stars, and it carried over to the press people who interviewed them, and the people who saw them play."

So, once you have even a slight toehold in fame, act like a real celebrity:

1. Make extravagant demands.
2. Manipulate your image.
3. Associate with people of the same or greater fame.
4. Traffic only in the right products, places, and pastimes.
5. Radiate *sprezzatura*.

1. MAKE EXTRAVAGANT DEMANDS

Famous people get what they want—so ask for a lot. Pay close attention to the perks that others enjoy, and demand the same or better.

Build up an entourage, with whatever attendants appropriate to your field: speechwriter, masseuse, personal trainer, media coach, chef, hairstylist, driver, bodyguard, astrologer.

Insist on the fastest, most convenient form of transportation. Demi "Gimme" Moore, while doing a voice for an animated Disney movie, balked at a recording session that conflicted with a PTA meeting. The studio arranged her transportation to the PTA meeting—but at the appointed time, Moore was astounded to learn that they'd only arranged for a limo. The PTA meeting, it turned out, was in *Idaho*. So the studio hired a private jet, at about $4,500 per hour, to take Moore to the meeting.

A necessary aspect of being a star is being stared at—but you demand otherwise. When Julia Roberts moved into an exclusive West Hollywood apartment complex, the other tenants were sent notices asking them not to make direct eye contact with her if they passed her in the halls or lobby. Madonna, too, wanted to avoid the stares of her fans; her bodyguards forbade hotel employees to speak her name, talk to, or even look directly at her. While working out at the gym, actress Sigourney Weaver and her personal trainer insisted that no one use the treadmills next to her.

Be imaginative in your demands, and don't hesitate to be specific. To get some ideas, consider the following: supermodel Claudia Schiffer insisted on mineral water and Skittles candies, with the odd requirement that all the purple ones be removed—perhaps inspired by the demand of the rock stars of Van Halen, who insisted on candy dishes filled with M&M's minus the brown ones. TV star Jane Seymour required her program, *Dr. Quinn, Medicine Woman*, to provide her with a weekly delivery of London rainwater, with which she washed her hair. Cost: $1,200 per shipment. When having her picture taken by the celebrity photographer Patrick Demarchelier, actress Ashley Judd demanded that her water be served at a precise seventy-two degrees. As part of his four-year, $52 million contract with the Arizona Diamondbacks, pitcher Randy Johnson not only got membership at the exclusive Desert Mountain golf club and ten year's worth of front-row seats to Phoenix Suns basketball games—he also won an exemption from the team's ban on facial hair.

Just the merest hint at your desires will set celebrity-foot-washers scrambling to please you. On the weekend before Clinton's second inauguration, Man A got into an elevator, already occupied by Man B, on the second floor of the Jefferson Hotel, a Washington power hotel. Man B cut a conspicuous figure in tuxedo and cowboy boots.

"You must be going to Black Tie and Boots," said Man A, referring to one of the big inauguration parties.

"That's right," Man B replied.

"I need to get a ticket to that," Man A mused aloud. "Somehow I didn't get one."

"I overbought by six," said Man B eagerly (the tickets must have been priced somewhere between $100 and $200), "if you need one."

"That'd be great," Man A answered, and stuck out his hand. "I'm Carl Bernstein."

"Yes, I recognize you, Mr. Bernstein," said Man B. "I'm with Michael Isikoff's group."

"How should I get the ticket? Who do I ask for?"

"Just ask for me . . ." the elevator doors opened. Man A and Man B walked out to discuss the arrangements. A need is satisfied—in the time it took to go from the second floor to the first floor.

Of course, at your level of fame, private jets and inaugural ball tickets may not be forthcoming. What can you demand? Insist on using complicated audiovisual equipment if this group wants you to address them (they must supply and run the equipment); require that a meeting be scheduled and rescheduled to suit you; demand that you travel to your interview at the local TV studio in a chauffeured car; insist that your country club serve your favorite water (*not* Evian, *not* Perrier, *not* Vittel, but Pellegrino). Remember the platinum rule: To whom much is given, more is given.

2. MANIPULATE YOUR IMAGE

Manage your image. Pursue the perfect haircut, agonize over the right tie, dress for the part. Follow the example of basketball star Scottie Pippen who, early in his years with the Bulls, wore glasses with noncorrective lenses—presumably to give himself a more serious look. Don't brush such details aside as trivial. Remember, a picture is worth a thousand words, so construct the visual image you want.

It's not enough just to hone your *appearance*. Help the press use your image to simplify, personalize, and dramatize complex matters. This makes their job much easier and allows you to advance yourself and your version of an issue. Emphasize your personality and your motivations. Say you're running for public office. Instead of droning on about the social costs of welfare or the theoretical underpinnings of the creative destruction of capitalism, emphasize your hardworking immigrant parents and the fact that you stand for solid American values. After her husband's assassination, Jackie Kennedy carefully fixed his image in the public mind through memorable pictures and phrases: for example, she prompted their young son, John, to salute his father's grave and suggested the term "Camelot" to historian Theodore H. White.

Convey your personality by adopting a signature symbol, like Kennedy's PT 109 pin, or allowing one to be created for you, like the bowls full of peanuts that staffers in the Carter White House kept on their desks. Humanize yourself—joke about your distaste for broccoli or your love for jelly beans. This technique works well for anyone at the center of a large group's attention. They want to know you, and you want to help them know you better than you can accomplish personally. They'll feel closer to you because they can laugh at the amount of Diet Pepsi you drink or your fanatic devotion to the racetrack.

If you adopt a signature gesture, make it memorable and engaging. Tycoon John D. Rockefeller softened his money-grubbing image by handing out shiny coins—dimes for adults, nickels for children—along with an exhortation to work hard.

Be careful not to undercut your image with juicy anecdotes or arresting pictures that are off-message. Learn from Lyndon Johnson's mistake: he was inundated with criticism from dog-loving Americans after news photos showed him pulling up his new beagle by the ears.

TIP: Describe yourself either as an ordinary person doing extraordinary things, or as an extraordinary person doing ordinary things.

Keep tight control of your image. Lyndon Johnson was furious with regret after he allowed himself to be photographed pulling his beagle up by the ears. Dog lovers across the world protested his cruelty. (AP/Wide World Photos)

Don't assume that people will appreciate your prominence—signal it. Surround yourself with bodyguards, or at least hire one for a special occasion. By showing you're the focus of threats, you show that you're the focus of interest. Snatch up (or create) any opportunity to be the subject of attention. Hire a writer to profile you—or even better, hire a camera crew to follow you around. Others will be impressed to see you shadowed by a disciple who is assiduously recording your every word and gesture.

Violate convention. If it fits the image you're creating, dress and act outrageously; or, if you don't want to be too daring, develop an inoffensively distinctive look. Instead of the standard business-suit-and-smile headshots that your colleagues submit for trade-publication announcements, turn in a photo of yourself sporting a sweatshirt and baseball cap.

Get professional help. A publicist will generate stories, steer reporters, improve editorial content, demand any needed airbrushing of your photographs. You've got to come across at your best.

TIP: If you've got a lot to hide, remember that your *press* agent also can act as your *suppress* agent.

3. ASSOCIATE WITH PEOPLE OF THE SAME OR GREATER FAME

You're judged by the company you keep, so be seen only with the right people. Before agreeing to appear on a panel at the year's biggest industry conference or to be interviewed for a feature on celebrity hobbies, ask who else is participating. If you're by far the biggest name they've got, decline. You can't associate with nobodies.

If you do decide to participate, make sure you're ranked as you deserve. Who's seated next to the big-name moderator? Who else is assigned to your table for lunch? Long before an appearance with Jay Leno or David Letterman, celebrities are wangling for the coveted first-interview slot. Guard your position.

If you've got an all-star connection, milk it for all it's worth. The easiest way to do this is by name-dropping—a practice that shows connection and access, even equality, to fame. But while name-dropping can be effective, it's tricky. Don't drop too many names in a single conversation (if you really knew these people, you wouldn't feel the need to prove it), hint at more than you reveal, and most important, *get the name right.* Use a nickname if appropriate: everyone knows to call Henry Louis Gates, Jr., "Skip." Don't make a nickname mistake, like those who affectionately referred to superagent Irving "Swifty" Lazar as "Swifty." They didn't realize that nobody who mattered called him "Swifty." "Magic" Johnson was "Magic" only to his fans and most sportswriters; those who knew him better called him Earvin (his given name); his teammates, and a few select others, used "Buck" (for young buck). And no real intimate called John F. Kennedy, Jr., "John John"—that name was the creation of a reporter who misheard a family conversation.

(How strange, now that you're famous, to be the subject of name-dropping. Distant acquaintances brag about their friendship with you, and they genuinely feel a connection—fame engenders a sense of intimacy that's felt only on one side. In faraway rooms, people slide your name into conversations. "He asked me to call him Pete, you know." They gather anecdotes. Ward Just's novel *Echo House* describes the process: "You listened to stories about 'Jack' all the time, what he liked to eat and drink, witty remarks that he made, his prowess on the golf course, his aches and pains; and other stories, none of them verifiable. Probably the same thing was true of the Pope or Chairman Mao, mysterious personalities whose offhand remarks proved that they were only human after all, with good close friends to prove it.")

Use your imagination to generate contact—or the appearance of contact—if you don't know anyone famous. Victor Good, a "nobody," invited perfect strangers to his wedding, for no other reason except that he wanted the pleasure of their company: Microsoft Chairman Bill Gates, gaming tycoon Stephen Wynn, AT&T chairman Robert Allen, and chief executives for more than a dozen other corporations. "I love to meet interesting people," Good explained. He got his fifteen minutes of fame when the *Wall Street Journal* wrote him up, plus a few wedding gifts and congratulatory letters, for his effort.

> **TIP:** If you're publishing a book or article, pack your acknowledgments with thanks to several stars in your field; you'll place yourself in their company and create the impression of a relationship. How could anyone know that you've never spoken to them? (See Acknowledgments page.)

4. TRAFFIC ONLY IN THE RIGHT PRODUCTS, PLACES, AND PASTIMES

Fame defines fashion; when enough famous people buy or do or say something, it becomes the fashion. Consider that even a practice as elemental as pregnancy can became trendy and written up with all the usual attendant hype, when such luminaries as Cindy Crawford and Aerin Lauder Zinterhofer take it up; or a subject as arcane as Jewish mysticism can become the fashion, when espoused by Madonna, Gwyneth Paltrow, and Michael Jackson (it's no surprise, then, when a scrambler like Marla Maples takes it up, as well).

Therefore, because fame defines fashion, to signal fame you must surround yourself with whatever is hottest, hippest, and most exclusive. Let's

> "[Being a rock star] gives me . . . *a license,*" he said. "So I can have my own style. . . . It means that if someone says it's not 'in' to wear that pair of shoes, they can look at me and see that I'm wearing the pair of shoes, and then they change their mind and say that it's 'in' to wear them, because I'm wearing them."
>
> BOB GREENE, *BILLION DOLLAR BABY*

say you're trying, like so many people, to signal your celebrity in Los Angeles. You make your appointments at the right salon in the right neighborhood, a salon where you can not only get a great haircut, but can take meetings. You talk about buying a place in the most sought-after new vacation spot. You riffle through jewelry in that little store in Beverly Hills—you know where to find it, despite the fact that it's on the second floor and has no sign. Your flowers come from the right shop. You've been training three days a week with this year's most celebrated new trainer. You used to go to A.A.; now you're going to anger-management classes.

Of course, you may be working to embody a fashion that seems less . . . *fashionable*. Maybe you're trying to be a Silicon Valley celebrity. You mention that you're meeting with firms on Sandhill Road about raising some more money. You lavish your fickle programmers with the latest, most outrageous perks to try to retain them (and to show your competitors that you can keep up with the perks race). You keep only one suit in your closet—and it's more than five years old. You're occasionally missing from work because you're adding to your collection of vintage tarot cards. You lace your conversation with industry words: "We're in that *space*," "How will we *incent* people to use our site?" "It lacks any good *functionalities*," "We want ads that will be very *impactful*." You immediately buy the latest digital camera (or even better, the company gives you a demo model).

5. RADIATE *SPREZZATURA*

Always behave as though your fame erupted spontaneously, without any effort or contrivance on your part. Of course the spotlight sought you out.

Decline, or at least pretend that you might decline, opportunities. That's how you show that you can afford to be choosy. Never seem desperate.

Never act as your own huckster; other people do that for you. Suppose the governor has an opening for a high-level post, and you want the job. Don't buttonhole his every minor factotum to trumpet yourself. Instead, hint to your law partners and friends to get the word out for you. Consider hiring a publicist—not only to generate coverage, but also to help you decide what to do and what *not* to do, which reporters to seek out and which to ignore.

Never reveal that you make any effort to stay in fashion—even while you're secretly clipping every "in and out" or "up and down" column you find. Cultivate the impression that you gravitate instinctively to what's hot and drop what's not—whether that's theories about global financial stability, hemlines, coffee bars, or Republican presidential candidates.

Never hint at how much you treasure your fame. It's no surprise that Hugh Hefner keeps scrapbooks—more than one thousand elaborately bound, museum-quality volumes, with captions written by Hef himself—but he would have been better off keeping his hobby a secret.

Appear to be so famous that you're trying (and failing) to pass unnoticed. Be ostentatiously clandestine. Wear sunglasses, even indoors; skulk behind tinted car windows; insist on being seated at a dim corner table—at a restaurant where you're bound to be seen, trying not to be seen. Surround yourself with bodyguards who (unsuccessfully) try to blend into the crowd. Leak the word to the press that you've hired a publicist to keep you out of the press. Tell everyone you've put your company in stealth mode, because "too many people seemed too interested in the ideas I was throwing around." Make your secretary sign a confidentiality agreement on the facts of your life—instantly everyone will be far more interested in you, now that it seems that you've got some secret to hide and presumably someone trailing you, seeking to uncover it.

• • •

Acting the part of a celebrity will build your fame. And that fame can be used, if you want, to build still more fame, as well as power, money, and sex.

CHAPTER SIXTEEN

FAME: A SOURCE OF MORE
FAME, POWER, MONEY, AND SEX

People value fame so highly that, manipulated correctly, it can yield ever greater fame, as well as power, money, or sex. Or all these things.

USE FAME TO WIN GREATER FAME

Once surfeited with applause in one arena, you want—you *deserve*—more recognition. Maybe you're a movie star who wants the cachet of politics, or you're an intellectual who craves the glamour of being mobbed by autograph seekers. The *snare of mounting expectations* compels you to boost your fame into new directions. That's easy. Fame in one area is readily leveraged into fame in another area.

Don't be bashful. Your fame justifies you, however you procured it. Although many judged Johnnie Cochran harshly for his defense of O. J. Simpson in the celebrity's murder trial, that doesn't stop him from being a successful TV analyst and commentator.

Pursue your dream and expand your fame into new territory. An actor or athlete? Follow the examples of Ronald Reagan, Fred Grandy, Sonny Bono, Jack Kemp, Bill Bradley, and Alec Baldwin, and plunge into politics. If you want to be known for your artistic expression, pursue your art. Sylvester Stallone and Donna Summer exhibited their paintings, Jerry Garcia designed neckties, Mickey Rourke sold his poster-sized poems for $2,000 each. Bill Gates, Madonna, Gene Hackman, Michael Eisner, Jamie Lee Curtis, and Fergie have all "written" books, and singers like Mariah Carey and Gloria Estefan have given movie stardom a shot. Maybe, like actresses Gwyneth Paltrow and Susan Sarandon, you want the honor of working as a guest editor of a magazine. Or maybe you want to polish your reputation with some conspicuous social activism. Emulate the group of models who started the improbably named DISHES philanthropy—Determined, Involved Supermodels Helping to End Suffering.

Vitalize your image with a *celebrity-splice.* Engraft your celebrity (based in politics or the arts or science or whatever) with a celebrity of a different genus. Actor Warren Beatty bartered his Hollywood glitz for politician Gary Hart's political gravitas. Author Truman Capote paid his way to the yachts and dinner tables of high society by lending, by his presence, his fame and intellectual achievement. The splice benefits both celebrities.

> **TIP:** As a celebrity, offer your support prudently. Grace a *new* or *fashionable* charity with your presence, but avoid yesterday's tired causes—the rain forest may have been the rage in 1992, but now it's hopelessly passé.

Celebrity-splice is easy, because once you reach the summit in one field, you're entitled to sit as an equal with the other masters of their domains—models mix with Nobel Prize winners, industry captains cultivate film directors. "In the aristocracy of success there are no strangers," declared S. J. Perelman. Well-known people all know (or pretend to know) each other, no matter how they came by their fame. That's why famous people don't hesitate to invite other famous people to parties or dinners, even if they've never met.

This wasn't always true. The mongrel aristocracy of success was launched, perhaps, at the Plaza Hotel in November 1966, at Truman Capote's Black and White Ball honoring *Washington Post* publisher Katharine Graham. There, 540 elites—from Harvard professor Arthur Schlesinger, Jr., to dress designer Oscar de la Renta—mingled together, glitterati alongside literati. Now all celebrities mix in an indiscriminate mass. The White House Correspondents' Association Dinner seats Washington jour-

> A good reason to be famous, though, is so you can read all the big magazines and know everybody in all the stories. Page after page it's just all people you've met. I love that kind of reading experience and that's the best reason to be famous.
>
> ANDY WARHOL, *THE PHILOSOPHY OF ANDY WARHOL (FROM A TO B AND BACK AGAIN)*

nalists with movie stars like Sean Penn and Melanie Griffith and scan-dalebrities like Paula Jones. *Time* magazine's seventy-fifth anniversary party jumbled together politicians and poets, jocks and journalists, sci-entists, pundits, actors. Hip-hop mogul Sean "Puffy" Combs had a twenty-ninth birthday party with an eclectic (and oversubscribed) guest list that included everyone from Martha Stewart to rapper Heavy D (Donna Karan, Muhammad Ali, and Sarah Ferguson had to wait in the cold behind police barricades).

SPOTLIGHT YOUR FAME TO BOOST YOUR POWER

Your fame provokes people to pay attention to what you say and do, and that gives you power. You have a *platform*. The ability to attract press attention is a philosopher's stone that can turn dross into gold.

Politicians stage frantic antics to raise their name recognition. Name recognition is so essential that ex-actors, ex-athletes, and relatives of ex-politicians are pushing the more obscure politicians out of the congressional ranks; it's hard to get elected without the boost of nonpolitical fame. Consider the startling success of for-mer pro-wrestler Jesse "The Body" Ventura (now he wants to be called "The Mind") in his first bid for office, as Minnesota gover-nor in 1998. People certainly recognized his name—and they voted for him.

Attention brings action. After a fall from a horse left him paralyzed, actor Christo-pher Reeve used his celebrity to draw attention and money to research on spinal-cord injuries. Reeve testified before Con-gress, and it voted a sixteen percent funding increase for NIH's research in the area; Reeve visited President Clin-ton and won an additional $10 million for research; and after Reeve joined the American Paralysis Association's board,

> Truman was said to be famous for calling up Johnny Carson when he had a real vendetta. He claims he could call up Johnny Carson and say, "I want to come on tonight. I want to be on this evening," because he had somebody he wanted to go after. . . . Now that's clout. And if you wanted to say something nasty about somebody, what more effective way than to go on television and tell millions of people who watched Johnny Carson. People feared Capote.
>
> GEORGE PLIMPTON, *TRUMAN CAPOTE*

its revenues were double the entire amount it had raised during its first thirteen years. A celebrity's misfortune is a boon to all fellow sufferers.

Don't worry if you lack expertise; your pet cause benefits much more from the help of your famous face than from the droning testimony of some dull, credentialed specialist. After all, more congressmen will show up to hear the testimony of—and to have photos taken with—a baseball star than an antitrust lawyer. The Washington-based service Cause Celebre matched celebrities with causes—usually for corporate clients who paid handsomely for the publicity. The cause gets the benefit of the attention you guarantee, and you benefit from the association with a "real" issue that gives you an aura of intellect and civic involvement.

Celebrity-Issue Quiz

Match the celebrities—mostly "actor-vists"—to the causes or candidates they've promoted:

a. Meryl Streep	1. Papparazzi restraint
b. Frank Sinatra	2. Animal rights
c. Linda McCartney	3. Boat safety
d. George Clooney	4. Apple safety
e. Veronica Webb	5. Anti-smoking
f. Walter Cronkite	6. Copyright protection
g. Rob Reiner	7. Land mines
h. Princess Diana	8. Early childhood development
i. Christy Turlington	9. Presidential campaign
j. Johnny Cash	10. Rock the Vote
k. Michael J. Fox	11. Parkinson's disease

Answers: a.-4; b.-9; c.-2; d.-1; e.-10; f.-3; g.-8; h.-7; i.-5; j.-6, k.-11.

Not famous yourself? Become friendly with celebrities to enjoy a glamorous power boost. Your guests are more impressed by the famous faces around your table than the expensive wines on your table. And, of course, relationships with famous people boost your own fame—and so enhance your power. Senator John Warner's marriage to Elizabeth Taylor was credited for his rapid political rise; she attracted enormous publicity that swept him from obscurity to the forefront as a serious political contender, and eventual winner, in the race for the U.S. Senate.

FAME AND FORTUNE

Fame sells. Your fame can be used to tout movies, books, concert tickets, TV shows, magazines, toys, clothing, diet plans, exercise videos, political candidates, or salad dressing.

Endorsements can mean millions. When Michael Jordan retired from basketball, he had endorsement deals worth tens of millions with Nike, Gatorade, Bijan, MCI Worldcom, Hanes, Ball Park Franks, and many others. Even if you don't rate a paid endorsement deal, cadge free products by promising to tout them. For a New York fall fashion week, designer Jill Stuart put up actress Ashley Judd at the Carlyle Hotel so she could attend Stuart's show, and even allowed Judd to choose about ten outfits out of her showroom. The implied endorsement is worth the cost of the clothes. Get yourself branded an "opinion maker"—maybe you're a columnist, prominent executive, government official, or TV personality—and you'll get an avalanche of free books from book publishers who send them in the hope of cranking up a buzz around this list's biggest offering.

Consider yourself a walking product placement opportunity. Let your salon know that you'd be pleased to refer clients in exchange for complimentary haircuts and manicures. Or hint that you'd be pleased to patronize the struggling new restaurant at least once a week, if only you didn't have to foot the cost of the wine.

Even better, use your fame to sell your own product. Rapper Jay-Z owns his own fashion label, Rocawear. Jerry Seinfeld's ex-girlfriend Shoshanna Lonstein created a trendy clothing line. Superstar actor Paul Newman markets Newman's Own lemonade, spaghetti

TIP: Looking for an easy way both to profit from your fame and to boost your cultural standing? Write a kids' book. You get the cachet and potential profits of authorship, but with less work (few pages, big type, illustrations to bolster the text). And your fame will land you the promo spots with Oprah, Rosie O'Donnell, or the *Today* show that you need to peddle your book. This technique has worked for John Travolta, Fergie, Shaquille O'Neal, Jamie Lee Curtis, Patrick Ewing, Debby Boone, and others.

sauce, popcorn, and salsa—all prominently labeled with his picture and sold to raise money for charity. Gennifer Flowers sells a line of cigars, El Presidente (a mixed reference—she wasn't the cigar girl), while Monica Lewinsky is selling her own line of cloth totes and purses.

Remember, the star-exploitation machine isn't concerned about why you're famous; exposure is the only thing that matters. The fashion designers Dolce & Gabbana sprang at the chance to provide a complete wardrobe for "Hollywood Madam" Heidi Fleiss to wear to her pretrial hearings. No point in letting those TV appearances go to waste.

What if, like most people, you're not famous? Exploit others' fame for profit—people will pay dearly for the opportunity to brush up against the famous. Every new store, restaurant, gallery, dress designer, or film needs the presence of stars to validate its latest offering, so become a celebrity bounty-hunter. New York's Stylefile got a fee for every star it persuaded to attend a client's event, with the fee calibrated to the fame of the attendee. Sports teams demand that star players put their fame to work for the team—graciously playing golf with starry-eyed corporate sponsors, dropping by luxury boxes, personally calling fans who haven't renewed their season tickets.

Other ways to turn someone else's fame into your fortune? If you can handle a camera, sell celebrity photos. The best-known fame-parasites are the paparazzi—the photographers who buzz around celebrities in pursuit of the front-page photo. Although the death of Princess Diana, after her car crashed while pursued by paparazzi, momentarily turned public opinion against these photographers, the public's appetite for tabloid pictures soon triumphed over the collective pangs of conscience. The paparazzi stop at nothing to try to snap the million-dollar shot. Once, the crush of photographers around Marilyn Monroe was so intense that a reporter jammed his microphone into her mouth and chipped her tooth. And now yesterday's still-photo paparazzi—like the notorious Ron Galella who hounded Jacqueline Onassis—have been joined by video "stalker-azzi," who use video cameras to capture tape for sale to the burgeoning slew of tabloid TV shows. Join them, and a single moment caught on film—a stolen toe-sucking, an ill-advised punch, a face with double chin and no eye makeup—could make your fortune.

What else? Be creative. Consider that the *National Enquirer* once ran a story, complete with photographs, about Madonna and Warren Beatty's garbage.

Or can you "discover" an untapped vein of celebrity gold in the mountains of anonymity? More celebrities mean more opportunities to make money. No one paid much attention to fashion models until Twiggy blazed the way to stardom—although the supremacy of supermodels is now waning, as they're replaced on magazine covers and in celebrity profiles by movie and TV stars. The 1980s marked the rise of the celebrity CEO, whose fortune brought him fame. The most successful cable channel, the sports network ESPN, has accelerated the celebrity-ization of sports; it provides nonstop sports coverage, with thrilling highlights, profiles, big-game promos, and jock-studded ads that help athletes like Michael Jordan and Ken Griffey, Jr., cross over into careers in commercials, television, and movies. TV fashion programs, like CNN's *Style with Elsa Klensch,* have made clothes designers into internationally recognizable stars. Publicists, naturally, have themselves become famous like the people who hire them—the old guard, like Howard Rubenstein, Bobby Zarem, John Scanlon, Nadine Johnson, and Peggy Siegal, and the younger set, like the "Power Girls" Lizzie Grubman, Elizabeth Harrison, Lara Shriftman, Ally b. (note the shortened name with lower case *b,* see Chapter 14), Jennifer Posner, Shari Misher, and Lauren London.

Celebrity hairdressers, photographers, book publishers, art dealers, pastry makers, fund managers, TV writers, have already been mined—what could be next? Celebrity computer programmers? Dog walkers? Look for events that can be exploited as rich sources of new faces, drama, and battle. Subject the National Association of Television Program Executives to the same breathless, dogged enthusiasm now devoted to New York Fashion Week. Don't worry if your new subjects don't strike you as particularly interesting; the cynosure effect is all that's needed to transform them from everyday folks into superstars worth watching.

If you boast a connection to someone famous—for whatever reason—exploit it. Lee Harvey Oswald's mother, Marguerite, was bitter that the rewards of being an assassin's mother didn't match her expectations: her son's diary and childhood photos didn't command the right price, she had no offers for her life story, and her speaking fees were low (her subject: "the American way of life"). She pointed out that while the other women involved in the case—the president's widow, Jackie, police officer Tippit's widow, and Oswald's wife, Marina—had each become "a very wealthy woman" as a result of her son's action, she hadn't. (But that was decades ago. Today, being Oswald's mother would surely guarantee fame, and with it, money.)

Tap into the value of proximity to fame. The remains of Marilyn Monroe rest in a vault in Westwood Memorial Park. The owners of the vacant vault next to hers put the space up for sale for $25,000—in the hope that eternal rest by Marilyn Monroe would be worth the premium to a fan. Mexico's Las Ventanas al Paraiso resort donated two-night stays at the resort's luxury rooftop suites to the presenters and entertainers from the Oscars. What a good investment—a few high-profile guests would more than pay for themselves with their presence.

Exploit celebrity even as you criticize or mock celebrity exploitation. *Brill's Content* used a glamour shot of JonBenét Ramsey, the six-year-old beauty-queen murder victim, as its cover for an issue featuring an article on the media's exploitation of JonBenét's lurid story. "Yes," the letter from the editor pointed out, "we're writing about media exploitation and putting a picture of JonBenét on the cover." This ironic pose is not new. In the late 1970s, at the height of the frenzy over Farrah Fawcett-Majors, the *New Times* magazine put her photograph on the cover with the bold caption, "In this issue: Absolutely nothing about Farrah Fawcett-Majors!" The magazine capitalized on Farrah's extraordinary ability to sell magazines even as it ridiculed the phenomenon.

Use celebrities to generate money for your favorite cause. A charity derives its prominence from the people associated with it, so enlist famous people to friend-raise and fund-raise. There's no cause so spiritual that it won't benefit from a celebrity association. The Church of Scientology coddles stars in its "Celebrity Centres" to enlist their help in spreading Scientology's message and bolstering its shaky credibility. This strategy seems to work. Members have included actors such as John Travolta, Kirstie Alley, and Tom Cruise, musician Isaac Hayes, and the TV legal analyst Greta Van Susteren.

EXPLOIT FAME FOR SEX

One of the consequences of fame is the adoring fans—the admirer who hands the screen idol a propositioning note or the groupie who shows up outside the rock star's hotel room late at night. Fame oils the way for sexual adventure.

Consider the example of one All-Star basketball player. After scanning the stands during a game, he'd point out a few spectators to the guard, who'd give each one the message that the player had invited her to visit the locker room. After the game, the athlete would show up in the small sauna room where the women he'd selected awaited him. He'd have sex with each of them, in turn—very quickly, because he had to return to the locker room in time to meet reporters. In a similar fashion, an ex-senator on the lecture circuit used his assistant to proposition attractive prospects he'd spotted from the lectern.

The thought of having sex with a celebrity is so titillating that the *New York Observer*'s classifieds, in the cagily named "Fitness and Fun" section, oozes with propositions by celebrity look-alikes. "Pamela Anderson & Kathy Ireland Look-Alikes" promised one ad, "Young Denzel Washington," promised another.

For some, sharing a sexual partner with a celebrity is the next best thing to having sex with a celebrity. Alex Adams, the famous Hollywood madam, reported that some men would ask for a particular prostitute because she'd been patronized by a famous client. A profile of forty-five-year-old entrepreneur Doug Elliott recounted that "Mr. Elliott noted that he had slept with women who had slept with famous men—among them John F. Kennedy, Jr., Keith Hernandez, Donald Trump and J. D. Salinger. He calls it his 'sharing list.'" Even a celebrity can enjoy sharing a sexual partner with a celebrity. Jack Kennedy refused to break off his dangerous affair with Judith Campbell Exner even after he became president; an important part of Exner's appeal was that she'd also been Frank Sinatra's lover—as well as the lover of Chicago mobster Sam "Momo" Giancana. (One enterprising human-egg donor tried to capitalize on the popular desire for a connection to fame by advertising: "I donated to a famous couple, WHY NOT YOU!"—this grammatically ambiguous enticement meaning, presumably, that your child and some celebrity's child would have the same stranger for a biological mother.)

· · ·

After you've planned and worked and clowned for fame, you discover that fame, too, brings its own peculiar blues. Would you relinquish your fame to cure them? No. But that fact doesn't soothe the blues away.

CHAPTER SEVENTEEN

FINAL NOTE: FAME BLUES

You're the center of attention, but you've lost the commonplace luxuries of privacy and anonymity. You want acclaim and attention on your own terms, but the greater your fame, the less you will be able to control it. And you're not transformed.

Your fame stirs up powerful emotions in other people. Your influence far exceeds your aim—your slang sweeps the country; your signature haircut sprouts on thousands of heads; store owners don't cash your checks, because they want to keep your autograph. Pundits opine about the things you've said and done, and they get all the facts wrong. If you want, you can generate legislation or rocket an obscure book onto the best-seller list or put an industry out of business. You arouse a frenzy of attention—people want to see how you look, what you're wearing, what you're doing, and with whom you're doing it. Many heads turn as you walk into a

> Three years before I would have been ready to kill for what I had now. I had envied published writers, envied and adored them. I had imagined them to be demigods, invulnerable to pain, blessed with a constant supply of love and self-assurance. Now I was learning about the other side of the fun-house mirror of fame. . . . There are the distortions of the press, the distortions of strangers who project their fantasies and frustrations on you, the distortions of all those people who envy you and imagine they would like to replace you. . . . They need to believe in the magic of that locked room. They need it in order to justify their own envy, their own climbing.
>
> ERICA JONG, *HOW TO SAVE YOUR OWN LIFE*

restaurant; everyone strains to overhear your conversation. Even your most casual remarks are perceived as profoundly meaningful, because of the reverence accorded to you, the source.

This intense interest strips you of your privacy. Foot-washers want to know your most intimate secrets—to see the inside of your house, to learn what books you read, to know whether you're on good terms with your mother. They want to watch.

The intensity of the public's interest in you gives them a claim on you. They want you to listen to them, to know them. One superstar musician said wearily, "Fucking groupies is so old. You could do it every night, there're always girls available. But if you're going to go to bed with one of them, that means that there's a whole stack of stories you have to listen to. At this point, I don't want to hear the stories of any of these girls' lives any more." Your public wants your *attention*.

But at the same time that people crave your notice and approval, they resent the sway you have over them. Their fervid enthusiasm, the feeling of wanting to draw near, is distressing when it's unsatisfied. And so your fame arouses jealousy and resentment. The people around you—your colleagues and competitors—vie to catch your notice and good opinion. Your children and old friends jealously measure the time you give them. Everyone clamors for your attention, and they resent you when you give them short shrift.

The fact is, you matter to other people far more than they matter to you. For them, you are the measure of every exchange. In her *Pillow Book*, Sei Shonagon included in the list of "Pleasing things" the entry: "A person of quality is holding forth about something in the past or about a recent event that is being widely discussed. Several peo-

> I was there to talk to [Robert Kennedy] about Vietnam, but, really, I just wanted to meet him. To have him know who I was. He was something of a hero to me then, in 1967, and I had only recently arrived at that point in my life where I was becoming aware that men who were heroes to others might someday become my friends.
> . . . But, listen: flying east, through the sadness and exhaustion, I felt pride. And a certain, possibly obscene, kind of excitement. *I had been there, on the inside, as a Kennedy had died.* It seemed the ultimate status symbol of the Sixties.
>
> JOE McGINNISS, *HEROES*

ple are gathered round him, but it is oneself that he keeps looking at as he talks."

They struggle to entertain you with their jokes, to impress you with their astute opinions, to entice you to glance with pleasure at their bodies. Consider the poignant imbalance in significance reflected in the eBay.com posting, placed soon after the death of JFK Jr. and his wife and sister-in-law, by someone auctioning off a pair of used airplane tickets: "These two airline tickets were given to me personally and before leaving the plane by John F. Kennedy

It's Friday night at the Bowery Bar. . . . There's Francis Ford Coppola at a table with his wife. There's an empty chair at Francis Ford Coppola's table. It's not just empty: It's alluringly, temptingly, tauntingly, provocatively empty. It's so empty that it's more full than any other chair in the place. And then, just when the chair's emptiness threatens to cause a scene, Donovan Leitch sits down for a chat. Everyone in the room is immediately jealous. Pissed off. The energy of the room lurches violently. This is romance in New York.

CANDACE BUSHNELL, *SEX AND THE CITY*

Jr. and Carolyn Bessette. They were sitting next to me the entire trip from Miami and New York, a trip that I will remember forever." (Asking price for the memento of this encounter? $4,850.)

Inevitably, you fail to satisfy their greed and leave them aching for more. Even celebrities suffer that painful starstruck feeling. Megastar Frank Sinatra craved Jack Kennedy's friendship, and in return for his tireless campaigning for Kennedy for president—even recording a version of his hit "High Hopes" as a campaign jingle—Sinatra asked only for Kennedy's friendship and company ("only"? that was quite a lot, of course). Sinatra's reverence for Kennedy was heartbreaking: he framed Kennedy's casual notes and mounted a gold plaque on the bedroom door in his house to mark where the candidate had slept. Sinatra planned that his Palm Springs compound would become JFK's Western White House, so he built a heliport and a guest house with a dining room that seated forty, erected a flagpole for the presidential flag, and installed an extensive communication system for the White House operators. But Kennedy, on the advice of his brother Attorney General Robert Kennedy, refused to stay there because of Sinatra's ties to organized crime. Sinatra flew into a rage, wrecked his new concrete helicopter pad with a sledgehammer, and never forgave the brush-off.

At the same time, you want to be loved and appreciated by the public not as a celebrity, but for your individual self. But are they responding to the "real" you? Do they respect your successes, or do they merely crowd around some fabricated image? In his best-selling autobiography, Lee Iacocca observed, "I certainly like being recognized for what I've done, but I'm always being reminded that my fame has little to do with my accomplishments. Am I famous for the Mustang? For guiding Ford through the most profitable years in its history? For having turned around Chrysler? It's a hell of a note, but I have a feeling I'm going to be remembered only for my TV commercials."

Your public persona becomes inextricable, yet detached, from your private personality. You feel misunderstood and underappreciated. You can't be seen as you really are. Andy Warhol, a master trick-

Supercelebrity Andy Warhol sits amid his books—he appears lost, isolated, drab—utterly different from his glamorous persona "Andy Warhol." Of course, Warhol constantly toyed with his image. (© Bettmann/CORBIS)

ster of celebrity, exploited the blinding effect of fame: he hired actor Alan Midgette to impersonate him on a lecture tour. Costumed in silver hairspray, makeup, a black leather jacket, and dark glasses, Midgette pulled it off beautifully. Why did Warhol hire someone to play Warhol? "Because he was better at it than I was."

> CLEOPATRA: "Since my lord
> Is Antony again, I will be Cleopatra."
>
> SHAKESPEARE,
> *ANTONY AND CLEOPATRA*

You as an actual person fade in importance—you become a figure for others to discuss and analyze. Eventually, you become their creation. Even *you* view *yourself* as an inscrutable phenomenon. Elvis Presley once confided, "I've always felt an unseen hand behind me, guiding my life, I mean, there has to be a purpose . . . there's got to be a reason . . . why I was chosen to be Elvis Presley." When opera diva Adelina Patti first heard her voice on a record, she kissed the phonograph's speaking-trumpet and cried, "Ah, *mon Dieu!* Now I understand why I am Patti. Oh yes. What a voice!" Recalling an event that took place in the distant past, when he was merely a Harvard professor, Henry Kissinger explained, "I wasn't Henry Kissinger yet."

According to his longtime colleague Stanley Levison, Martin Luther King, Jr., believed that he was "an actor in history at a particular moment that called for a personality, and he had simply been selected as that personality." You're the construction of other people—what they've seen in you, written about you, wanted from you.

Your reputation spreads, your image spreads, and soon your reality is diminished

> And so I was prominent and empty, and I had to begin life again; from now on, people who knew me would never be able to react to me as a person whom they liked or disliked in small ways, *for myself alone* (the inevitable phrase of all tear-filled confessions); no, I was a node in a new electronic landscape of celebrity, personality, and status. Other people, meeting me, could now unconsciously measure their own status by sensing how I reacted to them . . . now I had to guard against arousing the emotions of others, particularly since I had a strong conscience, and a strong desire to do just that—exhaust the emotions of others.
>
> NORMAN MAILER, *ADVERTISEMENTS FOR MYSELF*

beside your image. You have a dim sense, through a fog of vanity, of your irrelevance. You realize that it's not you, yourself, that attracts people, but their ideas about you.

And despite its drawbacks, the desire for fame is insatiable. You're caught in the snare of mounting expectations. As she walked into the Academy Awards, where her picture *The Sting* had been nominated in ten categories, producer Julia Phillips considered the retreating goal of fame: "There are barricades and cops and fans and photographers. Everywhere. We do not rate a flicker. There is nothing quite like being the only unknown in a bevy of luminaries. Unless it is to be the only name at a gathering of nobodies." The photographers and fans were clamoring at the stars around her; no one paid her any attention. "Nobody reaches out to us. No Army Archerd interview. No hail-fellow-well-met interchange with milling celebs. An all-time Humbler. A year or two before, I'd have been amazed to be here. Now that I am, I can see that the only way to attend one of these events is as a star." Once the intoxicant of applause enters your blood, you're addicted: you crave that heightened feeling of admiration and acceptance.

Maybe you feel like an impostor—all your success is attributable to luck, not merit. You're a star—you've achieved fabulous wealth, live in a fantasy world, see your face splashed everywhere, you inspire enormous reverence—but why were you chosen from all the others for this prize? The feelings of inadequacy that spurred you to great accomplishments aren't healed by your fame.

And what if, worst of all (worse than never having been famous), you've lost your place in the firmament? Former House Speaker Newt Gringrich declared in his heyday: "I have enormous personal ambition. I want to shift the entire planet. And I'm doing it. I am now a famous person." Where is he now? The fame-obsessed Norman Mailer recalled this humiliation: "My status dropped immediately—America is a quick country—but my ego did not permit me to understand that, and I went through tiring years of subtle social defeats because I did not know that I was no longer as large to others as I had been. I was always overmatching myself. To put it crudely, I would think I was dropping people when they were dropping me." You find yourself in a fury, demanding of strangers, *"Do you know who I am?"* They don't.

ILLUSTRATION: HOW BETH USED FAME

Beth recently opened a new restaurant, Zebra. She knew she was entering a risky business and was determined to make Zebra a success. Not only did she want her restaurant to be crowded, she wanted to establish herself as a well-known, well-respected figure in the city.

Beth named her restaurant Zebra because she loved any object with a zebra-hide design on it. She covered the tables, the booths, and her staff in zebra patterns. Beth herself wore some zebra-patterned item—a shirt, a skirt, a handbag, a headband—every day, whether she was in the restaurant or not.

Beth's first step was to hire a publicist to help generate positive stories about herself and her restaurant. One of the first ideas was to get Beth and her restaurant involved in charity work.

Every year, the city's most fashionable philanthropy, This City Cares, sponsored a glittering charity ball to raise money. Beth cajoled the benefit's chairwoman into having the pre-ball dinner (for top donors only) at Zebra. The dinner was a big hit.

Months later, This City Cares chose Zebra as the location for its annual awards ceremony. Beth immediately offered to host the event for free, as her personal contribution. Highlights of the event were broadcast on the local news, and the name "Zebra" and the distinctive zebra-hide pattern were prominently displayed. Soon other organizations were using the restaurant for similar events.

By the end of her first year in business, Beth and her restaurant were firmly entrenched in the public mind.

sex

CHAPTER EIGHTEEN

INTRODUCTION TO SEX

Using sex effectively isn't a simple matter. Sex is unlike the categories of power, money, and fame—less fluid, less controllable, more liable to disrupt the usual barriers of behavior and of social standing.

"Using" sex includes using it to achieve some goal—like gaining power or access to money or a shot at fame or emotional intimacy—whether consciously or unconsciously. It also includes sex for sensual gratification.

Even if you have no qualms about making the most use of power, money, or fame, the idea of using *sex* may make you uncomfortable. You're appalled at the thought of a "relationship" based on the desire to flaunt a conquest at a Christmas party or to procure a clothing allowance or to wangle an invitation to Aspen or to slake an evening's animal cravings. The level of calculation and strategy discussed in these chapters runs contrary to the customary expectations for sex—expectations of sincere affection, intimacy, or, at least, uncalculated mutual pleasure.

In any event, whether because they won't or because they can't, far fewer people exploit the strategic opportunities of sex than those of power, money, and fame. And certainly this strategy provokes more disapproval and indignation in onlookers.

But while you might never consider applying the principles discussed here yourself, read on to glean insight into other people's behavior. The fact that these sex strategies may be unattractive (who wants to consider whether men use power, money, and fame to get sex or whether women use sex to get power, money, and fame?) doesn't mean that they're ineffective. You should understand them even if you won't use them.

Of course, you may be thinking that your use for sex is no more complicated than the desire for physical pleasure. If so, examine your motives to make sure you're not actually prompted by the wish to accelerate emotional intimacy with your sexual partner—that's a losing strategy.

Except for the most dispassionate user, sex can be difficult to control; your emotions or your lusts may interfere with your self-interest. If you venture here, try to keep a clear head.

Quiz: Do you use sex?

You may be using sex without even realizing it. Answer "yes" or "no" to the following:

1. Have you ever stretched or flexed provocatively during a meeting to attract attention to yourself?

2. Do you go out of your way to be seen in public with an attractive date?

3. Do you compare the appearance or age or status or wealth of your date/spouse to that of others?

4. Have you ever consoled yourself in a confrontation with another man with the thought that you have a bigger penis than he does?

5. Have you ever lied about your age or exaggerated your height or your measurements?

6. Have you met someone and, upon discovering that this new acquaintance drove a Mercedes, regularly contributed to the *New York Times Magazine,* or had been invited to Julia Roberts's birthday party, felt a sudden throb of romantic interest?

7. In evaluating a mate, do you consider whether he or she would be useful in founding or continuing a strong family line?

8. Have you ever had sex, or refused to have sex, after a first or second date, not because that's what you really wanted to do, but because you thought doing so would increase the chances that you'd be going on another date?

If you answered "yes" to any of these questions, you're already using sex.

(The following chapters draw on the heterosexual model. If you're gay, the use of sex may be sufficiently different to warrant separate analysis not undertaken here.)

• • •

As demonstrated in the next two chapters, men and women use sex differently. Don't read only the chapter that pertains to your gender, however; it's useful to understand the strategies employed by the opposite sex.

CHAPTER NINETEEN

HOW TO USE SEX—FOR MEN

As noted, sex is less frequently exploited than power, money, or fame, but that doesn't mean it's ineffective. Use sex to signal—to women and to other men—your power, money, or fame. Because of the way women use sex (see next chapter), you'll find that as you acquire more power, money, and fame, your ability to attract women increases dramatically. Therefore you can use women's sexual attentions to signal onlookers of your attainments. Or, like many, you may want to use sex for nothing more than pure sensual gratification: sex for sex's sake. In either case—and make no mistake, the pleasure of being seen with a gorgeous woman on your arm is quite distinct from the pleasure of having sex with her—you'll find that a measure of power, money, or fame will help you achieve your goal.

People believe, and research proves, that high-status men attract women more easily than low-status men; so the woman at your side is a gauge. In one study, people examined photos of a couple and evaluated only the man: if the woman with him was attractive, he was perceived as smarter and more successful than if the woman was plain. After all, the reasoning goes, an unattractive guy must be very rich or very powerful or very famous to win the attention of a beautiful woman. The sex that accompanies your success is a nice perk for all your hard work—such a pleasant, convenient way to demonstrate the status you've achieved. A lesser man couldn't possibly hope to win the woman you have.

Sexual possession is ownership, and it enhances your reputation the way the acquisition of any important piece does—especially when you have the attention of a woman that other men want. They envy the pleasures they imagine you've won. Perception drives reality, and your status swells accordingly.

Impress other men by flaunting a status-symbol woman, whether a model or actress or resuméd executive or woman of pedigree (though men who use sex in this way probably signal more often with appearance than with accomplishment). The competition can be unspoken or explicit. Jonathan Farkas, the fifty-something Alexander's department store heir, reminisced about his younger days, "You only brought Ford models out with you, because that was the thing to do. And among the guys, we had this competition. Were you getting a $3,000-a-day model or a $4,000-a-day model?" Playboy developer Donald Trump bragged of one female companion, "When we walk into a restaurant, I watch grown men weep." He was watching other men's reaction to his date, not his date herself.

What kind of woman carries the right signal for you? A TV news commentator who's beautiful but also gives good dinner party; a busty ingenue on her first trip away from her home in the South; a blue-blooded WASP? (It's not that calculated, you're thinking. She's a lot of fun, and the sex *is* great.)

Push yourself to achieve a sexual benchmark, such as the popular aim of having sex with a large number of partners. Jack Kennedy reportedly often said that, "Once I get a woman, I'm not interested in carrying on, for the most part." He was pursuing conquests, not relationships. And Kennedy set the standard to beat. When people recounted tales of Kennedy's womanizing, LBJ—determined not to be outdone by his predecessor—would bang the table and say, "Goddamn it, I had more women by accident than he ever had by design!" (As majority leader of the Senate, Johnson maintained a "nooky room" in the Capitol for his illicit liaisons.) In the same way, actor Dustin Hoffman wanted to keep pace with his peers: "If anyone thinks that Jack Nicholson and I got laid less than Warren Beatty when we were single—they're wrong." Basketball star Wilt Chamberlain estimated he had sex with more than 20,000 women; Magic Johnson put his number at a still-astonishing 2,000. (Women are less numbers-

> "The fact that her name is Harrington must be just as sexually exciting to Sammy as that moist red mouth or those snooty boobs of hers."
>
> BUDD SCHULBERG, *What Makes Sammy Run?*

TIP: When flaunting your sexual activities, don't get carried away with showing off. New Line Production chief Mike DeLuca got a lot of negative attention after he was caught in a highly compromising position in the main room of a swanky Oscar night party. He forgot that even permissive Hollywood has its limits. On the other hand, the incident didn't seem to do him any real lasting harm.

oriented when it comes to sex, but there are exceptions—consider Annabel Chong, the adult-film star who in 1995 set a record by having sex with 251 men in a single day.)

Or you might try to have sex with a year's worth of *Penthouse* Pets of the Month, as one late investment banker did, or with a woman from every state, a favorite goal of frat boys. Consort with more than one woman at a time. Or pursue girls who are very young.

Don't worry if you don't have the time, energy, or interest actually to consummate relations with women. That doesn't matter. You can impress other men with your sexual opportunities without bothering with the actual sex. Henry Kissinger deliberately fabricated a "swinger" image to impress and intrigue other men. He made a point of lubricious public exhibition. He frequently joked about his taste for women. Even on the weekends, he'd bring a gorgeous blonde to the White House Mess to show off. These female companions confided, however, that Kissinger rarely if ever "did anything" with the women he escorted. That wasn't the point. As he explained in diplomat-ese to a journalist, this macho display was done merely for its signaling value: "I think that my playboy reputation has been and still is useful because it served and still serves to reassure people. To show them that I'm not a museum piece."

All the girls at our table were young. The Asian girl, Cromwell's girl, was younger than the other three, but Laurie was even younger than the Asian girl.

I had the youngest one there.

Laurie's youth was transformed into consumer goods, which I possessed.

It was I who had her youth, not she.

My popularity at the table was soaring. . . .

The vote was unanimous: I was fucking the youngest one there.
I was declared the unanimous winner of this night.

STEVE TESICH, *KAROO*

Hire "arm candy" to make a smashing appearance beside you. Other men will simmer with jealousy, and other women will be intrigued. You'll be the envy of everyone else in the room—and without the hassle that a more romantic relationship inevitably drags in.

But your use of sex isn't all for outward show; because sex is a form of conquest, it reinforces your sense of yourself as potent. You deserve this indulgence, now that you're rich, powerful, or famous. And you're going to have plenty of opportunity.

Do you find yourself thinking that now that you've made it, you're entitled to sex? You're caught in the snare of mounting expectations—on top of everything else, you deserve great sex with gorgeous girls. The platinum rule applies. It's not possible that you wouldn't be getting any—you get *everything*. Prominent New York divorce lawyer Raoul Felder has observed that mistresses are a direct function of the economy: as a man makes more money, he's more likely to have a mistress.

If you're not igniting the reaction from women you think you deserve, flaunt your status as rich, important, or famous so that they

> [Sammy] just went through the motions of relaxing because he was quick to discover and imitate how gentlemen of his rank were supposed to spend their leisure. It wouldn't have surprised me if this even extended to sex. He seemed to be a lusty little animal, but I think if Zanuck offered to give up his job to Sammy on the condition that Sammy never touch a woman again our hero would have gone impotent before you could say general-manager-in-charge-of-production.
>
> BUDD SCHULBERG, *WHAT MAKES SAMMY RUN?*

TIP: By reputation, the top five cities for sexual opportunity are Los Angeles, New York City, Chicago, Atlanta, and Houston.

> Why couldn't he (being a Master of the Universe) simply *explain* it to her? Look, Judy, I still love you and I love our daughter and I love our home and I love our life, and I don't want to change any of it—it's just that I, a Master of the Universe, a young man still in the season of the rising sap, deserve *more* from time to time, when the spirit moves me.
>
> TOM WOLFE, *THE BONFIRE OF THE VANITIES*

can recognize and respond to it. Then watch your colleagues' envious heads turn. (See also the chart in "Sex for Sex's Sake," later in this chapter.)

Signal your power. As Henry Kissinger is constantly quoted as having said, "Power is the ultimate aphrodisiac." Look for ways to brandish your powers. For example, President Nixon's counsel John Dean was interested in a woman who refused to give him her unlisted phone number. He was able to call her, and to give her an impressive display of his power, by putting the all-knowing White House operators to work to find her number.

Signal your money. Lavish money on everyday necessities, like clothes, car, and house. Make extravagant purchases—expensive gifts for her, as you might expect, make a particular impression. (You might as well give a gift that you can enjoy, too. Director Tony Scott was renowned for his "boobs and Bulgari" relationships: not only did he shower his women with jewelry from the Beverly Hills Bulgari showroom, he also paid for their breast augmentation surgery—presumably as much for his benefit as for theirs.) Hand over a credit card and tell the object of your affections that she has carte blanche. Buy the entire basket of roses, not just a single stem, when they're offered for purchase at a restaurant or bar.

TIP: Avoid calling explicit attention to the connection between *your* money and *her* favors. Don't follow the crass example of producer Don Simpson, who reportedly took out his American Express gold card and flashed it while he asked a woman, "Do you like me?" Be more subtle in your use of "fiscal foreplay."

Signal your fame. Actor Ben Affleck reflected that when you're famous, "you can be seriously disfigured and women are still attracted to you." Brat Pack actor Andrew McCarthy agrees: his 1980s fame changed nothing for him, except "chicks wanted to fuck me who didn't before." Extract the most from your fame. Make sure to go where you'll be recognized by your admirers, so your date will realize how important you are.

Remember, you need not be nationally famous to get the sex boost—you're judged by your fame within your own small pond (see Chapter 13). Patronize restaurants where you'll be recognized as a prized customer—the maitre d' calls you by name, ushers you to the best table, whisks "your usual" drink in front of you. Of course, all this presumes that you actually do have some measure of power, money, or fame. If you don't . . . time to work on your small talk and your waistline. And if you're using your money, power, or fame to get sex, don't expect, nevertheless, to be appreciated for your personality.

> And if a guy is rich—and he must be, or you wouldn't be with him—he takes his self-esteem from that, and sometimes it can result in a whopping, oversized ego. It can make him conveniently forget the little things, like why you're there with him in the first place. Other times, the fact that if he wasn't rich, you wouldn't be interested in him may eat him up.
>
> COERTE V. W. FELSKE, *THE MILLENNIUM GIRL*

Though less often than women, men also use their sexual relationships to win access to power, money, and prominence. New York real estate baron Mort Zuckerman dated a series of high-profile women such as Betty Rollins, Gloria Steinem, Nora Ephron, and Diane Von Furstenberg. U.S. Senator Bob Torricelli dated high-profile women like Patricia Duff and Bianca Jagger. As a student at Washington and Lee University, his classmates recalled, Virginia Senator John Warner looked through folders of the freshman classes of Sweet Briar, Mary Baldwin, and other girls' colleges, then checked names and faces against the *Social Register*. Whom did he marry? The daughter of multimillionaire philanthropist Paul Mellon, granddaughter of Andrew Mellon, Gulf Oil and Alcoa's founder. After their divorce, Warner dated other rich and famous women, such as TV interviewer Barbara Walters and Standard Oil heiress Page Lee Hufty, and married Elizabeth Taylor.

Even if you don't want to get married (because you're gay, for example), you can nevertheless use women for access to prominent events and people by acting as a "walker," an extra man, a man who escorts genteel ladies to events when husbands won't. Jerry Zipkin, famous as Nancy Reagan and other society women's escort, went everywhere.

You may have mixed feelings about being seen with a famous woman. On the one hand, if you're like most men, you don't like being eclipsed by a woman. You want to be the focus of the attention and respect. Candace Bushnell, the author of *Sex and the City*, who describes herself as "semifamous," observed from her experience, "The truth is, men don't like to be with a woman who gets more attention than they do." On the other hand, a celebrated woman is quite a trophy signal for you—with all her prestige, she wants you. And because she's famous, other men instantly recognize the prize you've won. That stirs their respect—and boosts your status by association.

EMASCULATION BY SEX

But just as sex can signal and boost your power, it can destroy it. Many high-powered men mix sexuality and power. They lust for the thrills of seduction and conquest. If this description fits you, guard against the traps that sex can set; it can strip away power by breeding scandal or precipitating your abdication.

Politicians face particular risks when they mix sex and power. Are politicians just caught more often than average philanderers because the very office that gives them greater sexual opportunity also subjects them to press scrutiny and public criticism? Or does the hunger for politics correspond to an insatiable appetite for sex? One study found a high correlation between political success and unusually vigorous sexual activity. The research suggested that men who achieve political success possess a sexual drive different in quantity and kind from the average citizen.

Politicians who espouse "family values" are particularly vulnerable to loss of power through sex. Opponents (and opportunists) eagerly look for misdeeds that contradict their high moral rhetoric. Congressmen who lambasted President Clinton for his moral failures found themselves pilloried as hypocrites when their own lapses came to light. Aggressive House Speaker Newt Gingrich, then fifty-six, was one of the harshest critics of the president's affair; when it emerged that Gingrich had been carrying on a six-year adulterous relationship with a thirty-three-year-old Capitol Hill aide, the contradiction between his words and his actions led to massive media coverage. As if this weren't enough of a blow to the family-values camp, the very man picked to succeed Gingrich, Robert Livingston, also tumbled from power after admitting that he'd "on occasion strayed from my marriage." Spurred by the threat that *Hustler* was going to publish details about his extramarital affairs, Livingston took the podium during the Clinton impeachment debate and announced that not only would he decline to stand for election to the Speaker position, he'd soon resign from his congressional seat.

How do politicians excuse these escapades? One justification is, improbably, that the sex is necessary for *health* reasons. President Kennedy told Democratic operator Bobby Baker, "I get a migraine headache if I don't get a strange piece of ass every day." (He made a similar observation to England's prime minister Harold Macmillan.) And Martin Luther King, Jr., used sex to relieve the pressures of the spotlight—he once remarked that "Fucking's a form of anxiety reduction." But this form of "anxiety reduction" left him vulnerable to exposure by J. Edgar Hoover's FBI, which had bugged his hotel rooms and made incriminating tapes.

Expect scorn, ridicule, and salacious prying if sexual misdeeds threaten your power. Think of Antony after Cleopatra. Former Republican senator Bob Packwood was expelled for sexual mis-conduct—the groping and chasing and tonguing of at least seven-teen women. And, of course, Bill Clinton suffered impeachment—and a year of intense scrutiny and humiliation from everyone from Jay Leno to Maureen Dowd to Don Imus to the commentators on *The View*—because of his dalliances with his impassioned and indis-creet twenty-three-year-old intern.

If discovered, your satyriasis may be deemed to reflect your lack of the critical quality of *self-possession*—that even when the stakes were at their highest, and you had the most to lose, you couldn't control your private needs. This recklessness suggests you're unfit for political position. Why would you jeopardize your public goals for so little? And your actions show that you believe you're above the laws or immune from censure. During his bid for the presidency in 1987, Gary Hart challenged reporters investigating reports of his womanizing: "If anybody wants to put a tail on me, go ahead. They'd be very bored." In fact, they weren't bored. Hart had dared the press to follow and watch him, and yet continued to pursue an affair with Donna Rice. And this man, people asked, wants to be president?

TRUE RULE

Don't let sex strike you impotent.

Scandal forever links a person with a particular image in the public mind. Match the scandalous alleged acts with the perpetrators:

CAUGHT	ALLEGED ACT
a. New York judge Sol Wachtler	i. exposing himself in an X-rated theater
b. Sportscaster Marv Albert	ii. toe-sucking with a prostitute
c. Televangelist Jim Bakker	iii. engaging in suspicious activities with a child
d. Politician Nelson Rockefeller	iv. dying in the arms of a young female friend while "working on a book on art"
e. Actor Pee-Wee Herman	v. having sex with a twenty-one-year-old church secretary
f. Singer Michael Jackson	vi. engaging in quasi-incest
g. Political consultant Dick Morris	vii. making threats against the daughter of a woman who rejected him
h. Actor and director Woody Allen	viii. indulging in a fetish for ladies' underwear

Answers: a-vii; b-viii; c-v; d-iv; e-i; f-iii; g-ii; h-vi.

SEX-LINKED ATTRIBUTES

- Penis size
- Hair
- Height

Penis size

If you're like many men, you associate your penis size with both your sexual power and your worldly power. In both respects, you're concerned with the length, girth, and liveliness of your penis.

Surprisingly, a man who worries about his penis is probably more concerned about what other men—not women—will think. In one study of three hundred men approved for penis-enhancing surgery, a majority were motivated by "locker room phobia," that is, a sense of discomfort in front of other men. Fewer than a third came as a result of complaints from female sexual partners.

Are you considering a penis enlargement? You're not alone. It's a hot new cosmetic surgery specialty. Or you can take less drastic measures, like using weights to stretch your penis. Before taking action, consider that you may have unrealistic expectations. Reportedly, men think an erect penis averages ten inches, while women think it averages four inches. The actual average is 5.1 inches.

Some men are enormously encouraged by their enhanced presentation. One confided, "I go out on a limb more than I did before with business. Now [when] I go into business meetings, I'm thinking, 'If you guys had just half of what I have.'"

If you feel the urge toward raw exhibitionism, however, squelch it. (Unless, however, you can use such an episode to prove your impunity, see "Power," Chapter 3. Apple Computer's Steve Jobs reportedly wore loose-fitting shorts, with no underwear, to interview a young woman for a job—an outfit that didn't stop him from uncrossing his legs and flashing the interviewee.) Men's fascination with male genitalia is not limited to their own equipment. Greek tycoon Aristotle Onassis's yacht *Christina* boasted barstools upholstered with the skin of a whale's testicles.

Hair

If you're like most men, you worry about losing your hair. Hair is associated with youth and power. One study examined people's perceptions of bald men contrasted with men with full heads of hair. The study showed that both sexes assumed that balding men were weaker and found them less attractive. Men realize this: of bald men

TIP: If you're going bald, consider shaving your head.

interviewed, seventy-five percent said they felt self-conscious about their baldness. This preoccupation is nothing new. According to his valet, when Napoleon met with Russia's Czar Alexander, they strayed from the topic of European politics to compare baldness cures.

Height

You're also likely to be preoccupied with your height—and if you're short, you're right to worry. If you're a man, the taller you are, the better. Men of stature tend to be men of status; they're more apt to get better jobs, make more money (according to a 1990 study, average yearly salary rose at a rate of $1,300 an inch), and win the attention of better-looking women.

Height pays off in terms of money, sex, and power. Money: More than half of the CEOs in American Fortune 500 companies are six feet or taller, and only three percent are five feet seven or under. Sex: One study found that women prefer a man at least six inches taller than themselves. Power: For seven straight decades, the United States elected the taller of the two presidential candidates. Richard Nixon broke the run. When Jimmy Carter and President Gerald Ford debated in 1976, the Carter campaign wisely opposed the prospect of their candidate standing beside the six-foot-one president. They were turned down when they asked that the candidates be seated for the debates, but in the end, the two camps agreed to lecterns placed far apart. In return for that concession, the Ford contingent required that the background be changed to disguise Ford's encroaching baldness. At the end of the 1988 televised presidential debates, George Bush made a point of standing near the shorter Michael Dukakis, to underscore the disparity in height. In fact, in almost all presidential races to date, the taller candidate has triumphed.

So, if you're short, take measures to disguise your height. Of course, the simplest disguise is exaggeration—and, in fact, seventy-one percent of the time people slightly overestimate their height. But you may want to take more elaborate measures. The power-hungry FBI director J. Edgar Hoover didn't approach six feet, but kept visitors looking up at him by seating them on a low couch and placing his desk and swivel chair on a raised platform, with the chair screwed to the maximum height. As head of distribution of Paramount, height-challenged Frank Yablans split his Gulf and Western office into two levels, with his desk on a six-inch platform, so he could gaze down at his visitors.

On the other hand, shortness may drive you to compensate— the "Napoleon" complex, named after the power-hungry conqueror of Europe who stood only five feet two inches.

Even if you're worried about some aspect of your appearance, remember the importance of *sprezzatura*. Especially as a man, never reveal any concern for your appearance. Senator Bob Packwood became an instant target of ridicule when the country read his March 1992 diary entry: "I didn't use any jell [sic] on it at all. I just blew it until it was about dry, combed it, and if it didn't come out looking just right. It had just the right amount of bounce to it, and wave to it. I came back rather confident. I now think we can beat a political opponent." The public expected a senator to be preoccupied with different matters than his wonderment over the efficacy of the hair dryer; his anxiety about his appearance made him look weak.

SEX FOR SEX'S SAKE

I'm not interested in all these complicated goals, you may be thinking. I just want sex for the pure pleasure of having sex. In fact, it may be that the chief reason you want power, money, or fame is to improve your prospects for sex. Because women are powerfully attracted to power, money, and fame, the more of these you have, the more easily you'll have casual sex. The prominent director, rapper, politician, executive, or football player has his pick of sexual partners.

For most men, however, casual sex is difficult to obtain; because more men want it, there's a shortage of willing women, and unlike men, women demand much of the same qualities for a fling as they do for a permanent relationship.

If you're just a regular fellow and can't rely on power, money, or fame to make conquest easy, how can you succeed in your quest for casual sex? Consider these pointers:

Appearance

- Although women put much less emphasis on appearance than men, they do appreciate height. Look as tall as possible.

- Because women look for signs of prosperity, dress well whether at work, at a bar, or in the park. Your clothes should be of high quality, clean, and loose.

- Try to look physically strong and athletic. Emphasize your physical prowess by casually mentioning your rigorous workout routine or helping to rearrange her furniture. Remember that women much prefer a lean build to a bulky, muscle-bound physique.

- Concentrate on your speaking voice. Women are attracted to a low, resonant voice with consistent pitch.

- A symmetrical face is more attractive than asymmetrical. Keep your sideburns even; if your nose leans right, part your hair on the left to add balance; make sure one eyebrow hasn't sprouted more vigorously than the other.

- Hair on your head is good; much hair almost anywhere else, bad. Trim protruding nose hair, ear hair, or beetling eyebrows. (A furry back unfortunately requires more drastic measures.)

- Consider contact lenses or surgery to correct bad vision. Studies show that while men in glasses are considered smarter and more sensitive, women find them less physically appealing. If you've had the same frames for several years, it's time to get a new pair. And wear sunglasses— they're sexy and will improve your looks if your eyes are deep set or too close together.

Action

- Demonstrate your resources and your generosity by buying drinks, buying gifts, handing out large tips.

- Confidence in front of a group signals social success, so work the crowd. Draw favorable attention to yourself by perfecting some skill, like skiing, sleight of hand, or poker, and develop your sense of humor—women love funny guys. (If you're no good at telling jokes, learn to laugh at yourself.)

- Show interest and affection for children. Why do you think politicians kiss babies? Signal that you'll be an attentive father and that you're generally a caring person.

- Make use of "subliminal touching," touching a person so unobtrusively that it's not noticed. Studies show that subliminal touching dramatically increases that person's sense of well-being and positive feelings toward you, the toucher. Keep it subtle, however; women hate being pawed by strangers.

- Act protective—insist on walking her to her car, lend her your jacket if the restaurant is cold, intervene if anyone starts hassling her.

Attitude

- Women are attracted to ambition and industriousness. Drop hints about your many achievements. Confide your life goals.

- As always, radiate *sprezzatura*. Your demeanor should communicate supreme confidence, even a dash of machismo.

- Attentiveness is one of the secrets to seduction, so make eye contact, avoid eye stray, and center the conversation on her.

Commentator Elizabeth Drew observed
that "[Clinton] listened and focused on
what guests or other casual acquaintances
said. . . . He looked at the other person
intently, seemingly utterly focused on what
he or she was saying."

- Women value dependability and
trustworthiness, so keep your cool—
moodiness suggests you can't handle stress.
Kindness is universally attractive.

But I've tried all that, you may be thinking. Still need additional
pointers? Try following the example set by legendary seducer
Casanova. His detailed memoir contains principles of sexual conquest that can be applied today:

EXCITE CUPIDITY WITH A SHOWER OF PRESENTS.
*After I had bought a very fine watch, I thought of ear-rings, of a fan,
and of many other pretty nicknacks. Of course I bought them all at
once. She received all those gifts offered by love with a tender delicacy
which overjoyed me.*

APPRAISE YOUR COMPETITION.
*I wanted only to ascertain, for the sake of form and etiquette, whether
the officer was her husband, her lover, a relative or a protector, because,
used as I was to gallant adventures, I wished to know the nature of the
one in which I was embarking.*

PROMISE MARRIAGE.
*I had thought of marrying her when I loved her better than myself
[before sex], but after obtaining possession the balance was so much on
my side that my self-love proved stronger than my love for Christine.*

IF SEDUCTION IS IMPOSSIBLE, MOVE ON.
*In the heart of a libertine, a love without solid nourishment dies of ina-
nition, as women with some experience well know.*

• • •

Like men, women use sex, but their purposes and methods are different.

CHAPTER TWENTY

HOW TO USE SEX—FOR WOMEN

You can incorporate sex into your strategy whether you're pursuing a *jackpot*—a man through whom you'll gain access to power, money, or fame—or whether you're seeking sheer sexual gratification. Don't, however, make the common mistake of using sex to accelerate a relationship's intimacy.

SEX FOR THE JACKPOT

Some women—granted, a small minority—use sex to win the favors of a *jackpot*, a man from whom they can gain access to power, money, or fame.

If you're like most women, you're excited—even if only subconsciously—by a man's command, his high salary, his respectful treatment by his colleagues, his nationally recognized face. One Washingtonian observed: "You'd be amazed at how many women throw themselves at the feet of a U.S. Senator as opposed to how many throw themselves at the feet of a C.P.A." Your ardor is genuine (but if he loses his job, will your interest fade?).

Some sociologists argue that it's because women have historically been prohibited from winning power, money, and fame themselves that they work to acquire it vicariously, through powerful, rich, celebrated men.

Evolutionary psychologists argue instead that it's the evolutionary advantages afforded to their children that drive women to seek out high-resource men. Women, the argument goes, desire men who can offer them and their children protection from harm, social status, and an investment of attention and resources—the necessary ingredients for survival and success beginning in prehistoric days.

The certainty that she could marry Percy Gryce when she pleased had lifted a heavy load from her mind, and her money troubles were too recent for their removal not to leave a sense of relief which a less discerning intelligence might have taken for happiness. Her vulgar cares were at an end. She would be able to arrange her life as she pleased, to soar into that empyrean of security where creditors cannot penetrate. She would have smarter gowns than Judy Trenor, and far, far more jewels than Bertha Dorset. She would be free forever from the shifts, the expedients, the humiliations of the relatively poor. Instead of having to flatter, she would be flattered; instead of being grateful, she would receive thanks. There were old scores she could pay off as well as old benefits she could return. And she had no doubts as to the extent of her power.

EDITH WHARTON, *THE HOUSE OF MIRTH*

Whatever the reason, women swarm toward money and power and fame, and to associated qualities such as ambition, industriousness, height, and high rank.

You, however, may be one of the far rarer sort who pursues a jackpot as an absolute goal. You're not much concerned with a potential jackpot's character and personal history, except as they affect his bank account or who invites him (and with him, you) to dinner. You're quite frank about the fact that you're only interested in a specific quality of man—high school teachers and public interest lawyers shouldn't bother asking for your phone number. "Mayflower Madam" Sydney Biddle Barrows offered this encouragement for those pursuing a jackpot: "Trying to land a wealthy, powerful man takes a great deal of dedication, perseverance, and hard work. It's a high-stakes game, and the woman who is the most committed and focused has the best chance of winning. Not everyone has the interest, the disposition, or the tolerance to dedicate herself to pursuing this type of relationship, of course. But it can be done, and history is filled with hundreds of examples of women who have made their dream of untold riches come true."

Never admit that you're working to win over a jackpot. The illusion of romance is important; no man wants to admit that without his worldly success, he wouldn't have a chance. Don't worry about plausibility—just insist on your devotion. Topless dancer Anna Nicole Smith, twenty-seven, had no trouble convincing Houston oil tycoon J. Howard Marshall II, eighty-nine, of her true love (his $500 million had nothing to do with her feelings, she protested when people suggested she might have married for money). And of course, the fact that you've hit a jackpot doesn't mean that you don't have true feelings of love. You might, or you might not.

Always try to marry your jackpot. Your access to money, power, or fame is more secure if concretized in a legal bond (even an eventual divorce will leave you better off than before).

Money jackpot

Are there any guides to help a woman seeking to find that money jackpot? Yes. There are many candid and . . . *unsentimental* sources of instruction:

- *How to Meet the Rich: For Business, Friendship, or Romance* (1999) and *How to Marry the Rich* (1991), Ginie Polo Sayles
- *How to Snare a Millionaire,* Lisa Johnson (1995)
- *How to Marry Money: The Rich Have to Marry Someone—Why Not You,* Susan Wright (1995)
- *How to Marry a Millionaire* (1951), updated to *How to Marry a Billionaire* (1984), Doris Lilly
- *Cosmopolitan* magazine covers this topic extensively
- Coerte V. W. Felske's novel *The Millennium Girl* (1999) minutely details the life of a "Digger" in hot pursuit of "Walletmen"

If you don't want to take the time to read all the materials listed above, here are highlights of their advice for the upwardly marital:

Who A woman of dependent means wants a man with plenty of money—but old or new? Old money is more distinguished; new money is more indulgent.

Your best choice of jackpot is a recent widower of a happy marriage. Move in fast—maybe even provide comfort and support during the wife's final illness, and in the first period of mourning.

Where

Go where the action is: the first-class section on airplanes, gallery openings, museum benefits, auctions, the right conferences, the right funerals. Move to Silicon Valley, home to the most single, highly eligible men per single woman. Play the right sports, such as tennis, squash, skiing, and sailing, and work out at the best gym. Vacation in the right spots: Aspen, Gstaad, Saint Bart's, Martha's Vineyard. Master gambling games, such as baccarat, blackjack, bridge. Settle for the tiniest apartment in order to live in the right neighborhood. Scrimp, if necessary, to send your children to the best private schools—a great place to meet rich divorced dads.

How

Be creative and persistent. An enterprising young woman had set her sights on one of the richest men in New York. She wangled an invitation to a formal dinner party at his house and then secretly rearranged the place cards so she was sitting to his left. Within months she had her million-dollar engagement ring. Marla Maples hung out in front of Donald Trump's building until she got the opportunity accidentally to bump into him (literally).

Investigate

Research your potential jackpot to make sure he's the real thing—don't take his word for it. Use the Internet to look up his company. Estimate the value of his car, clothes, neighborhood, vacations. Size up his friends and colleagues—his social set reflects his standing.

Keep in mind that the same qualities that made your jackpot what he is might make him an unpleasant companion. Make sure the winnings are worth the price.

TRUE RULE

Those who marry for money earn every penny.

Special note on the explicit use of sex for money

Of course, prostitution is the most direct way to use sex for money. But in this field, the more lucrative and perhaps easier route is to play pander instead of prostitute.

While the public despises male pimps as exploiters of women, female procurers are viewed more warmly. Somehow, when a woman makes the arrangements, sex for money seems more acceptable: entrepreneurial, warmhearted, even fun. In her account of founding her business, "Mayflower Madam" Sydney Biddle Barrows emphasized the closeness of her "girls," with descriptions of them meeting in her office, making popcorn as they waited for their assignments, celebrating birthday parties each month. Other renowned real-life procuresses include Xaviera Hollander, the "Happy Hooker"; Hollywood's Alex Adams and Heidi Fleiss; and Edna Milton, immortalized in the Broadway musical and movie *The Best Little Whorehouse in Texas*. (For a madam or prostitute, as for those in every other line of work, servicing a celebrity clientele will speed your way to fame and fortune. The arrest of Heidi Fleiss set off a tabloid frenzy because of the A-list stars who supposedly were her customers.)

Those who want to exchange sex for money, but who aren't interested in the prostitution business, sometimes turn to child support. A man might leave or demand a prenuptial agreement, but he can't refuse to support a child. One lucky one-night stand with a rich man could be the guarantee of a healthy monthly income for eighteen years. Even just a credible *threat* of paternity may mean a multimillion-dollar settlement if the rich potential father is also prominent and married, with much to lose from any salacious publicity.

Athletes make attractive targets. Professional athletes' lives abound with temptations—and indulgences. Sonics guard Gary Payton had two sons, born within four months of each other: son Gary Payton II, born to Payton's future wife, and son Gary Payton, Jr., born to another woman. First baseman Steve Garvey was successfully sued in a paternity suit by a former fiancée; it emerged in the proceedings that he'd fathered children with two women out of wedlock (in addition to his two children with his ex-wife). Knicks player Larry Johnson supported five children by four women—only two of whom were born to his wife. And these are just a few illustrations.

The choicest target among sports teams? Basketball players. They enjoy a lot of free time on the road (with five times as many road games as NFL players). They make a lot of money; the NBA pays an average of a couple million dollars, more than other sports. And players are easy to spot—they tower above anybody else, their faces familiar from the TV set. As the notorious Chicago Bulls star Dennis Rodman crowed in his autobiography, "Fifty percent of life in the NBA is sex. The other fifty percent is money."

Well, this is preposterous, you're most likely thinking. Who decides to run out and get pregnant with some basketball player's baby! Child support can nevertheless be used as an indirect way to secure considerable income for yourself. Consider that an issue in the custody suit between the prominent and well-connected Patricia Duff and billionaire Ronald Perelman was whether a payment of $38,000 would be an adequate yearly *clothing* allowance for their four-year-old daughter.

Power jackpot

Perhaps you've got your heart set on a jackpot who offers power. Remember: Vicarious power is more precarious than vicarious wealth. Your jackpot can readily and permanently transfer money to you, but he'll find it much harder to give you power. Sure, Kate Capshaw has some power in Hollywood, and she gets more work acting and producing than she would if she weren't married to Steven Spielberg, but her status as "wife of" can't win her the power of Jodie Foster or Madonna. (Note, too, that while houses, jewelry, or blue-chip stocks can be stockpiled in your name, vicarious power disappears along with the jackpot who dies, divorces you, or plummets from high position.)

Other people are suspicious of any power that is acquired by sexual means—even if your sexual relationship long predates the power you've acquired. A first lady wields power because of her association with a president, and she poses a threat to officials who hold their power by conventional means. Consider the controversy fired by Rosalynn Carter's insistence on attending cabinet meetings, and by Nancy Reagan's engineering of Chief of Staff Donald Regan's ouster. First ladies with even more explicit public power, such as Hillary Rodham Clinton and Eleanor Roosevelt, come under constant attack. "Pillow power" is perceived as illegitimate and threatening.

In addition to this illegitimacy problem, holding vicarious power as a strong wife leads the public to assume your husband is weak. In the 1994 Senate race in California, Arianna Huffington's drive was so visible that people speculated that she was just using her then-husband, Michael, as a vehicle for her own ambition. She seemed to be far more interested in winning the campaign than he did, and her forcefulness emphasized his inadequacy.

Also, because women now are expected to be able to achieve power without making use of sexual relationships, you will raise the ire of both women and men who disapprove of your methods.

But despite these drawbacks, a power jackpot can help you gain access to power. Just remember that a power jackpot is better able to buttress your existing power than to bestow power from scratch.

(Don't, like some unsophisticated people, make the mistake of assuming that a jackpot who is rich must also

If she was restless now, it was not that she wanted an affair for lust's sake, for she had a genuine distaste for sexual intimacy and hated to sacrifice a facial appointment for a mere frolic in bed; but there were so many things to be gained by trading on sex and she thought so little of the process that she itched to use it as currency once again, trading a half-hour in bed for a flattering friendship, a royal invitation; power of whatever sort appealed to her.

DAWN POWELL, *A Time to Be Born*

have power and status. "He's a *very important* man!" How could he be rich and not important?)

Fame jackpot

Of course, sex with a famous man—the most extreme example of fame frottage—can bring you fame. Who'd heard of Monica Lewinsky before she tangled with Bill Clinton, or Shoshanna Lonstein before Jerry Seinfeld? The fame jackpot brings power and money in his wake. Your vicariously derived fame can help you win attention for your new business, land an endorsement deal, make an appearance on a TV talk show . . . The list is endless, but short-lived, unless you manage to perpetuate interest in your sex life and yourself.

The "casting couch" is a cliché in Hollywood (where fame and power are inextricably linked), because wannabe starlets work to hit the fame/power jackpot by winning the sponsorship—or at least the momentary attention—of the powerful director, leading man, or executive. Director John Singleton reportedly entertained a steady stream of female extras in his trailer on a movie set. (He didn't approach them himself, but had an assistant explain that "Mr. Singleton would like to see you in his trailer.") By turning the camera on a favorite, he could transform her from extra into star—and women eagerly vied to try to win his approval, however possible.

Maybe you want to use sex to hit the jackpot, but you want to maintain, at the same time, your sexual unavailability. Is this possible? Absolutely. In fact, the challenge of overcoming your inaccessibility is a powerful enticement for men. Apply La Rochefoucauld's observation: "Coldness in a woman, like a gaud, is something put on to increase the allure."

TRUE RULE

Sex—to use it, refuse it.

A mere hint of sex sparks interest in you. Use subtle signals to attract attention and approval. For example, methods of sexhibitionism for the workplace include:

- languid stretching or flexing, to call attention to your body ("I'm so stiff this morning");
- socializing casually with those of higher rank, in a way that your male peers can't do (that group of VPs asked if you wanted to join them for drinks but didn't bother to invite your office-mate, John);
- highlighting intimacy with a few male favorites by whispering, passing notes, sharing food or drinks, borrowing clothing, cadging car rides;
- dropping suggestive references to your boyfriend or husband, especially if he's rich, powerful, or famous enough to excite prurient interest and feelings of competition;
- finding plausible ways to strip down, such as parading through the office in spandex on your way to the gym, or taking off a jacket to reveal a silky, wispy camisole.

It's a common belief that women use sex to win access to rich, powerful, famous men, and that men are susceptible to women's seduction. As a result, institutions that capitalize on women's sexuality will try to circumscribe women's behavior. Don't be fooled by the explanation that such rules are in place to protect women. Often they're in place for two quite different reasons: to protect men who might get snared, and to tantalize men by preserving the women's unavailability. Consider:

- Dallas Cowboys Cheerleaders were forbidden, on pain of losing their jobs, to date, or "fraternize," with football players.
- Playboy Bunnies working as waitresses in the clubs couldn't be seen meeting men and couldn't date customers *except* (significantly) #1 Keyholders, which included executives, reporters, big shots. They also had to be tested for venereal disease. Why? The only explanation was that it was "for everyone's good" and "your own protection."

- Historically, from the moment they arrived, contestants in the Miss America Pageant were forbidden to be alone with a man— even with their own fathers.

SEX FOR SEX'S SAKE

I don't have any agenda, you may be saying to yourself. Who needs a jackpot? I just want to have sex for the sake of sex. Casual sex is easier for a woman to obtain than for a man; women tend to be more interested in long-term relationships. But if you want a quick fling, consider these pointers:

Appearance
- Men are attracted by signs of fecundity, so aim to look youthful and bursting with health.

- Tastes differ, but most men have a preference for women who are busty, tall, with long, usually blonde, hair.

- Your clothes don't have to be on the cutting edge of fashion, but you should look nicely put together.

- Signal your availability by wearing tight clothes that reveal a lot of skin.

Action
- A man is eagerly looking for a sign that you're interested. Make suggestive gestures: suck seductively on a straw, lick your lips, stroke your own arms or legs.

- Look intently into his eyes, and let him catch you staring at him.

- Move your body to afford him a good view of your figure.

- Wear sunglasses. Research shows that you'll feel more confident, attractive, and also emboldened to do things you normally wouldn't do, like sunbathe topless. Use sunglasses as a flirt prop, by dropping them to the end of your nose to reveal your eyes, by taking them off to show you wish to connect, or brushing them against your lips.

- As noted in the previous chapter, use subliminal touching to give him a feeling of satisfaction and warmth. Or be more obvious about your touching; men aren't as put off by it as women are.

Attitude

- Make it easy for a man to start up a conversation. Wear an unusual piece of jewelry; drive a crazy car; carry a controversial book.

- Suggestive conversation drives men wild. If you're on an airplane, drop hints about your secret desire to join the Mile High Club. If you're at a party, confess with a glass of champagne in your hand that champagne always makes you misbehave.

- Radiate *sprezzatura*—act nonchalant and lighthearted.

- Energy is attractive, so speak with animation and put a bounce in your step.

- Hang on every word. Your intense interest will make him feel brilliant and sexy. Pamela Harriman was renowned for her extraordinary, laserlike attentiveness to the objects of her desire—invariably, rich or powerful men.

- Men and women alike appreciate the quality of kindness.

TRUE RULE

To enliven sex's commonplace pleasures, violate a prohibition.

TIP: Copy Marilyn Monroe's secret for a sexy walk—rumor has it that she cut a quarter-inch off one shoe's heel, so that she'd wiggle spectacularly when she walked.

Do you find enticements like a tight sweater or a flirtatious gaze too tame? Drive a man wild by promising that you want to make his most lascivious taboo fantasies come true. Whisper in his ear about how aroused you are—and why. Tap into what Sigmund Freud called "the charm of forbidden things":

- *Exhibitionism.* Dress or act provocatively. Wear a trench coat over your naked body, wear a business suit without underwear, suggest sex in front of a window with no shades.
- *Novelty.* Familiarity breeds boredom. Propose an unusual place or position for sex. Although "swapping" and "key-parties" are outmoded, the excitement that comes from trying a new partner or new situation will never go out of fashion.
- *Orgy,* including ménage-à-trois, or threesome. Suggest combining the pleasures of exhibitionism, voyeurism, and novelty by having sex with several people at once.
- *Risk.* Take a risk: sex in the bathroom of a restaurant, on the conference-room desk at work, in a car on the highway. When one South Carolina congressman asked his new wife to meet him during a late-night session of Congress, she arrived wearing a mink coat, high heels, and little else. They had sex standing between the columns of the (aptly named) Members Portico, overlooking the city.
- *Talk dirty.* Describe sex as it's taking place, or share your sexual fantasies. Phone sex, of course, burst into the spotlight when Monica Lewinsky confided that she and the president had done it. In fact, she bought him a copy of *Vox*, Nicholson Baker's novel about phone sex (when this fact emerged, the book's sales quadrupled).
- *Sadomasochism.* Excite your partner with the suggestion that you've experimented with, or are open to, S&M. (Don't confuse

S&M with brute violence. Signs of real S&M? Role-playing, consensuality, dominance and submission, verbal humiliation, and bondage.)

This dirty-girl strategy has its risks. As Casanova warned: "Too easy conquest often points to a depraved nature, and this men do not like, however depraved they themselves may be."

Note that even if you're not interested in sex for sex's sake but are actually pursuing some other goal, you may want a man to *think* that all you want is sex—for example, if you want to use child support as a way to get money.

SEX FOR INTIMACY

Have you ever found yourself having sex in the early stages of a relationship because you wanted to feel more settled as a couple, or to establish your claim over a quasi-boyfriend, or to please someone of whose affections you weren't certain? If so, you've used physical intimacy to try to accelerate emotional intimacy. You wanted to hurry things along toward emotional connection and secure coupledom, with the sweet promises of dinner-and-a-movie, surprise birthday parties, brunch with parents, and borrowed clothing. So you had sex.

Big, big mistake. This strategy is notoriously unsuccessful—not only futile, but actually counterproductive, and upsetting as well. Don't assume that by dropping your defenses and offering yourself up, you can force a new sexual partner, by some law of amordynamics, to make a counterpoising move toward intimacy. Go ahead and sleep with that casual acquaintance if you're just in it for raw sexual experience—just don't expect that he'll feel like, or act like, your lover in the morning.

In a relationship that isn't emotionally intimate, sexual intercourse wreaks a dramatic shift in power—before a couple has sex, the balance of power rests with the woman; after sex, power shifts to the man. (*Only* sexual intercourse does it; no need to debate whether gray areas "count," as arose in the Clinton-Lewinsky affair, because they don't.) The less emotional intimacy in the relationship, the more abrupt is the power transfer; a strong emotional connection keeps power in balance. By allowing sex to precede emotional connection, you significantly weaken your power status—and there's no payoff in emotional intimacy, no matter what you hope.

The fact is that despite countless attempts by women to use sex as a shortcut to emotional closeness, sex rarely has such accelerating effect. Or rather, it has a lopsided effect. After sex, you're more vulnerable and eager for affection and approval: you feel the pressure of his unspoken judgment (your performance, your thighs), you feel exposed to risk (no condom can totally erase the risk of pregnancy, AIDS, VD), you feel emotionally insecure (rejection *now* will hurt far worse than rejection before sex). But your sexual partner probably won't feel any corresponding rush to connect. In fact, just when you feel most in need of reassurance, he may feel just the opposite: distant, satisfied with a conquest, uneasy about the gusher of expectations that you release.

Do you use sex for intimacy? Consider whether you've relied on any of these rationalizations for rushing into sex:

- "I was swept away by passion. After all, women have strong sexual desires, too." (Was it actually physical lust or romantic hope that urged you on?)
- "He really wanted to have sex, and I didn't really care, and I didn't want it to become some big *issue.*" (How did you feel about it a week later?)
- "I liked him a lot, so I wanted him to feel that we had a perfect evening." (What difference would it have made if the evening weren't "perfect"?)
- "After he'd spent so much on the date, I felt bad turning him away at my door." (Why does it matter how much he spent?)
- "I'm not shackled by prefeminist notions of chastity and feminine restraint—I can be spontaneous and wild, just the way men are." (Are you really as carefree as you pretend?)

TIP: If you realize you've made the mistake of having sex to spur intimacy, counteract the misstep by staying emotionally distant, thereby maintaining equilibrium. Get up in the middle of the night and leave.

SEX-LINKED ATTRIBUTES

Breasts

If you're like many women, you're acutely aware of your breasts—and of men's fascination with breasts. You want to make a big impression.

If you're considering having your breasts "done," don't forget that, like everything, fashions in breasts change. Don't be fooled by Silicone Valley advertisements that bigger is necessarily better. Large, round breasts atop a tiny waist were the rage in 1900; then in the 1920s, a flat bosom was considered sexiest; in the 1940s, large, pointy breasts came into style; and then in the 1960s Twiggy made the boyish figure fashionable again. In the 1970s, shape and size mattered less than going "natural" without a bra. So, because style counts, even in breast size, adapt to the style that's right for your situation. In the 1990s, bigger was better in places in the South, like Texas or Las Vegas, while the fashion in the North tended toward a more natural, subtle enhancement. Trends are sure to change in the new millennium.

• • •

The use of sex doesn't require *actual* sex; the tantalizing suggestion of sex is enough. Or you can use sex in the context of a date, a fling, an affair, a romance. It's marriage—the permanent sexual relationship—that allows you to take advantage of sex in ways that more casual liaisons don't permit. Marriage allows you to join the establishment, to draw on the social position of your partner, to build a dynasty.

CHAPTER TWENTY-ONE

MARRIAGE: THE PERMANENT SEXUAL RELATIONSHIP

Money, power, and celebrity can't win everything. Fame and fortune are the rewards of an individual, but success in society is a family matter. Use marriage (the permanent sexual relationship) to secure your place, and your children's place, in society.

Marriage allows you to join yourself to family-based institutions. There is a long tradition of *purse* marrying *pedigree*—an exchange in which purse attains blue-blooded social distinction (one of the few

Use marriage to acquire what you can't yourself achieve. In the controversial Onassis marriage, pedigree married purse. (© Bettmann/CORBIS)

things that can't directly be bought) and pedigree attains the money necessary to maintain its position.

It is faintly ridiculous to design your own family crest or to devise a new family tweed, but marry into the right family and all such impedimenta will be yours. Marriage allows you to join the company of the "right" families and to swaddle your common or disreputable lineage in social eminence. At last you have a charming house on Martha's Vineyard ("it's been in the family for years"), a country-club membership, friendly interviews in places you might like to work. You move in lofty circles—you're accepted, or at least tolerated.

> Charlie knew very well, when he was being honest with himself, that if it hadn't been for Martha, he would never have gotten in. Martha was from Richmond, and in Atlanta things *Richmond* (like things *New York,* when it came to the arts) had *authenticity.* Charlie kept telling himself that he couldn't care less about the Driving Club one way or the other; but had he been excluded, his Hard Cracker resentment would have known no bounds. It was the very fact that it was . . . there . . . that mattered so terribly much.
>
> TOM WOLFE, *A MAN IN FULL*

If you're angling to marry up, don't be discouraged by an undistinguished background. Marriage isn't impossible, and once accomplished it will (mostly) erase your past. Patricia Kluge's past—including appearing in an X-rated movie and penning a sex column for a British skin magazine, *Knave*—didn't stop billionaire John Kluge from marrying her.

To cement your social position, an actual marriage is essential, with its guarantee of secure social position and constant financial support—or entitlement to money upon a breakup. Avoid settling for less permanent relationships, if possible.

And, of course, marrying the boss's daughter or son is a great way to get into business—just look at Philip Graham (married into the Meyer *Washington Post* publishing family) or Arthur Sulzberger (married into the Ochs *New York Times* publishing family).

> Lady Ailesbury, the incarnation of worldly wisdom, used to say: "We should always be civil to unmarried girls, we do not know whom they may marry."
>
> PHILIPPE JULIAN, *THE SNOB SPOTTER'S GUIDE*

As women achieve their own high position at work, the *power couple* is becoming increasingly common, in which a marriage provides husband and wife with mutual career support. Consider such intimidating couples as Harold Evans and Tina Brown, Bob and Elizabeth Dole, David Kelley and Michelle Pfeiffer, John Gregory Dunne and Joan Didion, James Rubin and Christiane Amanpour, Mike Nichols and Diane Sawyer, Richard Phillips and Dana Hoey, Ben Bradlee and Sally Quinn, Ken Auletta and Amanda Urban. The whole is greater than the sum of the two parts. (Although it offers great benefits, one disadvantage to being in a power couple is that because power couples often work in the same field, they occasionally face conflicts of interests: working for competitors, maintaining trade secrets, taking a government post where a spouse is a regulated party, and the like.)

Marriage is a particularly effective method of celebrity-splice. Sharon Stone, the actress best known for her pantyless leg-crossing scene in *Basic Instinct,* was taken much more seriously after she married Phil Bronstein, executive editor of the *San Francisco Examiner.* The marriage of Marilyn Monroe to baseball legend Joe DiMaggio

Marriage is an effective way to exploit celebrity-splice. The marriage of actress Marilyn Monroe and baseball hero Joe DiMaggio enhanced the legend of both. (AP/Wide World Photos)

and then to playwright Arthur Miller, and the marriage of actress Jane Fonda to politician Tom Hayden and then to media tycoon Ted Turner, burnished the fame of both husband and wife. Political consultants and power couple James Carville (Democrat) and Mary Matalin (Republican) made a more interesting pundit package together than apart.

The marriage that's most visible to the public is the marriage of the President and the First Lady, and there is always intense curiosity about whether that partnership is a merely a businesslike arrangement, maintained for appearances as part of a politician's permanent campaign, or whether it retains sexual and romantic vitality. Of these First Families, who did or didn't share bedrooms? Test your knowledge by checking in the appropriate column.

PRESIDENT & FIRST LADY	DID SHARE	DID NOT
a. Bill and Hillary Clinton		
b. George and Barbara Bush		
c. Ronald and Nancy Reagan		
d. Jimmy and Rosalynn Carter		
e. Gerald and Betty Ford		
f. Richard and Pat Nixon		
g. Lyndon and Lady Bird Johnson		
h. Jack and Jackie Kennedy		
i. Dwight and Mamie Eisenhower		

Answers: Bill and Hillary Clinton didn't share; George and Barbara Bush did share; Ronald and Nancy Reagan did share; Jimmy and Rosalynn Carter did share; Gerald and Betty Ford did share; Richard and Pat Nixon didn't share; Lyndon and Lady Bird Johnson didn't share; Jack and Jackie Kennedy didn't share; Dwight and Mamie Eisenhower did share.

DYNASTY

Once you reach a certain level of power, money, or fame, you may feel the urge to establish a dynasty to secure the prominence of your name and the security of your descendants—and you need a marriage to do so. What else do you need? An examination of some of the most prominent American dynasties—Rockefellers, Kennedys, Fords, and Bushes—contains some hints:

- A founding fortune;
- Subsequent cleansing of that fortune, if necessary, through high-profile philanthropy or public service;
- Prominent and honorable position, with some continuity (within the same field or company) over two or more generations;
- Repetition of family names (Senior, Junior, III, IV) to jog the public's memories;
- A willingness actually to work hard yourself, and to boost your powers through the retention of talented, loyal, self-sacrificing staff;
- An occasional whiff of sexual or financial scandal to keep the public's interest piqued;
- The naming of a prominent institution after your family (either by you or by the government), to keep the name in the public mind.

Note that three generations is all that's needed to make a "dynasty"; indeed, most dynasties begin to disintegrate after the fourth generation.

If you're eager for the dynasty you founded to assume an aristocratic air, you're going to have to wait a few generations. Not you, but your descendants will enjoy the steady, inexorable exposure to money that confers the inimitable air of carelessness

> The millionacracy . . . is not at all an affair of persons and families, but a perpetual fact of money with a variable human element. . . . Of course, this trivial and fugitive fact of personal wealth does not create a permanent class, unless some special means are taken to arrest the process of disintegration in the third generation. This is so rarely done, at least successfully, that one need not live a very long life to see most of the rich families he knew in childhood more or less reduced.
>
> OLIVER WENDELL HOLMES, SR.,
> *ELSIE VENNER: A ROMANCE OF DESTINY*

and belonging. (And one day, after your fortune has been depleted, your progeny will cling to that gentility and to the memory of ease and luxury.)

The dynastic ideal is so powerful that even public companies, which might be expected to demonstrate an unsentimental reluctance to respect family lines, capitulate: Seagram, with the Bronfman family; News Corp., with the Murdoch family; Ford Motor Company, with the Ford family; AIG with the Greenberg family. However, not just any CEO can install a child as heir. To succeed, pack the board with your supporters; pick a successor who, if not the best candidate, isn't a preposterous choice; and you must also be considered the institution's *moral* owner (even if it's a public company) by dint of founding or transforming it, so that it seems appropriate that you be allowed to bequeath your title within your family line. And remember to retain a controlling share of the stock.

Like anything taken to the extreme, the dynastic impulse—particularly as expressed through the dynastic name—can become ridiculous. Of the nine children fathered by boxing heavyweight champion George Foreman, four are named George. Michael Jackson has two children: Prince Michael Jackson and Paris-Michael Jackson. When passing on your dynastic name, try to limit yourself to naming just one child after yourself.

APPLYING THE PRINCIPLE OF DIS-EXPECTATION

As always, apply the principle of dis-expectation to demonstrate complete triumph. Men: If the men around you are trading in their wives for newer models, you stick with your wife of twenty-five years. Women: Flout the instinct to be impregnated by a husband who has higher status than you. Stars like Jodie Foster and Madonna don't feel the need to have a man of equal prominence to father their babies, or to be married. Foster's partner is unknown; Madonna chose a "nobody" (personal trainer Carlos Leon) as the father of her first child.

TRUE RULE

Simplicity and modesty can be the
most effective way to demonstrate complete triumph.

• • •

Using sex for money, for power, for fame is made easier by the fact that these worldly passions convey a tantalizing erotic charge to their possessors. The presence of power, money, fame electrify the intercourse between a man and a woman; their influence is wordless, primitive, irresistible.

CHAPTER TWENTY-TWO

THE EROTICISM OF POWER, MONEY, AND FAME

Power, money, and fame ignite a sexual glow that attracts admirers. Of course, part of the attraction is that some people, unable to win these worldly prizes themselves, want to enjoy them vicariously through a sexual partner. That's enticing. But it's not just greed; money, power, and fame gleam with their own erotic luster, and you feel a real sexual quiver.

The cynosure effect is partly responsible: the spotlight shining on the rich, powerful, and famous makes them alluring. So many people watch them, discuss them, defer to them—so much attention makes them sexy, and the prospect of you yourself being at the center of their attention is delicious. And the pleasure of foot-washing also contributes to the enticement: placing yourself (being invited to place yourself) at the service of the great is thrilling.

An imbalance of power and money and fame is erotic. Professors and students, law partners and paralegals, doctors and nurses—how many of these lovers would be together if they'd met at a bar or a family party? Few. It's the thrill of disparity (and, often, proximity) that fuels their passion.

Dreams of power, money, and fame perfume the fantasies of both men and women. At the core, men's fantasies center on their desire *to teach* and *to protect* and *to acquire* and *to impress*. Women's fantasies focus on their desire *to inspire* (either as a muse or savior) and *to excite* and *to sacrifice* and *to be raised up*.

TRUE RULE

Money, power, and fame are the ultimate aphrodisiacs.

That moment, when Caroline had collapsed against him, weeping, bruised, he had felt swept by tenderness, the wish to protect her. She had seemed vulnerable, he had felt strong. All this had risen up in him, urgent, turbulent. A kind of love; he had thought it the real one.

ROXANA ROBINSON, *THIS IS MY DAUGHTER*

Power is erotic: it includes the thrill of winning, or being won. As a man, you dream about the power to dominate and to protect, to ride up on a white horse to rescue a beautiful maiden.

The woman you desire is surrounded by suitors vying for her attention and her favors—but she loves only you. Other men watch as you bear her away, in triumph. In *The Technique of the Love Affair*, Doris Langley Moore advised, "A man does not often want what nobody else would have. He tends rather to covet what others have already found desirable, especially in the way of women. The more proofs he has that you are sought after, the more convinced he will be that you are worth seeking."

As a woman, you feel the power of being the trophy that is won. Men battle for your hand—you, the desired one, inspiring envy. And dependence, being swept into the shelter of someone more powerful, exerts its own seduction. "Power is an aphrodisiac," wrote Barbara Amiel, "because it protects and offers a shield from the world. . . . Power is sexy, not simply in its own right, but because it inspires self-confidence in its owner and a shiver of subservience on the part of those who approach it." You savor the satisfaction of commanding one who commands.

Sally Quinn analyzed the sexual architecture of the "Washington Affair": "For the mistress there is the pleasure of having and exerting power over a man who is powerful himself. For the wife, there is the title, the social status and the money. And for the man himself, there is the satisfaction of having his needs met by two women. In the Washington Affair there is something for everyone."

This kind of multiple benefit isn't limited to a "Washington affair," however. Imagine two ambitious management consultants: he's older, very senior in the company; she's younger, not quite so senior. No one knows for sure if they're having an affair, but even the speculation works to the couple's benefit. He's perceived to be vital, active, able to make an impressive conquest; she's perceived to have access to, and influence at, the highest levels. Their affair is perceived to be a reflection of their achievement.

Money permits the thrill of *paying for*, or *being paid for*.

For men, there's a deep satisfaction in laying spoils at the feet of a woman. You fasten a diamond necklace around a woman's throat and appear with her, adorned by you, at your side. It was Daisy who inspired the wealth of the great Gatsby; it existed only to please and glorify her.

At the same time you demonstrate your wealth, you put yourself in command. Superstar Hugh Grant mystified his public when he was caught with Divine Brown, a twenty-dollar Sunset Strip prostitute. Why, people wondered, would he pay for a cheap hooker, when he was getting gorgeous Elizabeth Hurley for free? But that's precisely the point. There is a thrill and domination and ease in *paying for*. In her memoir *Slow Motion*, Dani Shapiro recalled her rich, older lover Lenny: "All Lenny really wanted to do was go somewhere where we could rip our clothes off. He didn't care if that place was a $300-a-night hotel room or my apartment. In fact, he probably preferred hotel rooms, with their faint whiff of sex for money."

And there's a concomitant pleasure, of *being paid for*. The intoxication of purchase envelops you—you inspire the money spent on you; you're expensive and therefore valuable. You gather in the treasure that is heaped on you, that is dedicated to you.

"Not any stuffy pension in the rue de l'Université," Sylvia was saying, "and not any back seat in the Comédie listening to Racine. I want to go to Foyot's and then to the Folies Bergère."

"Would you like me to take you there?" Willis asked.

"Yes," she said, "on the *Mauretania*."

"All right," he said, "I'll take you some day, Sylvia. . . . Where's the best place to buy dresses in Paris?" he asked.

"I'd rather go to Worth's than any other," she said.

"Don't worry. I'll take you there," he told her.

It had seemed natural to kiss her then, and she had clung to him, and then she hid her face on his shoulder.

J. P. MARQUAND, *SINCERELY, WILLIS WAYDE*

I couldn't remember the last time a man had bought me clothing. Something in me wanted to refuse the gift: the fear of being bought, of being paid for sex. And what that meant about my being owned, about my time being at the disposal of a lover. A lover with money. My time in sexual thrall to a man. But I couldn't help being excited by a man going into a store, an expensive store, carrying the image of my body in his mind, the costliness of the gift a sign of my power.

MARY GORDON, *SPENDING*

If you're like most women, you're genuinely sexually attracted to power, money, and fame; your feelings are completely sincere, but perhaps a bit impersonal—originally inspired not by a personality but by a status. ("But he just wouldn't be himself, the man I truly love, if he weren't rich/powerful/famous. That's part of who he is!" you're protesting.) Jessica Sklar met Jerry Seinfeld about two months after she'd gotten married to someone else—and her marriage soon dissolved amid reports of her affair. Sure, her love is real, but would Seinfeld have been able to lure her from her new husband so quickly if the superstar comic had been just another ordinary guy? Doubtful.

"Don't you know what I'm after? Don't you know what I want? A real relationship. With you. I want to mean something to you. I want you, with all your fame and success, to care about me."

JOE MCGINNISS, *THE DREAM TEAM*

Special note on fairy tales of sex:

Fairy tales of sex. For both men and women, fairy tales of sex reflect secret, unacknowledged, or even repudiated desires—of rescue, transformation, and conquest. There is a deep satisfaction in enacting these stories, in seeing yourself as the triumphant prince or the saved maiden. Shape your encounters into one of these stimulating archetypes (even if only in your own mind). Cast yourself as Beauty or as the Beast.

But remember: Picking the wrong person to enact your fairy tale can lead to serious disappointment. Do you really believe that the man who works down the hall will be able to teach you and to lift you up to unseen heights? After you've gone to the trouble of rescuing that woman you met in a bar, will she reward you with affection and gratitude? Maybe. Maybe not.

- *Pygmalion*—*After King Pygmalion fell in love with the beautiful statue he fashioned himself, Aphrodite brought it to life. Pygmalion then married his creation.*

  A man discovers a woman, whom he molds and improves; having won her gratitude and love, he's the envy of every man around.

  Examples from film: *My Fair Lady. Pretty Woman.*

- *Lancelot and Guinevere (with a dash of Oedipus)*—*The young Sir Lancelot stole away King Arthur's lovely wife Guinevere.*

  The hero wins a desirable woman away from a rival of greater established power and position.

  Examples from film: *The Philadelphia Story. The Graduate.*

- *Cinderella*—*Cinderella, trapped in rags and drudgery, won the handsome Prince's heart as soon as she showed up wearing the right dress at the right party.*

  A woman manages to remake herself, and thus transformed, meets the right people and is "discovered" by a prince.

  Examples from film: *Working Girl. Sabrina.*

- *Rapunzel*—*The fair Rapunzel was locked in a high tower, with no doors and only a small window, until her rescue by the young, handsome Prince.*

  A woman is trapped in a boring job or an unhappy relationship until a man appears to free her from her daily cares. Actor Eli Wallach reflected on Marilyn Monroe's allure: "Every man who met her had the feeling that they could rescue her. She was a princess in a locked castle, and they could help her escape."

  Examples from film: *An Officer and a Gentleman. While You Were Sleeping.*

- *Beauty and the Beast*—*After feeling initial repulsion, a virtuous maiden befriended an ugly beast, discovered his hidden virtues, and by her love, transformed him into a handsome prince.*

With love and attention lavished by a persistent woman, a beastly man changes into a lover ready for commitment.

Examples from film: *Jerry McGuire. As Good As It Gets.*

• • •

This sex business doesn't interest me very much, you may be think-ing; as much as people go on and on about it, sex just doesn't hold my interest the way that power and money and fame do. Fine. Even if you're not fascinated by sex, other people are—and their fascina-tion is your opportunity. Exploit sex to achieve your own goals.

CHAPTER TWENTY-THREE

SEXPLOITATION

Tap into the boundless fascination with sex for your own gain—without shedding a stitch of clothing. Instead of using a sexual relationship with a particular man or woman, capitalize on the widespread fixation on the idea of sex.

Of course, in one of its rawest forms, sex in the form of pornography sells. At $10 billion a year, adult entertainment is one of America's fastest growing industries. What's the best way to get in on the action these days? Set up shop on the Internet—you'll offer your customers an unprecedented level of convenience, access, and anonymity that will entice them in droves. Consider that, as of 1999, about one in six of the millions of Internet surfers visited adult entertainment sites. And you'll be able to charge for your content; people will pay for reputable information from the *Wall Street Journal* or *Consumer Reports,* and they'll pay to see a black lace push-up bra in spike heels, but not much else. Some surfers find cyber-sex better than the real thing: with its offer of total control, without commitment or rejection; constantly new faces and bodies; its promise that every desire (however adventurous, kinky, or embarrassing) can be explored.

Another prurient taste serviced by the Internet, with revolutionary ease, is voyeurism. On her site jennicam.com, Jennifer Ringley, a twenty-something woman in Washington, D.C., webcasts every minute of her life—eating, sleeping, dressing, having sex with her boyfriend—over the Internet to millions of onlookers. She's her own paparazzo. Jennicam.com has spawned dozens of imitators, and if you have a taste for exhibitionism and the money for some cameras, you can cultivate your own cyber-following.

But can you use sex without actually being a porn purveyor?

Absolutely. Merchants of Venus use sex to sell everything from soap to cars.

If your nonporn product lends itself to a soft-porn approach, exploit that. Lingerie maker Victoria's Secret scored a publicity coup by webcasting its Spring Fashion Show live over the Internet. The computers failed when more than a million Web surfers tried to log on to watch models slink down the runway dressed in silk and skin. One enterprising website creator decided to piggyback on Victoria's Secret's sex-success by naming a site "**VICTORIA'S SECRET FASHION SHOW** is something I don't have here." The site proclaimed: "In a crass effort to garner hits on my web site, I have decided to pretend that I am Victoria's Secret Fashion Show, which two million Internet viewers tried to see on Feb. 3, 1999."

Use sex to sell your product by pumping your ad campaign with suggestive words and steamy pictures: "It's better in the Bahamas"; "Nothing comes between me and my Calvins"; "Take it off, take it all off." Play a woman's orgasmic moans to sell your herbal shampoo, or advertise your perfume amidst hazy glimpses of an orgy. What else? Clothes, cars, food, music, anything.

To focus on just one example, magazines are notoriously dependent on sexploitation. This trend extends far beyond obviously sexploitative magazines like *Playboy, Penthouse,* or *Juggs,* or "lad mags" like *Maxim* or *Details.* The covers of even the tamest check-out-aisle magazines blare with "The best sex I ever had!"; "Have the best sex of your life—starting now!"; "Have sex like you're single!" *Esquire* dedicated an issue to "Breasts! The Triumph of Cleavage Culture" with a cover showing Pamela Anderson Lee squeezing her bosoms together—using breasts to sell a magazine with an article arguing that breasts had become America's predominant sales tool. As editor of *Vanity Fair,* Tina Brown put an Annie Leibovitz photograph of actress Demi Moore on the cover—very pregnant, nearly naked, instantly notorious. And of course *Sports Illustrated's* swimsuit issue, with its full-page photos of bikini-clad models basking in the surf, is the magazine's best-selling issue each year.

To use sex to sell your magazine, be *exotic, erotic,* and *demotic:*

- combine sex with the other surefire topics (sex and sports, sex and clothes, travel, fitness, grooming, personal advice—even better, could you combine sex with the story of a climbing or sailing expedition turned fatal? Or astounding weight loss through sex?);

- offer a sex list: the ten best positions; the five secrets of the orgasm; the fifty sexiest men in Hollywood; fifteen tips on how to get her into bed;
- include lots of seductive photos of naked or near-naked sleek bodies, preferably posed in spectacular scenery;
- unveil new sexual information: unexpected positions (learn from the *Kama Sutra*!), overlooked erogenous zones (do you know where your G-spot is?), medical facts (sex keeps you looking toned!).

Are you a reporter? The same advantages of sexploitation apply. The news media use sex to sell their product whenever possible. The Monica Lewinsky sex scandal was a gold mine, with an astounding cast of characters, several sensational story lines complete with props, heroes (for example, Betty Currie) and villains (for example, Linda Tripp), and a suspenseful story arc of a quality not seen since the O. J. Simpson trial. The controversy allowed news anchors to neglect, in good conscience, soporific topics like Bosnia and health-care reform; instead, they were able to debate newsworthy questions such as whether oral sex "counts" as sex and whether a certain cigar had been just a cigar. Words and practices never before mentioned on TV or in the newspapers became the subject of sober commentary.

Given a lurid story with good pictures, there's no limit on the amount of news coverage the public will devour. Consider the non-stop coverage of the 1996 murder of JonBenét Ramsey, the six-year-old beauty queen. Innumerable TV news segments and magazine covers played up her image, tarted up with makeup, teased hair, and a moist smile like a Playmate-of-the-Month. The case would never have attracted such attention without those sexually charged photos.

Of course, as a journalist covering a sensational sex story, you may find it prudent to agonize in print, from time to time, whether this story's news value justifies your extensive coverage, or whether the serious, mainstream press is losing the journalistic culture battle to the tabloids.

TIP: Keep sexploitation up to date. *Playboy* and Playboy Clubs were a huge hit in the 1950s and 1960s, but became outmoded. Viewership of the quaint Miss America pageant has plunged. (At some point, unfashionable sexploitation may emerge as retro and breathe a second life, as *Playboy* is attempting.)

Magazines are just one example of where sex can profitably be used. There are countless others. Use sex as a platform for fame. Dr. Ruth Westheimer is a household name (fame note: Dr. Ruth uses her accent as an ear-tag). Candace Bushnell used the combination of "sex and the city" as a way to get noticed in print, then in television (the TV show based on her columns and book about a New York City sex columnist, *Sex and the City,* is also known as "dirty-something"). Prostitute Tracy Quan drew on her own experience as a basis for her fictional column, "Nancy Chan: Diary of a Manhattan Call Girl" for online magazine *Salon.* Proclaim yourself a sexpert—a particularly successful route on the Internet, with its insatiable hunger for content providers and specialists.

• • •

If sexploitation is your only use for sex, you may escape the blues; for you, it's just another commodity, another branding device, another set of images for the ad agency to play with. But if you use sex for pleasure or conquest, you find that you can't sustain that forever; sooner or later you're struck with the sex blues. The passions of the body give way to the mind's melancholy.

CHAPTER TWENTY-FOUR

FINAL NOTE: SEX BLUES

Sex is fleeting; it cannot be sustained. You must make conquest after conquest, otherwise yesterday's prize turns into tomorrow's familiar companion, and you find yourself sunk in a homely routine, with responsibilities, aggravations, limitations.

You married a powerful, rich older man; you thrilled at his mastery of foreign travel, wine lists, architects; you couldn't believe the important people who were his friends. But now you realize that he can't really afford to build that boat he's been talking about for years, and you've learned as much about wine as he has. His knees are so bad that he has trouble climbing even the shortest flight of stairs.

Or the gorgeous woman you've been squiring about has a brother who's got cancer; she's fatally allergic to nuts and carries an emergency shot of adrenaline with her; she wants you to take her jewelry shopping this weekend. And she thinks it's time for you to get a haircut.

Sex, because of its promise of intimacy and affection, works only to underscore calculation when it's put to use for power, money, fame—or even for the sheer pleasure of sex, which too dulls in time, with familiarity.

> There must be thousands of men like him, rich businessmen who over the past ten or fifteen years had divorced their old wives of two to three decades' standing and taken on new wives, girls a whole generation younger. . . . What if a man goes through all that, the separation, the divorce, all that agony, that struggle, that hellish expense, that . . . that . . . that *guilt* . . . and one day, or one night, he wakes up and wonders, Who the hell is this in the bed next to me? Why is she here? Where did she come from? What does she want? Why won't she leave?
>
> TOM WOLFE, *A MAN IN FULL*

ILLUSTRATION: HOW JOHN USED SEX

John's computer business succeeded far beyond his wildest hopes. In fact, he was featured in a *City Magazine* cover story about "Thirty-five under thirty-five" as one of the city's rising stars. (John was actually thirty-seven, but he'd lied when they'd asked his age.)

John now felt an obligation to keep up a certain image—young, dynamic, rich, enterprising. And although John was consumed with ambition and worked constantly, he feigned a casual, easygoing attitude toward business and appeared at every event and social occasion. To underscore this image, John cultivated a string of tall, luscious twenty-somethings who were glad to play the latest adoring girlfriend. He didn't have any sort of relationship with these women—he didn't have the time or energy for that—but he wouldn't have wanted to show up alone.

His competitive spirit was gratified by the jealous looks he got from his more settled peers. As he became known for having a different gorgeous woman on his arm every night, photographers from the newspaper's society pages and from *City Magazine* began to feature him regularly as a prominent playboy. This coverage raised John's profile, helped break the ice when he met with potential clients (all of whom had heard of him), and kept women interested in him.

ILLUSTRATION: HOW TINA USED SEX

Tina worked the bar at Zappy's, a seedy bar in L.A. frequented by millionaire rock star Thor. Night after night Tina smiled provocatively and wore her tightest, most revealing clothing, and finally Thor asked her out. The two dated briefly, but broke up when Thor found out Tina was pregnant and refused to have an abortion as he wanted. (Tina hadn't tried to get pregnant, but she hadn't tried to prevent it, either.) After their son, Dragon, was born, Thor didn't contest paternity and now pays Tina $7,000 a month for Dragon's support. Tina quit her bartending job and moved with Dragon to Santa Monica to be near the beach.

conclusion

POWER MONEY FAME SEX

Congratulations! You've mastered the rules for exploiting power, money, fame, and sex—now it's time to apply these tools yourself. You know what you need to do. Where will you start? By changing where you sit at the conference table? where you get your hair cut? what you'll wear on your next blind date?

But you've gained more than a guide for your *own* behavior; you've gained the key that cracks the code to explain what *others* are doing, and why. You understand the people around you—better, perhaps, than they understand themselves. Why does that person namedrop? or flash $100 bills? or refuse to wear any shoes except sneakers? You know—and your knowledge robs such gestures of their force.

Your mind overflows with plans. "Soon, soon," you promise yourself. "Soon I'll hit that next level, where I'll be with all the right people, and have all the right possessions, with all the attention and power I require." The world's incomplete and ready pleasures bestir you, and you're eager for new things. A new car, a new identity, a new childhood. You hide *Power Money Fame Sex* beneath some papers in a desk drawer (remember, *sprezzatura*) and resolve to start applying these principles tomorrow to make sure you get what you want.

But consider: Can you ever have enough?

"Now you're going to tell me that money won't buy happiness, or that no honors can substitute for a loving family or good health," you say, and shake your head in exasperation. "Sure, okay. But don't tell me that achieving my worldly ambitions wouldn't make me happier. I *would* be happier if I were running the company. If I could fly first-class. If I got the respect that I crave." True, having attained those rungs brings you some relief—but *then* what would you want? Something else, certainly.

Contentment can't be supplied from outside yourself. Consider Plutarch: "For dealing with the blessings which come to us from outside we need a firm foundation based on reason and education; without this foundation, people keep on seeking these blessings and heaping them up but can never satisfy the insatiable appetites of their souls." Your ambition has caught you in the snare of mounting expectations. Your successes only whet the appetites you're working to slake.

And no matter how absorbing the contest, sometimes you catch a glimpse of what else might have been. Sometimes you think, "If only I got . . . if I could give . . ." But you don't know what you want to give, or who could give it to you.

Ah! *Vanitas Vanitatum!* Which of us is happy in this world? Which of us has his desire? or, having it, is satisfied? —Come children, let us shut up the box and the puppets, for our play is played out.

WILLIAM THACKERAY, *VANITY FAIR*

SELECT BIBLIOGRAPHY

For readers who want to continue their study of power, money, fame, or sex, a select bibliography follows. (The publication date provided is the date of original publication.)

A

Adams, Alex, with William Stadiem, *Madam 90210: My Life as Madam to the Rich and Famous* (1993).

Adams, Henry, *Democracy* (1880).

Aldrich, Nelson W., Jr., *Old Money* (1988).

Amende, Carol, *Hollywood Confidential* (1997).

Amis, Martin, *Money* (1984).

Amory, Cleveland, *Who Killed Society?* (1960).

Andersen, Kurt, *The Real Thing* (1980).

———, *Turn of the Century* (1999).

Anderson, Christopher, *Madonna Unauthorized* (1991).

Arlen, Michael, *The Camera Age* (1981).

Atholl, Desmond, *At Your Service: Memoirs of a Majordomo* (1992).

Auchincloss, Louis, *Portrait in Brownstone* (1962).

———, *The Rector of Justin* (1964).

———, *The Vanderbilt Era* (1989).

Auletta, Ken, *Greed and Glory on Wall Street: The Fall of the House of Lehman* (1987).

B

Balsan, Consuelo Vanderbilt, *The Glitter and the Gold* (1973).

Barrows, Sydney Biddle, with William Novak, *Mayflower Madam: The Secret Life of Sydney Biddle Barrows* (1986).

Bataille, Georges, *The Accursed Share,* vol. 1, *Consumption* (1991).

Beaverbrook, William Maxwell Aitken, Baron, *The Abdication of King Edward VIII* (1966).

Beck, Mary Giraudo, *Potlatch* (1993).

Beran, Michael Knox, *The Last Patrician: Bobby Kennedy and the End of American Aristocracy* (1998).

Bingham, Sallie, *Passion and Prejudice* (1989).

Birmingham, Stephen, *Our Crowd* (1967).

———, *Carriage Trade* (1993).

———, *The Wrong Kind of Money* (1997).

Biskind, Peter, *Easy Riders, Raging Bulls: How the Sex, Drugs and Rock'n'Roll Generation Saved Hollywood* (1998).

Blair, Gwenda, *Almost Golden: Jessica Savitch and the Selling of Television News* (1988).

Boorstin, Daniel J., *The Image: A Guide to Pseudo-Events in America* (1987).

Botton, Alain de, *How Proust Can Change Your Life: Not a Novel* (1997).

Boyer, Peter J., *Who Killed CBS* (1988).

Bradlee, Benjamin C., *Conversations with Kennedy* (1975).

———, *A Good Life: Newspapering and Other Adventures* (1995).

Brammer, Billy Lee, *The Gay Place* (1961).

Braudy, Leo, *The Frenzy of Renown* (1986).

Brenner, Marie, *Intimate Distance: Some Private Views of Public Lives* (1983).

Brock, David, *The Seduction of Hillary Rodham* (1996).

Bronson, Po, *Bombardiers* (1995).

———, *The First Twenty Million is Always the Hardest* (1997).

———, *The Nudist on the Late Shift* (1999).

Brown, Claude, *Manchild in the Promised Land* (1965).

Brownstein, Ronald, *The Power and the Glitter: The Hollywood-Washington Connection* (1990).

Bruck, Connie, *The Predators' Ball* (1988).

———, *Master of the Game: Steve Ross and the Creation of Time Warner* (1994).

Bruno, Jerry, and Jeff Greenfield, *The Advance Man* (1971).

Buckley, Christopher, *Thank You for Smoking* (1994).

———, and John Tierney, *God Is My Broker: A Monk-Tycoon Reveals the 7 1/2 Laws of Spiritual and Financial Growth* (1998).

Buckley, William F., Jr., *Overdrive: A Personal Documentary* (1983).

Burrough, Bryan, and John Helyar, *Barbarians at the Gate: The Fall of RJR Nabisco* (1990).
Bushnell, Candace, *Sex and the City* (1996).
Buss, David, *The Evolution of Desire* (1994).

C

Campbell, Colin, Lady, *Diana in Private: The Princess Nobody Knows* (1992).
Capote, Truman, *Breakfast at Tiffany's* (1958).
Carnegie, Dale, *How to Win Friends and Influence People* (1936).
Caro, Robert, *The Power Broker: Robert Moses and the Fall of New York* (1974).
———, *The Years of Lyndon Johnson: Path to Power* (1981).
———, *The Years of Lyndon Johnson: Means of Ascent* (1990).
Casanova, Giacomo, *Memoirs* (1797).
Castiglione, Baldesar, *The Book of the Courtier* (1528).
Chapple, Steve, and David Talbot, *Burning Desires: Sex in America* (1989).
Chernow, Ron, *Titan: The Life of John D. Rockefeller, Sr.* (1998).
Chesterfield, Philip Dormer Stanhope, Earl of, *Letters to His Son: On the Fine Art of Becoming a Man of the World and a Gentleman* (1774).
Churchill, Winston, Sir, *Great Contemporaries* (1937).
———, *A Roving Commission: My Early Life* (1939).
———, *The Second World War,* Vols. 1–6 (1948).
Cialdini, Robert B., *Influence: The Psychology of Persuasion* (1993).
Cunningham, Mary, *Powerplay: What Really Happened at Bendix* (1984).

D

Davies, Nicholas, *Diana: A Princess and Her Troubled Marriage* (1992).
Dean, John, *Blind Ambition: The White House Years* (1976).
Deaver, Michael, with Mickey Herskowitz, *Behind the Scenes* (1987).
Didion, Joan, *Slouching Towards Bethlehem* (1961).
———, *After Henry* (1993).
Doctorow, E.L., *Billy Bathgate* (1989).

Drew, Elizabeth, *On the Edge: The Clinton Presidency* (1994).

Duchin, Peter, *Ghost of a Chance: A Memoir* (1996).

Dunne, Dominick, *The Two Mrs. Grenvilles* (1985).

————, *People Like Us* (1988).

————, *The Mansions of Limbo* (1991).

E

Ehrlichman, John, *Witness to Power: The Nixon Years* (1982).

Ellis, Joseph J., *American Sphinx: The Character of Thomas Jefferson* (1996).

Epstein, Joseph, *Ambition: The Secret Passion* (1980).

Etcoff, Nancy, *Survival of the Prettiest: The Science of Beauty* (1999).

Evans, Robert, *The Kid Stays in the Picture* (1994).

F

Fairchild, John, *Chic Savages* (1989).

Farrow, Mia, *What Falls Away* (1997).

Felske, Coerte V.W., *The Millennium Girl* (1999).

Fitzgerald, F. Scott, *The Great Gatsby* (1925).

————, *Tender Is the Night* (1933).

Flem, Lydia, *Casanova: The Man Who Really Loved Women* (1995).

Fleming, Charles, *High Concept: Don Simpson and the Hollywood Culture of Excess* (1998).

Fraser, Kennedy, *The Fashionable Mind* (1981).

————, *Ornament and Silence* (1996).

Freud, Sigmund, *Totem and Taboo* (1918).

————, *Civilization and Its Discontents* (1929).

Fussell, Paul, *Class* (1983).

G

Gabler, Neal, *Winchell: Gossip, Power, and the Culture of Celebrity* (1994).

Gaines, Steven S., *Philistines at the Hedgerow: Passion and Property in the Hamptons* (1998).

————, and Sharon Churcher, *Obsession: The Lives and Times of Calvin Klein* (1994).

Galella, Ron, *Jacqueline* (1974).

Gallagher, Mary Barelli, *My Life With Jacqueline Kennedy* (1969).

Garrow, David J., *Bearing the Cross: Martin Luther King, Jr., and the Southern Christian Leadership Conference* (1986).

Gilbert, Martin, *Churchill: A Life* (1991).

Goldman, William, *Hype and Glory* (1990).

Goodwin, Doris Kearns, *Lyndon Johnson and the American Dream* (1976).

————, *No Ordinary Time: Franklin and Eleanor Roosevelt: The Home Front in WWII* (1994).

Gordon, Barbara, *Jennifer Fever: Older Men, Younger Women* (1988).

Gordon, Mary, *Spending* (1998).

Graham, Katharine, *Personal History* (1997).

Graham, Sheilah, *How to Marry Super Rich, or, Love, Money, and the Morning After* (1974).

Greene, Bob, *Billion Dollar Baby* (1974).

Greene, Robert, and Joost Elffers, *The 48 Laws of Power* (1998).

Gross, Michael, *Model: The Ugly Business of Beautiful Women* (1995).

Guralnick, Peter, *Last Train to Memphis: The Rise of Elvis Presley* (1994).

————, *Careless Love: The Unmaking of Elvis Presley* (1999).

H

Halberstam, David, *The Powers That Be* (1979).

————, *Playing for Keeps: Michael Jordan and the World He Made* (1999).

Hamilton, Nigel, *JFK: Reckless Youth* (1992).

Harrison, Rosina, *Rose: My Life in Service* (1975).

Hart, Josephine, *Damage* (1991).

Hayward, Brooke, *Haywire* (1977).

Hazlitt, William, *Table Talk* (1824).

————, *Characteristics: In the Manner of Rochefoucault's Maxims* (1837).

Heidenry, John, *What Wild Ecstasy: The Rise and Fall of the Sexual Revolution* (1997).

Holmes, Oliver Wendell, Sr., *Elsie Venner: A Romance of Destiny* (1891).

Hoving, Thomas, *Making the Mummies Dance* (1993).

I

Iacocca, Lee, *Iacocca* (1984).
Isaacson, Walter, *Kissinger* (1992).
Ishiguro, Kazuo, *The Remains of the Day* (1989).

J

Janus, Samuel S., and Cynthia L. Janus, *The Janus Report on Sexual Behavior* (1993).
Johnson, Lisa, *How to Snare a Millionaire* (1995).
Jong, Erica, *How to Save Your Own Life* (1977).
Julian, Philippe, *The Snob Spotter's Guide* (1958).
Just, Ward, *Honor, Power, Riches, Fame, and the Love of Women* (1973).
———, *Jack Gance* (1989).
———, *Ambition and Love* (1994).
———, *Echo House* (1997).

K

Kalman, Laura, *Abe Fortas* (1990).
Kaplan, Louise J., *Female Perversions: The Temptations of Emma Bovary* (1991).
Katzenbach, Maria, *The Grab* (1978).
Kelley, Kitty, *Jackie Oh!* (1978).
———, *Elizabeth Taylor: The Last Star* (1981).
———, *Nancy Reagan: The Unauthorized Biography* (1991).
———, *The Royals* (1997).
Kenmore, Carolyn, *Mannequin: My Life as a Model* (1969).
Kessler, Ronald, *Sins of the Father: Joseph P. Kennedy and the Dynasty He Founded* (1996).
Kirkland, Gelsey, *Dancing on My Grave* (1986).
Klapp, Orrin, *Symbolic Leaders: Public Dramas and Public Men* (1964).
Klein, Edward, *All Too Human: The Love Story of Jack and Jackie Kennedy* (1996).
Koestenbaum, Wayne, *Jackie Under My Skin: Interpreting an Icon* (1995).
Korda, Michael, *Power! How to Get It, How to Use It* (1975).
———, *Success!* (1977).

————, *Another Life* (1999).

Kornbluth, Jesse, *Highly Confident: The Crime and Punishment of Michael Milken* (1992).

Krantz, Judith, *Scruples* (1978).

Kureishi, Hanif, *Intimacy* (1998).

Kurtz, Howard, *Spin Cycle: How the White House and the Media Manipulate the News* (1998).

L

Lanchester, John, *The Debt to Pleasure* (1996).

Lapham, Lewis, *Lapham's Rules of Influence* (1999).

La Rochefoucauld, François, Duc de, *Moral Reflections, Sentences, and Maxims* (1665).

Leaming, Barbara, *Marilyn Monroe* (1998).

Lefevre, Edwin, *Reminiscences of a Stock Operator* (1923).

Lewis, C.S., *The Weight of Glory* (1949).

————, *Screwtape Letters* (1950).

Lewis, Michael, *Liar's Poker* (1989).

————, *The Money Culture* (1991).

————, *The New New Thing: A Silicon Valley Story* (2000).

Long, Rob, *Conversations With My Agent* (1997).

Lowenstein, Roger, *Buffett: The Making of an American Capitalist* (1995).

M

Machiavelli, Niccolò, *The Prince* (1517).

Mackay, Charles, *Extraordinary Popular Delusions and the Madness of Crowds* (1841).

Maier, Thomas, *Newhouse* (1994).

Mailer, Norman, *Advertisements for Myself* (1959).

Maraniss, David, *First in His Class* (1995).

Marcus, George, *Lives in Trust: Fortunes of Dynastic Families in Late Twentieth Century America* (1992).

Marquand, J.P., *The Late George Apley* (1937).

————, *H.M. Pulham, Esquire* (1943).

————, *B.F.'s Daughter* (1946).

————, *Point of No Return* (1949).

————, *Sincerely, Willis Wayde* (1955).

Martin, Ralph, *The Woman He Loved: The Story of the Duke and Duchess of Windsor* (1973).

Marx, Karl, *Capital* (1867).

Matthews, Christopher, *Hardball* (1988).

Mauss, Marcel, *The Gift: Forms and Functions of Exchange in Archaic Societies* (1967).

McBride, Joseph, *Steven Spielberg: A Biography* (1997).

McClintick, David, *Indecent Exposure: A True Story of Hollywood and Wall Street* (1982).

McGinniss, Joe, *The Selling of the President 1968* (1969).

————, *The Dream Team* (1972).

————, *Heroes* (1976).

McNeill, Elizabeth, *Nine and a Half Weeks* (1978).

McPherson, Harry, *A Political Education* (1972).

Melville, Herman, *Moby Dick* (1851).

Miller, Russell, *Bunny: The Real Story of Playboy* (1984).

Monaco, James, ed., *Celebrity: Who Gets It, How They Use It, Why It Works* (1978).

Moore, Doris Langley, *The Technique of the Love Affair* (1928).

Morris, Dick, *Behind the Oval Office* (1997).

————, *The New Prince* (1999).

Morris, Sylvia Jukes, *Rage for Fame: The Ascent of Clare Boothe Luce* (1997).

Musashi, Miyamato, *A Book of Five Rings* (1645).

N

Nixon, Richard, *Six Crises* (1962).

Noonan, Peggy, *What I Saw at the Revolution* (1990).

O

Ogden, Christopher, *Life of the Party: The Biography of Pamela Digby Churchill Hayward Harriman* (1994).

Oppenheimer, Jerry, *Martha Stewart: Just Desserts* (1997).

O'Toole, Patricia, *Money and Morals in America* (1998).

Ovid, *The Art of Love* (c. 1 B.C.).

P

Paley, William, *As It Happened* (1979).

Phillips, Julia, *You'll Never Eat Lunch in This Town Again* (1991).
Plimpton, George, *The X Factor* (1995).
————, *Truman Capote* (1997).
Plutarch, *Lives* (c. 100).
Podhoretz, Norman, *Making It* (1967).
Powell, Dawn, *A Time to Be Born* (1942).
Powers, Richard, *Gain* (1998).
Price, Richard, *Clockers* (1992).

Q
Quinn, Sally, *We're Going to Make You a Star* (1975).
————, *Regrets Only* (1986).
————, *Happy Endings* (1991).
————, *The Party* (1997).

R
Regan, Donald, *For the Record: From Wall Street to Washington* (1988).
Reich, Robert, *Locked in the Cabinet* (1997).
Remnick, David, *King of the World: Muhammad Ali and the Rise of an American Hero* (1998).
Rhodes, Richard, *Making Love* (1992).
Robinson, Roxana, *This Is My Daughter* (1998).
Rose, Phyllis, *The Year of Reading Proust* (1977)
Rollins, Ed, with Tom DeFrank, *Bare Knuckles and Back Rooms: My Life in American Politics* (1996).
Rush, Norman, *Mating* (1991).

S
Safire, William, *Before the Fall: An Inside View of the Pre-Watergate White House* (1975).
Sayles, Ginie Polo, *How to Marry the Rich* (1991).
Scholz, Suzette, Stephanie, and Sheri, with John Tullins, *Deep in the Heart of Texas: Reflections of Former Dallas Cowboy Cheerleaders* (1991).
Schulberg, Budd, *What Makes Sammy Run?* (1941).
Sennett, Richard, *The Fall of Public Man* (1977).
Shakespeare, William, *Henry IV* (c. 1597).

————, *Henry V* (c. 1598).

————, *Julius Caesar* (c. 1599).

————, *King Lear* (c. 1605).

————, *Antony and Cleopatra* (c. 1607).

Shapiro, Dani, *Slow Motion* (1998).

Shaw, Maud, *White House Nannie: My Years with Caroline and John Kennedy, Jr.* (1966).

Shields, David, *Remote* (1996).

Slater, Philip, *Wealth Addiction* (1980).

Smith, Sally Bedell, *In All His Glory: The Life of William S. Paley* (1990).

————, *Reflected Glory: The Life of Pamela Churchill Harriman* (1996).

Sontag, Susan, *The Volcano Lover* (1992).

Spencer, Scott, *Men in Black* (1995).

Stanley, Thomas, and William Danko, *The Millionaire Next Door* (1996).

Steel, Dawn, *They Can Kill You But They Can't Eat You* (1993).

Stephanopoulos, George, *All Too Human: A Political Education* (1999).

Stockman, David, *The Triumph of Politics* (1986).

Suetonius, *The Twelve Caesars* (c. 110).

Summers, Anthony, *Goddess: The Secret Lives of Marilyn Monroe* (1985).

————, *Official and Confidential: The Secret Life of J. Edgar Hoover* (1993).

Sun-tzu, *The Art of War* (c. 500 B.C.).

Susann, Jacqueline, *Valley of the Dolls* (1966).

T

Taylor, John, *Circus of Ambition: The Culture of Wealth and Power in the '80s* (1989).

————, *Falling: The Story of One Marriage* (1999).

Thackeray, William Makepeace, *Vanity Fair* (1848).

Timm, Uwe, *Headhunter* (1991).

Toobin, Jeffrey, *The Run of His Life: The People v. O. J. Simpson* (1996).

V

Veblen, Thorstein, *The Theory of the Leisure Class* (1919).
Vreeland, Diana, *D.V.* (1984).

W

Wagner, Bruce, *I'm Losing You* (1996).
Warhol, Andy, *The Philosophy of Andy Warhol (From A to B and Back Again)* (1975).
Warren, Robert Penn, *All the King's Men* (1950).
Whalen, Richard, *The Founding Father: The Story of Joseph P. Kennedy* (1964).
Wharton, Edith, *The House of Mirth* (1905).
———, *The Reef* (1912).
———, *The Custom of the Country* (1913).
———, *The Age of Innocence* (1920).
White, Theodore H., *Breach of Faith: The Fall of Richard Nixon* (1975).
Wills, Garry, *The Kennedy Imprisonment: a Meditation on Power* (1982).
———, *Certain Trumpets: The Call of Leaders* (1994).
———, *John Wayne's America: The Politics of Celebrity* (1997).
Wilson, Mike, *The Difference Between God and Larry Ellison* (1997).
Woodward, Bob, *The Agenda: Inside the Clinton White House* (1994).
———, and Carl Bernstein, *The Final Days* (1976).
Wolfe, Tom, *The Kandy-Kolored Tangerine-Flake Streamline Baby* (1965).
———, *Radical Chic and Mau-Mauing the Flak Catchers* (1970).
———, *The Bonfire of the Vanities* (1987).
———, *A Man in Full* (1998).
Woolf, Virginia, *Mrs. Dalloway* (1925).
———, *Diaries* (1915-1941).
Wright, Susan, *How to Marry Money: The Rich Have to Marry Someone—Why Not You* (1995).

INDEX

Fox News Channel, 147
Frank, Anne, 162
Frankfurter, Felix, 56
Franklin, Benjamin, 70
Freud, Sigmund, 3, 248
friends, rewarding, 55–56
frottage, 167–69, 181, 182, 204, 244
"Furs and Station Wagons," 94

Galella, Ron, 205
Gandhi, Mohandas, 35
Garcia, Jerry, 199
Garfunkel, Art, 160
Garvey, Steve, 242
Gates, Bill, 4
    blues and, 151
    books and, 199
    charity and, 146
    frottage and, 169, 196
    house of, 130–31
    Leonardo da Vinci and, 95
    sycophancy and, 26, 62
Gates, Henry Louis, Jr., 195
Gaulle, Charles de, 69
Geffen, David, 62, 71, 95, 126
General Electric Company, 57, 58
George VI, 49
Gere, Richard, 175
Germond, Jack, 24, 164
Getty, J. Paul, 149
Giancana, Sam "Momo," 208
gift-giving, 127–28, 186, 226, 235,
    236, 261, 262
Gingrich, Newt, 52, 176, 214, 228
Glorious Food, 123
Glucksman, Lew, 139
gold, 142–43, 144
Goldman Sachs, 44, 146
Good, Victor, 196
Goodwin, Dick, 24
Gordon, Mary, 262
Gordon, Shep, 190
Gottlieb, Robert, 57
grab, the, 138–40

Graduate, The (film), 263
Graham, Katharine, 144, 200
Graham, Philip, 253
Graham, Stedman, 168
Grandy, Fred, 199
Grant, Hugh, 261
Great Gatsby, The (Fitzgerald), 136
Greenberg family, 257
Greene, Bob, 168, 196
Greenspan, Alan, 28, 161
Grey, Lord de, 130
Griffey, Ken, Jr., 205
Griffith, Melanie, 201
Grove, Andy, 72
Grubman, Lizzie, 205
Gucci, 93, 99, 108
Guggenheim, Solomon R., 149
guidance counselors, college, 147
Guinness Book of World Records, 170
Gulf and Western, 233
Gulf Oil Company, 227
Gulfstream, 128, 177
Gumbel, Bryant, 165
Gutfreund, Susan, 109, 125

Hackman, Gene, 199
Haig, Alexander, 76
hair, 231–32, 234
Haldeman, H. R., 21, 24, 49, 66,
    72
Hamm, Mia, 161
Hammer, Armand, 47
Hammer Codex, 95
Hanaka, Marty, 16
handshake, 68
happiness, 5, 273–74
Harper's Bazaar, 180
Harriman, Averell, 25
Harriman, Pamela, 4, 18, 25, 103,
    168, 247
Harris, Eric, 172–73
Harrison, Elizabeth, 205
Hart, Gary, 21, 200, 229
Harvard University, 92, 200, 213

Knave, 253
Knowles, Harry, 181
Koch, Julia, 102, 109
Korda, Michael, 4, 57–58
Korine, Harmony, 178
Krantz, Judith, 98, 139
Kuczynski, Alex, 159

lagniappe, 138
Lake, Anthony, 52
Lake, Ricki, 172
Lanchester, John, 137
La Rochefoucauld, 5, 80, 244
Las Ventanas al Paraiso, 206
Lauer, Matt, 157
Lauren, Ralph, 98, 108, 126
Lawford, Peter, 178
Lawrence, D. H., 135
Lawrence, T. E., 35
Lazar, Irving, 178, 195
Lee, Jennifer 8., 177
Lee, Pamela Anderson, 266
Lee, Robert E., 185
Lee, Spike, 161
Lehman Brothers Kuhn Loeb, 59,
   139
Leibovitz, Annie, 266
leisure, 105–06, 113–16
Leitch, Donovan, 211
Lennon, John, 162
Leno, Jay, 195, 229
Leon, Carlos, 257
Leonardo da Vinci, 95
Léron, 101
Letterman, David, 165, 195
Letters to His Son (Chesterfield), 42
leverage, 57
Levin, Gerald, 72
Levison, Stanley, 213
Lewinsky, Monica, 164, 169, 204,
   229, 244, 248, 249, 267
Lewis, C. S., 22
Library of Congress, 37
Lincoln, Abraham, 149, 162

Lindbergh, Charles, 163
Lindsay, John, 160
Lives (Plutarch), 4, 26, 48
Livingston, Robert, 228–29
L. L. Cool J., 100
Loehmann's, 103
London, Lauren, 205
Lonstein, Shoshanna, 203, 244
Los Angeles County Museum of Art,
   147
lotteries, 140
Louis, Joe, 162–63
Love, Courtney, 177
Lovett, Lyle, 175
Lowe, Rob, 178
Lucas, George, 67, 127
luxury, 119–22, 132–34

Machiavelli, Niccolò, 4, 5
MacDonald, William, 126
MacKinnon, Catharine, 166
Macmillan, Harold, 229
Madonna, 153
   books and, 199
   child of, 257
   colorfulness of, 175
   fashion and, 196
   garbage of, 205
   image and, 188
   perks of, 4, 58
   power of, 191, 242
   signaling and, 97
Magdalene, Mary, 32
Maguire, Tobey, 178
Mailer, Norman, 173, 213, 214
Malcolm X, 177
Manchester, William, 36
Manchild in the Promised Land
   (Brown), 71
Man In Full, A (Wolfe), 253, 269
Manson, Charles, 165
Mantle, Mickey, 176
Mao Tse-Tung, 196
Maples, Marla, 132, 172, 196, 240